FRACTAL MARKET ANALYSIS

WILEY FINANCE EDITIONS

FRACTAL MARKET ANALYSIS
Applying Chaos Theory to Investment and Economics

Edgar E. Peters

JOHN WILEY & SONS, INC.

New York • Chichester • Brisbane • Toronto • Singapore

This text is printed on acid-free paper.

Copyright © 1994 by John Wiley & Sons, Inc.

All rights reserved. Published simultaneously in Canada.

Reproduction or translation of any part of this work beyond
that permitted by Section 107 or 108 of the 1976 United
States Copyright Act without the permission of the copyright
owner is unlawful. Requests for permission or further
information should be addressed to the Permissions Department,
John Wiley & Sons, Inc., 605 Third Avenue, New York, NY
10158-0012.

This publication is designed to provide accurate and
authoritative information in regard to the subject
matter covered. It is sold with the understanding that
the publisher is not engaged in rendering legal, accounting,
or other professional services. If legal advice or other
expert assistance is required, the services of a competent
professional person should be sought. *From a Declaration
of Principles jointly adopted by a Committee of the
American Bar Association and a Committee of Publishers.*

Library of Congress Cataloging-in-Publication Data:

Peters, Edgar E., 1952–
    Fractal market analysis : applying chaos theory to investment and
economics / Edgar E. Peters.
        p. cm.
    Includes index.
    ISBN 0-471-58524-6
    1. Investments—Mathematics. 2. Fractals. 3. Chaotic behavior in
systems. I. Title. II. Title: Chaos theory.
HG4515.3.P47 1994
332.6'01'51474—dc20   93-28598

Printed in the United States of America

10 9 8 7 6 5 4 3 2

To Sheryl

Preface

In 1991, I finished writing a book entitled, *Chaos and Order in the Capital Markets*. It was published in the Fall of that year (Peters, 1991a). My goal was to write a conceptual introduction, for the investment community, to chaos theory and fractal statistics. I also wanted to present some preliminary evidence that, contrary to accepted theory, markets are not well-described by the random walk model, and the widely taught Efficient Market Hypothesis (EMH) is not well-supported by empirical evidence.

I have received, in general, a very positive response to that book. Many readers have communicated their approval—and some, their disapproval—and have asked detailed questions. The questions fell into two categories: (1) technical, and (2) conceptual. In the technical category were the requests for more detail about the analysis. My book had not been intended to be a textbook, and I had glossed over many technical details involved in the analysis. This approach improved the readability of the book, but it left many readers wondering how to proceed.

In the second category were questions concerned with conceptual issues. If the EMH is flawed, how can we fix it? Or better still, what is a viable replacement? How do chaos theory and fractals fit in with trading strategies and with the dichotomy between technical and fundamental analysis? Can these seemingly disparate theories be united? Can traditional theory become nonlinear?

In this book, I am addressing both categories of questions. This book is different from the previous one, but it reflects many similar features. Fractal Market Analysis is an attempt to generalize Capital Market Theory (CMT) and to account for the diversity of the investment community. One of the failings of traditional theory is its attempt to simplify "the market" into an average prototypical rational investor. The reasons for setting out on this route were noble. In the tradition of Western science, the founding fathers of CMT attempted to learn something about the whole by breaking down the problem into its basic components. That attempt was successful. Because of the farsighted work of Markowitz, Sharpe, Fama, and others, we have made enormous progress over the past 40 years.

However, the reductionist approach has its limits, and we have reached them. It is time to take a more holistic view of how markets operate. In particular, it is time to recognize the great diversity that underlies markets. All investors do not participate for the same reason, nor do they work their strategies over the same investment horizons. The stability of markets is inevitably tied to the diversity of the investors. A "mature" market is diverse as well as old. If all the participants had the same investment horizon, reacted equally to the same information, and invested for the same purpose, instability would reign. Instead, over the long term, mature markets have remarkable stability. A day trader can trade anonymously with a pension fund: the former trades frequently for short-term gains; the latter trades infrequently for long-term financial security. The day trader reacts to technical trends; the pension fund invests based on long-term economic growth potential. Yet, each participates simultaneously and each diversifies the other. The reductionist approach, with its rational investor, cannot handle this diversity without complicated multipart models that resemble a Rube Goldberg contraption. These models, with their multiple limiting assumptions and restrictive requirements, inevitably fail. They are so complex that they lack flexibility, and flexibility is crucial to any dynamic system.

The first purpose of this book is to introduce the Fractal Market Hypothesis—a basic reformulation of how, and why, markets function. The second purpose of the book is to present tools for analyzing markets within the fractal framework. Many existing tools can be used for this purpose. I will present new tools to add to the analyst's toolbox, and will review existing ones.

This book is not a narrative, although its primary emphasis is still conceptual. Within the conceptual framework, there is a rigorous coverage of analytical techniques. As in my previous book, I believe that anyone with a firm grounding in business statistics will find much that is useful here. The primary emphasis is not on dynamics, but on empirical statistics, that is, on analyzing time series to identify what we are dealing with.

THE STRUCTURE OF THE BOOK

The book is divided into five parts, plus appendices. The final appendix contains fractal distribution tables. Other relevant tables, and figures coordinated to the discussion, are interspersed in the text. Each part builds on the previous parts, but the book can be read nonsequentially by those familiar with the concepts of the first book.

Part One: Fractal Time Series

Chapter 1 introduces fractal time series and defines both spatial and temporal fractals. There is a particular emphasis on what fractals are, conceptually and physically. Why do they seem counterintuitive, even though fractal geometry is much closer to the real world than the Euclidean geometry we all learned in high school? Chapter 2 is a brief review of Capital Market Theory (CMT) and of the evidence of problems with the theory. Chapter 3 is, in many ways, the heart of the book: I detail the Fractal Market Hypothesis as an alternative to the traditional theory discussed in Chapter 2. As a *Fractal* Market Hypothesis, it combines elements of fractals from Chapter 1 with parts of traditional CMT in Chapter 2. The Fractal Market Hypothesis sets the conceptual framework for fractal market analysis.

Part Two: Fractal (R/S) Analysis

Having defined the problem in Part One, I offer tools for analysis in Part Two—in particular, rescaled range (R/S) analysis. Many of the technical questions I received about the first book dealt with R/S analysis and requested details about calculations and significance tests. Parts Two and Three address those issues. R/S analysis is a robust analysis technique for uncovering long memory effects, fractal statistical structure, and the presence of cycles. Chapter 4 surveys the conceptual background of R/S analysis and details how to apply it. Chapter 5 gives both statistical tests for judging the significance of the results and examples of how R/S analysis reacts to known stochastic models. Chapter 6 shows how R/S analysis can be used to uncover both periodic and nonperiodic cycles.

Part Three: Applying Fractal Analysis

Through a number of case studies, Part Three details how R/S analysis techniques can be used. The studies, interesting in their own right, have been selected to illustrate the advantages and disadvantages of using R/S analysis on different types of time series and different markets. Along the way, interesting things will be revealed about tick data, market volatility, and how currencies are different from other markets.

Part Four: Fractal Noise

Having used R/S analysis to find evidence to support the Fractal Market Hypothesis, I supply models to explain those findings. Part Four approaches market activity from the viewpoint of stochastic processes; as such, it concentrates on fractal noise. In Chapter 13, using R/S analysis, different "colored" noises are analyzed and compared to the market analysis. The findings are remarkably similar. In addition, the behavior of volatility is given a significant explanation. Chapter 14 discusses the statistics of fractal noise processes, and offers them as an alternative to the traditional Gaussian normal distribution. The impact of fractal distributions on market models is discussed. Chapter 15 shows the impact of fractal statistics on the portfolio selection problem and option pricing. Methods for adapting those models for fractal distributions are reviewed.

Part Four is a very detailed section and will not be appropriate for all readers. However, because the application of traditional CMT has become ingrained into most of the investment community, I believe that most readers should read the summary sections of each chapter, if nothing else, in Part Four. Chapter 13, with its study of the nature of volatility, should be of particular interest.

Part Five: Noisy Chaos

Part Five offers a dynamical systems alternative to the stochastic processes of Part Four. In particular, it offers noisy chaos as a possible explanation of the fractal structure of markets. Chapter 16, which gives R/S analysis of chaotic systems, reveals remarkable similarities with market and other time series. A particular emphasis is placed on distinguishing between fractal noise and noisy chaos. A review is given of the BDS (Brock–Dechert–Scheinkman) test, which, when used in conjunction with R/S analysis, can give conclusive evidence one way or the other. Chapter 17 applies fractal statistics to noisy chaos, reconciling the two approaches. An explanation is offered for why evidence of both fractal noise and noisy chaos can appear simultaneously. The result is closely tied to the Fractal Market Hypothesis and the theory of multiple investment horizons.

Chapter 18 is a review of the findings on a conceptual level. This final chapter unites the Fractal Market Hypothesis with the empirical work and theoretical models presented throughout the book. For readers who understand a problem better when they know the solution, it may be appropriate to read Chapter 18 first.

The appendices offer software that can be used for analysis and reproduce tables of the fractal distributions.

While reading the book, many of you will wonder, where is this leading? *Will this help me make money?* This book does not offer new trading techniques or find pockets of inefficiency that the savvy investor can profit from. It is not a book of strategy for making better predictions. Instead, it offers a new view of how markets work and how to test time series for predictability. More importantly, it gives additional information about the risks investors take, and how those risks change over time. If knowledge is power, as the old cliché goes, then the information here should be conducive, if not to power, at least to better profits.

EDGAR E. PETERS

Concord, Massachusetts

Acknowledgments

I would like to thank the following people for their invaluable advice and assistance: From PanAgora Asset Management: Richard Crowell, Peter Rathjens, John Lewis, Bruce Clarke, Terry Norman, Alan Brown, and Clive Lang. Also Warren Sproul, Earl Keefer, Robert Mellen, Guido DeBoeck, and Ron Brandes for help, ideas, and references. Thanks also to Kristine ("with a K") Lino, David Arrighini, Jim Rullo, and Chuck LeVine of the PanAgora Asset Allocation team, for their indulgence and help.

I would also like to thank, belatedly, my original Wiley editor, Wendy Grau, who persuaded me to write both books and saw me through the first publication. I would also like to thank Myles Thompson, my current editor, for seeing me through this one.

Finally, I would once again like to thank my wife, Sheryl, and my children, Ian and Lucia, for their continued support during the many hours I needed to myself to complete this project.

E.E.P.

Contents

PART TWO   FRACTAL (R/S) ANALYSIS

PART THREE   APPLYING FRACTAL ANALYSIS

PART FIVE   Noisy Chaos

PART ONE
FRACTAL TIME SERIES

1
Introduction to Fractal Time Series

Western culture has long been obsessed by the smooth and symmetric. Not all cultures are similarly obsessed, but the West (meaning European derived) has long regarded perfect forms as symmetric, smooth, and whole. We look for patterns and symmetry everywhere. Often, we impose patterns where none exists, and we deny patterns that do not conform to our overall conceptual framework. That is, when patterns are not symmetrical and smooth, we classify them as illusions.

This conflict can be traced back to the ancient Greeks. To describe our physical world, they created a geometry based on pure, symmetric, and smooth forms. Plato said that the "real" world consisted of these shapes. These forms were created by a force, or entity, called the "Good." The world of the Good could be glimpsed only occasionally, through the mind. The world we inhabit is an imperfect copy of the real world, and was created by a different entity, called the "Demiurge." The Demiurge, a lesser being than the Good, was doomed to create inferior copies of the real world. These copies were rough, asymmetric, and subject to decay. In this way, Plato reconciled the inability of the Greek geometry, later formalized by Euclid, to describe our world. The problem was not with the geometry, but with our world itself.

FRACTAL SPACE

Fractal geometry is the geometry of the Demiurge. Unlike Euclidean geometry, it thrives on roughness and asymmetry. Objects are not variations on a few perfect and symmetrical forms, but are infinitely complex. The more closely they are examined, the more detail is revealed. For example, a tree is a fractal form. Imagine a pine tree like the Douglas fir, commonly used for Christmas trees. Children often draw Douglas firs as triangles (the branches) with rectangular bases (the tree trunks), giving the trees as much symmetry as possible. Logos of Christmas trees have the same appearance or may substitute cones for the triangles. Yet, Douglas firs are not triangles or cones. They are a network of branches qualitatively similar to the shape of the overall tree, but each individual branch is different. The branches on branches (successive generations of branches) become progressively smaller. Yet, within each generation there is actually a range of sizes. And, *each tree is different.*

Euclidean geometry cannot replicate a tree. Using Euclidean geometry, we can create an approximation of a tree, but it always looks artificial, like a child's drawing or a logo. Euclidean geometry recreates the *perceived* symmetry of the tree, but not the variety that actually builds its structure. Underlying this perceived symmetry is a controlled randomness, and increasing complexity at finer levels of resolution. This "self-similar" quality is the defining characteristic of fractals. Most natural structures, particularly living things, have this characteristic.

A second problem, when we apply Euclidean geometry to our world, is one of dimensionality. We live in a three-dimensional space, but only solid forms are truly three-dimensional, according to the definitions that are the basis of Euclidean geometry. In mathematical terms, an object must be differentiable across its entire surface. A wiffle ball, for instance, is not a three-dimensional object, although it resides in a three-dimensional space.

In addition, our *perception* of dimension can change, depending on our distance from an object. From a distance, a Douglas fir looks like a two-dimensional triangle. As we come closer, it appears as a three-dimensional cone. Closer still, we can see its branches, and it looks like a network of one-dimensional lines. Closer examination reveals the branches as three-dimensional tubes. Euclidean geometry also has difficulty with the dimensionality of creations of the Demiurge and with increasing complexity. By contrast, Euclidean structures become simpler at smaller and smaller scales. The three-dimensional solid reduces to a two-dimensional plane. The two-dimensional plane is made up of one-dimensional lines and, finally, nondimensional points. Our perception of the tree, on the other hand, went from two-dimensional to three-dimensional to one-dimensional, and back to three-dimensional. This is different from the Euclidean perception.

Euclidean geometry is only useful as a gross simplification of the world of the Demiurge. Fractal geometry, by contrast, is characterized by self-similarity and increased complexity under magnification. Its major application as a geometry of space has been in generating realistic looking landscapes via computers.

The Demiurge created not only fractal space but fractal time as well. Although our primary focus will be on fractal time series, fractal space will help us understand fractal time. We will see the difference between the smoothness of the Euclidean world and the roughness of our world, which limits the usefulness of Euclid's geometry as a method of description.

FRACTAL TIME

This conflict between the symmetry of Euclidean geometry and the asymmetry of the real world can be further extended to our concept of time. Traditionally, events are viewed as either random or deterministic. In the deterministic view, all events through time have been fixed from the moment of creation. This view has been given a theological basis by denominations such as the Calvinists, and scientific endorsement by certain "big bang" theorists. In contrast, nihilist groups consider all events to be random, deriving from no structure or order through time.

In fractal time, randomness and determinism, chaos and order coexist. In fractal shapes, we see a physical representation of how these opposites work together. The pine tree has global structure *and* local randomness. In general, we know what a pine tree looks like, and we can predict the general or global shape of any pine tree with a high degree of accuracy. However, at the individual branch level, each branch is different. We do not know how long it is, or its diameter. Each tree is different, but shares certain global properties. Each has local randomness and global determinism. In this section, we will examine how the concept of fractal time evolved, and what it means.

Most cultures favor the deterministic view of time. We like to think that we have a place in the universe, that we have a destiny. Yet, we see random, catastrophic events that can thwart us from fulfilling our purpose. Natural disasters can destroy our environment. Economic disasters can take what we own. Individuals we do not know can rob us of our lives, by accident or with malice. Conversely, good fortune can arrive by being at the right place at the right time. A chance meeting can open new doors. Picking the right lottery numbers can bring us a fortune.

Great events also seem to rest on chance. Newton saw an object falling (legend says it was an apple) and formulated the calculus and the laws of gravity. Fleming left a petri dish exposed and discovered penicillin. Darwin decided to go on a voyage and formulated a theory of evolution because of his experiences on the journey.

These and similar events seemed to happen by chance, and they changed history. Yet, Liebnez developed the calculus independently of Newton, at almost the same time—in fact, we use Liebnez's notation. Wallace developed the theory of natural selection independently of Darwin, though later. Because of a paper by Wallace, Darwin found the energy to write *Origin of Species* so he would receive credit as the theory's original developer. In our own field of financial economics, what is known as the Capital Asset Pricing Model (CAPM) was developed independently by no fewer than three people—Sharpe (1964), Lintner (1965), and Mossin (1966)—at almost the same time. This would imply that these discoveries were meant to happen. History demanded it. It was their destiny.

It has been difficult to reconcile randomness and order, chance and necessity, or free will and determinism. Is this dichotomy once again the Demiurge imperfectly copying the Good?

Events are perceived as either random, and therefore unpredictable, or deterministic, and perfectly predictable. Until the beginning of this century, it was generally accepted that the universe ran like a clock. Eventually, scientists were to discover the equations underlying the universe, and become able to predict its eventual course. Time was of no consequence in Newtonian mechanics; theoretically, time could be reversed, because Newton's equations worked fine whether time ran forward or backward. Irreversible time, the first blow to this deterministic view, came in the mid-19th century from the emerging field of thermodynamics.

Thermodynamics began as the study of heat waste produced by machines. It was some time before thermodynamics, an applied science, was taken seriously by scientists. The initial study focused on how energy is converted into useful work. In a system such as the steam engine, steam turns wheels and performs a function such as powering a boat's paddle wheel. Not all the energy produced is converted into work. Some is lost or is dissipated as friction. The study of these "dissipative systems" eventually grew to include fluid dynamics. Fluid dynamics, which investigated the heating and mixing of fluids, gave us time-irreversible systems.

Suppose two liters of fluid are separated by a waterproof, removable partition. On one side is a liter of red fluid; on the other, a liter of blue. We decide to use the term *entropy* as the measure of the degree of mixing of the red and blue fluids. As long as the partition is in place, we have low entropy. If we lift the partition, the red and blue fluids will flow into one another, and the level of entropy will rise as the fluids become more mixed. Eventually, when the red and blue become thoroughly mixed, all of the fluid will become purple.

When fully mixed, the fluid has reached a state of equilibrium. It cannot become "more mixed." It has reached a level of maximum entropy. However, we cannot "unmix" the fluid. Despite the fact that the mixing of the fluids is understandable in dynamical terms, it is time-dependent and *irreversible*. The fluid's state of high entropy, or *uncertainty,* which comes from the maximum mixing of two states (in this case, the states are labeled "red" and "blue"), cannot be described by time-reversible, Newtonian equations. The fluid will never become unmixed; its entropy will never decline, even if we wait for eternity. In thermodynamics, time has an arrow that points only toward the future. The first blow had been struck against the clockwork view of the universe.

The second blow came with the emergence of quantum mechanics. The realization that the molecular structure of the universe can be described only by states of probability further undermined the deterministic view. But confusion remained. Was the universe deterministic or random?

Slowly, it has become apparent that most natural systems are characterized by local randomness and global determinism. These contrary states must coexist. Determinism gives us natural law. Randomness induces innovation and variety. A healthy, evolving system is one that not only can survive random shocks, but also can absorb those shocks to improve the overall system, when appropriate.

For instance, it has been postulated by West and Goldberger (1987) that physical fractal structures are generated by nature because they are more error-tolerant than symmetrical structures in their creation. Take the mammalian lung. Its main branch, the trachea, divides into two subbranches. These two halves continue branching. At each branching generation, the average diameter decreases according to a power law. Thus, the diameter of each generation is dependent on the diameters of the previous generation. In addition, each branch generation actually has a range of diameters within it. The average diameter of each generation scales down according to a power law, but any individual branch can be described only probabilistically. We have global determinism (the average branch size) and local randomness (the diameter of individual branches). Why does nature favor this structure, which appears in all mammalian lungs? West and Goldberger have shown that this fractal structure is more stable and error-tolerant than other structures. Remember that each branch generation is dependent on the generations before it. If diameters scaled exponentially, not only would an error in the formation of one generation affect the next branching generation, but the error would grow with each successive generation. A small error might cause the lung to become malformed and nonfunctional. However, by fractal scaling, the error has less impact because of the power law, as well as the local probabilistic structure. Because each generation has a range of diameters, one malformed branch has less impact on the formation of the others. Thus, the fractal structure (global determinism, local randomness) is more error-tolerant during formation than other structures.

To look ahead, if we change this concept from a static structure (the lung) to a dynamic structure like the stock market, we can make some interesting conjectures. Change branch generation to "investment horizon." The stock market is made up of investors, from tick traders to long-term investors. Each has a different investment horizon that can be ordered in time. A stable market is one in which all the participants can trade with one another, each facing a risk level like the others', adjusted for their time scale or investment horizon. We will see in Chapter 2 that the frequency distribution of returns is the same for day traders as it is for one-week or even 90-day returns, once an adjustment is made for scale. That is, five-minute traders face the same risk of a large event as does a weekly trader. If day traders have a crash at their time scale, like a four-sigma event, the market remains stable if the other traders, who have different trading horizons, see that crash as a buying opportunity, and step in and buy. Thus, the market remains stable because it has no characteristic time scale, just as the lung had no characteristic diameter scale. When the market's entire investment horizon shortens, and everyone becomes a one-minute trader (investors have lost their faith in long-term information), the market becomes erratic and unstable. Therefore, the market can absorb shocks as long as it retains its fractal structure. When it loses that structure, instability sets in. We will discuss this concept more fully in Chapter 3.

A different time-dependent example is found in the formation of living creatures such as mammals and reptiles. Once again, we see local randomness and global determinism. When a fetus is formed, an initial cell subdivides a number of times. At some point (exactly why is not known), some cells form the heart, some the lungs, and so on. These cells migrate to their proper positions; a deterministic process of some kind causes this specialization. As the cells travel, most reach the appointed position, but some die. Thus, at the local cell level, whether an individual cell lives or dies is completely probabilistic, while globally, a deterministic process causes the migration of cells necessary to organize life.

Another example is a fluid heated from below. At low levels, the fluid becomes heated by convection, eventually reaching an equilibrium level of maximum entropy. All of the water molecules move independently. There is both global and local randomness. However, once the heat passes a critical level, the independent molecules behave coherently, as convection rolls set in. The fluid heated from below rises to the upper levels, cools, and falls again in a circular manner. The individual molecules begin behaving coherently, as a group. Scientists know precisely when these convection rolls (called Raleigh–Bayard convections) will begin. What is unknown is the direction of the rolls. Some move right, some move left. There is no way to predict which direction the roll will travel. Once again, we have global determinism (the temperature convection rolls begin) and local randomness (the direction of a particular roll).

Finally, we have the development of society and ideas. Innovations, such as the development of CAPM, often arise spontaneously and independently. The probability that any individual will create such an innovation is random, no matter how promising the person's abilities. Yet, for any system to evolve and develop, such innovations must be expected to occur on a global basis—whether in science, government, the arts, or economics—if the system is expected to survive.

In the world of the Demiurge, randomness equates with innovation, and determinism explains how the system exploits the innovation. In markets, innovation is information, and determinism is how the markets value that information.

Now we have the third blow to Newtonian determinism: the science of chaos and fractals, where chance and necessity coexist. In these systems, entropy is high but never reaches its maximum disorderly state because of global determinism, as in the Raleigh–Bayard convection cells. Chaotic systems export their entropy, or "dissipate" it, in much the way that mechanical devices dissipate some of their energy as friction. Thus, chaotic systems are also dissipative and have many characteristics in common with thermodynamics—especially the arrow of time.

FRACTAL MATHEMATICS

All this conceptual distinction between the world of the Demiurge and the Euclidean geometry of the Good is interesting, but can it be made practical? After all, the main advantage of Euclidean geometry is its elegant simplicity. Problems can be approximated using Euclidean geometry, and solved for optimal answers. Models can be easily generated, even if they are gross simplifications. Can these ever increasingly complex forms that we have called fractals also be modeled?

The answer is Yes. Strangely, they can be modeled in a fairly simple manner. However, fractal math often seems counterintuitive as well as imprecise. It seems counterintuitive because all of us, even nonmathematicians, have been trained to think in a Euclidean fashion. That is, we approximate natural objects with simple forms, like children's drawings of pine trees. Details are added later, independent of the main figure. Fractal math seems imprecise because traditional mathematical proofs are hard to come by and develop: our concept of a "proof" is descended, again, from ancient Greek geometry. Euclid developed the system of axioms, theorems, and proof for his geometry. We have since extended these concepts to all other branches of mathematics. Fractal geometry has its share of proofs, but our primary method for exploring fractals is through numerical experiments. Using a computer, we can generate solutions and explore the implications of our fractal formulas. This "experimental" form of exploring mathematics is new and not yet respectable among most pure mathematicians.

THE CHAOS GAME

The following example of a mathematical experiment was used in my earlier book, *Chaos and Order in the Capital Markets* (1991a), as well as in other texts. It was originally devised by Barnesley (1988), who informally calls it the *Chaos Game*.

To play the game, we start with three points that outline a triangle. We label the three points (1,2), (3,4), and (5,6). This is the playing board for the game, and is shown in Figure 1.1(a). Now pick a point at random. This point can be within the triangle outline, or outside of it. Label the point P. Roll a fair die. Proceed halfway from point P to the point (or angle) labeled with the rolled number, and plot a new point. If you roll a 6, move halfway from point P to the angle labeled C(5,6) and plot a new point (Figure 1.1(b)). Using a computer, repeat these steps 10,000 times. If you throw out the first 50 points as transients, you end up with the picture in Figure 1.1(c). Called the Sierpinski triangle, it is an infinite number of triangles contained within the larger triangle. If you increase the resolution, you will see even more small triangles. This self-similarity is an important (though not exclusive) characteristic of fractals.

Interestingly, the shape is not dependent on the initial point. No matter where you start, you always end up with the Sierpinski triangle, despite the fact that two "random" events are needed to play the game: (1) the selection of the initial point, and (2) the roll of the die. Thus, at a local level, the points are always plotted in a random order. Even though the points are plotted in a different order each time we play the game, the Sierpinski triangle always emerges because the system reacts to the random events in a deterministic manner. Local randomness

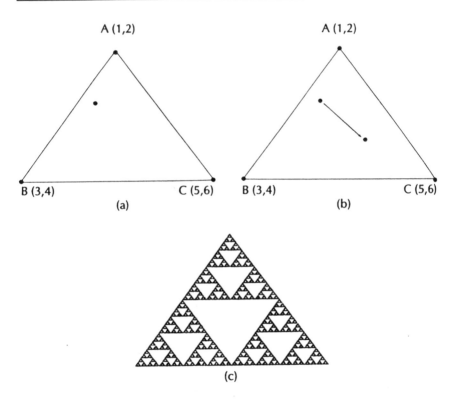

FIGURE 1.1 The Chaos Game. (a) Start with three points, an equal distance apart, and randomly draw a point within the boundaries defined by the points. (b) Assuming you roll a fair die that comes up number 6, you go halfway to the point marked C(5,6). (c) Repeat step (b) 10,000 times and you have the Sierpinski triangle.

and global determinism create a stable structure. Appendix 1 includes a BASIC program shell for creating the Sierpinski triangle. You are encouraged to try this yourself.

The Chaos Game shows us that local randomness and global determinism can coexist to create a stable, self-similar structure, which we have called a fractal. Prediction of the actual sequence of points is impossible. Yet, the odds of plotting each point are *not* equal. The empty spaces within each triangle have a zero percent probability of being plotted. The edges outlining each triangle have a higher probability of occurring. Thus, local randomness does not equate with equal probability of all possible solutions. It also does not equate with independence. The position of the next point is entirely dependent on the current point, which is itself dependent on the previous points. From this, we can see that "fractal statistics" will be different from its Gaussian counterpart.

At this point, a relationship to markets can be intuitively made. Markets may be locally random, but they have a global statistical structure that is nonrandom. In this way, traditional quantitative theory would tend to support local randomness. Tests on "market efficiency" have long focused on whether short-term predictions can be made with enough accuracy to profit. Typically, quantitative studies have shown that it is difficult to profit from short-term (weekly or less) market moves. Yet, lengthening our time horizon seems to improve our predictive ability.

WHAT IS A FRACTAL?

We have not yet defined the term *fractal*. No precise definition actually exists. Even mathematics, the most concise of all languages, has trouble describing a fractal. It is similar to the question posed by Deep Thought in *The Hitchhiker's Guide to the Galaxy* by Douglas Adams. Deep Thought is a supercomputer created by a superrace to answer "The Ultimate Question of Life, the Universe, and Everything." Deep Thought gives an answer (the answer is "42"), but no one knows how to pose the question so that the answer can be understood.

Fractals are like that. We know them when we see them, but we have a hard time describing them with enough precision to understand fully what they are. Benoit Mandelbrot, the father of fractal geometry, has not developed a precise definition either.

Fractals do have certain characteristics that are measurable, and properties that are desirable for modeling purposes.

The first property, *self-similarity,* has already been described at some length. It means that the parts are in some way related to the whole. This similarity can be "precise," as in the Sierpinski triangle, where each small triangle is geometrically identical with the larger triangle. This precise form of self-similarity exists only mathematically.

In real life, the self-similarity is "qualitative"; that is, the object or process is similar at different scales, spatial or temporal, statistically. Each scale resembles the other scales, but is not identical. Individual branches of a tree are qualitatively self-similar to the other branches, but each branch is also unique. This self-similar property makes the fractal *scale-invariant:* it lacks a characteristic scale from which the others derive.

The logarithmic spiral, which plays a prominent role in Elliott Wave theory, is one example of a characteristic scaling function. A nautilus shell is a logarithmic spiral because the spiral retains its original proportions as the size increases. Therefore, the nautilus grows, but does not change its shape, because it grows according to a characteristic proportion—it has a characteristic scaling feature. The logarithmic spiral is not fractal. Neither is Elliot Wave theory.

Likewise, early models to explain the construction of the mammalian lung were based on an exponential scaling mechanism. In particular, the diameter of each branching generation should decrease by about the same ratio from one generation to the next. If z represents the generation number, and d_z is the average diameter of branch generation z, then:

$$d_z = q*d_{z-1}d_0 \tag{1.1}$$

Weibel and Gomez (1962) estimated $q = 2^{-1/3}$, so equation (1.1) can be rewritten as:

$$\overline{d}_z = d_0*2^{-z/3} \tag{1.2}$$

where d_0 = diameter of the trachea (the main branch of the lung)

Thus, this model has a characteristic scaling parameter, $q = 2^{-1/3}$. Each branching generation scales down, according to an exact ratio, to the way the previous generation scaled down. This is a characteristic scale.

Equation (1.1) can be rewritten in a more general form:

$$d_{z,\alpha} = d_0*e^{-\alpha*z} \tag{1.3}$$

where $\alpha = -\ln(q) > 0$

As West, Valmik, and Goldberger (1986) state: "Thus, if a single parameter α characterized this process, then d(z,α) is interpreted as the average diameter in the zth generation for the scaling parameter α." Note the exponential form of equation (1.3) using a characteristic scale.

However, modeling the lung based on a characteristic scale ignores other properties. Within each generation, the actual diameters have a range: some are larger and some are smaller than the average. In addition, the exponential scaling law fits only the first ten branching generations. After that, there is a systematic deviation from the characteristic scaling function.

Figure 1.2 is taken from West and Goldberger (1987). If equation (1.3) holds, then a plot of the log of the diameter against the generation number should result in a straight line. The slope of this semi-log plot should be the

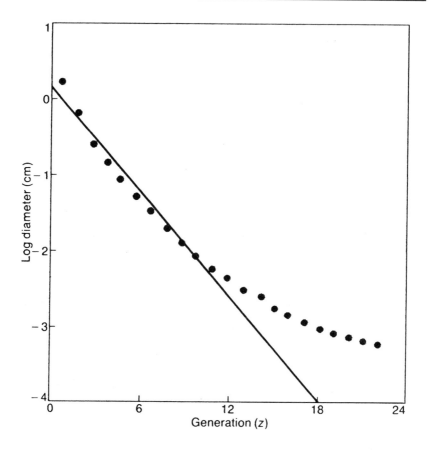

FIGURE 1.2 The lung with exponential scaling. (From West and Goldberger (1987); reproduced with permission from *American Scientist.*)

scaling factor. We can see that the exponential scaling feature does not capture the full shape of the lung. However, a log/log plot (Figure 1.3), using the log of the generation number, does yield a wavy line that trends in the right direction. But what does the log/log plot mean?

The failure of the semi-log plot to capture the data means that the exponential scaling model is inappropriate for this system. The model should use a power law (a real number raised to a power) rather than an exponential (e raised to a power). This power law scaling feature, which does explain the scaling structure of the lung, turns out to be the second characteristic of fractals, the *fractal dimension*, which can describe either a physical structure like the lung or a time series.

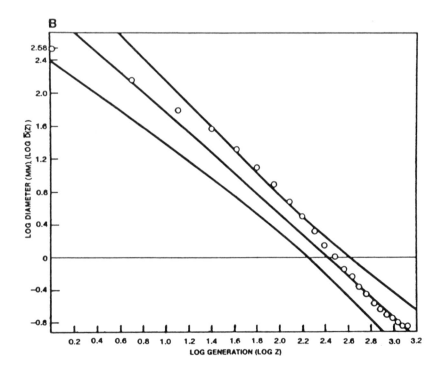

FIGURE 1.3   Log/Log plot.

THE FRACTAL DIMENSION

To discuss the fractal dimension, we must return to the conflict between the Good and the Demiurge. A primary characteristic of Euclidean geometry is that dimensions are integers. Lines are one-dimensional. Planes are two-dimensional. Solids are three-dimensional. Even the hyperdimensions developed in later eras are integer-dimensional. For instance, the space/time continuum of Einstein is four-dimensional, with time as the fourth dimension. Euclidean shapes are "perfect," as can be expected from the Good. They are smooth, continuous, homogeneous, and symmetrical. They are also inadequate to describe the world of the Demiurge, except as gross simplifications.

Consider a simple object—a wiffle ball. It is not three-dimensional because it has holes. It is not two-dimensional either, because it has depth. Despite the fact that it resides in a three-dimensional space, it is less than a solid, but more than a plane. Its dimension is somewhere between two and three. It is a noninteger, a fractional dimension.

Now consider a mathematical construct like the Sierpinski triangle, which is clearly more than a line but less than a plane. There are, within it, holes and gaps shaped like triangles. These *discontinuities* classify the Sierpinski triangle as a child of the Demiurge, and, like the wiffle ball, its dimension is a fraction.

The fractal dimension characterizes how the object fills its space. In addition, it describes the structure of the object as the magnification factor is changed, or, again, how the object scales. For physical (or geometric) fractals, this scaling law takes place in space. A fractal time series scales statistically, in time.

The fractal dimension of a time series measures how jagged the time series is. As would be expected, a straight line has a fractal dimension of 1, the same as its Euclidean dimension. A random time series has a fractal dimension of 1.50. One early method for calculating the fractal dimension involves covering the curve with circles of a radius, r. We would count the number of circles needed to cover the curve, and then increase the radius. When we do so, we find that the number of circles scales as follows:

$$N*(2*r)^d = 1 \tag{1.4}$$

where N = the number of circles
    r = radius
    d = the fractal dimension

Because a line would scale according to a straight linear scale, its fractal dimension would be equal to 1. However, a random walk has a 50–50 chance of rising or falling; hence, its fractal dimension is 1.50. However, if the fractal dimension is between 1 and 1.50, the time series is more than a line and less than a random walk. It is smoother than a random walk but more jagged than a line. Using logarithms, equation (1.4) can be transformed into:

$$d = \log(N)/\log\left(\frac{1}{2*r}\right) \tag{1.5}$$

Once again, the fractal dimension can be solved as the slope of a log/log plot. For a time series, we would increase the radius as an increment of time, and count the number of circles needed to cover the entire time series as a function of the time increment. Thus, the fractal dimension of a time series is a function of scaling in time.

The circle counting method is quite tedious and imprecise for a long time series, even when done by computers. In Part Two, we will study a more precise method called rescaled range analysis (R/S).

The fractal dimension of a time series is important because it recognizes that a process can be somewhere between deterministic (a line with fractal dimension of 1) and random (a fractal dimension of 1.50). In fact, the fractal dimension of a line can range from 1 to 2. At values $1.50 < d < 2$, a time series is *more* jagged than a random series, or has more reversals. Needless to say, the statistics of time series with fractal dimensions different from 1.50 would be quite different from Gaussian statistics, and would not necessarily be contained within the normal distribution.

FRACTAL MARKET ANALYSIS

This book deals with this issue, which can be summarized as the conflict between randomness and determinism. On the one hand, there are market analysts who feel that the market is perfectly deterministic; on the other, there is a group who feel that the market is completely random. We will see that there is a possibility that both are right to a limited extent. But what comes out of these partial truths is quite different from the outcome either group expects.

We will use a number of different analyses, but the primary focus of this book is R/S, or rescaled range analysis. R/S analysis can distinguish fractal from other types of time series, revealing the self-similar statistical structure. This structure fits a theory of market structure called the Fractal Market Hypothesis, which will be stated fully in Chapter 3. Alternative explanations of the fractal structure are also examined, including the possible combining of the well-known ARCH (autoregressive conditional heteroskedastic) family of processes, with fractal distributions. This reconciliation ties directly into the concept of local randomness and global determinism.

First, we must reexamine, for purposes of contrast, existing Capital Market Theory (CMT).

2

Failure of the Gaussian Hypothesis

When faced with a multidimensional process of unknown origin, scientists often select an independent process such as brownian motion as a working hypothesis. If analysis shows that prediction is difficult, the hypothesis is accepted as truth. Fluid turbulence was modeled in this manner for decades. In general, markets continue to be modeled in this fashion.

Brownian motion has desirable characteristics to a mathematician. Statistics can be estimated with great precision, and probabilities can be calculated. However, using traditional statistics to model the markets assumes that they are games of chance. Each outcome is independent of previous outcomes. Investment in securities is equated with gambling.

In most games of chance, many degrees of freedom are employed to make the outcome random. In roulette, the spin of the wheel in one direction and the release of the ball in the opposite direction bring into play a number of nonrepeatable elements: the speed of the wheel when the ball is released, the initial velocity of the ball, the point of release on the wheel, and, finally, the angle of the ball's release. If you think that it would be possible to duplicate the conditions of a particular play, you would be wrong. The nonlinearity of the ball's spiral descent would amplify in a short time to a completely different landing number. The result is a system with a limited number of degrees of freedom, but with inherent unpredictability. Each outcome, however, is independent of the previous one.

A shuffled deck of cards is often used as an exemplary random system. Most card games require skill in decision making, but each hand dealt is independent of the previous one. A "lucky run" is merely an illusion, or an attempt by a player to impose order on a random process.

An exception is the game of blackjack, or "21." Related examples include baccarat and chemin de fer, games beloved of European casinos and James Bond enthusiasts. In blackjack, two cards are dealt to each player. The objective is to achieve a total value of 21 or lower (picture cards count as ten). A player can ask for additional cards. In its original form, a single deck was played until the cards were exhausted, at which point the deck was reshuffled.

Edward Thorpe, a mathematician, realized that a card deck used in this manner had a "memory"; that is, the outcome of a current hand depended on previous hands because those cards had left the system. By keeping track of the cards used, he could assess the shifting probabilities as play progressed, and bet on the most favorable hands. Upon discovering this "statistical memory," casinos responded by using multiple decks, as baccarat and chemin de fer are played, thus eliminating the memory.

These two examples of "games of chance" show that not all gambling is necessarily governed by Gaussian statistics. There are unpredictable systems with a limited number of degrees of freedom. In addition, there can be processes that have a long memory, even if they are probabilistic in the short term.

Despite these exceptions, common practice is to state all probabilities in Gaussian terms. Plato said that our world was not the real world because it did not conform to Euclid's geometry. We say that all unpredictable systems must be Gaussian, or independent processes. The passage of almost 2,500 years since Plato has not diminished our ability to delude ourselves.

CAPITAL MARKET THEORY

Traditional Capital Market Theory (CMT) has been largely based on fair games of chance, or "martingales." The insight that speculation can be modeled by probabilities extends back to Bachelier (1900) and continues to this day. My earlier book (Peters, 1991a) elaborated on the development of CMT and its continuing dependence on statistical measures like standard deviation as proxies for risk. This section will not unduly repeat those arguments, but will instead discuss some of the underlying rationale in continuing to use Gaussian statistics to model asset prices.

It has long been conventional to view security prices and their associated returns from the perspective of the speculator—the ability of an individual to profit on a security by anticipating its future value before other speculators do. Thus, a speculator bets that the current price of a security is above/below its future value and sells/buys it accordingly at the current price. Speculation involves betting, which makes investing a form of gambling. (Indeed, probability was developed as a direct result of the development of gambling using "bones," an early form of dice.) Bachelier's "Theory of Speculation" (1900) does just that. Lord Keynes continued this view by his famous comment that markets are driven by "animal spirits." More recently, Nobel Laureate Harry Markowitz (1952, 1959) used wheels of chance to explain standard deviation to his audience. He did this in order to present his insight that standard deviation is a measure of risk, and the covariance of returns could be used to explain how diversification (grouping uncorrelated or negatively correlated stocks) reduced risk (the standard deviation of the portfolio).

Equating investment with speculation continued with the Black–Scholes option pricing model, and other equilibrium-based theories. Theories of speculation, including Modern Portfolio Theory (MPT), did not differentiate between short-term speculators and long-term investors. Why?

Markets were assumed to be "efficient"; that is, prices already reflected all current information that could anticipate future events. Therefore, only the speculative, stochastic component could be modeled; the change in prices due to changes in value could not. If market returns are normally distributed "white" noise, then they are the same at all investment horizons. This is equivalent to the "hiss" heard on a tape player. The sound is the same regardless of the speed of the tape.

We are left with a theory that has assumed away the differentiating features of many investors trading over many investment horizons. The risks to each are the same. Risk and return grow at a commiserative rate over time. There is no advantage to being a long-term investor. In addition, price changes are determined primarily by speculators. By implication, forecasting changes in economic value would not be useful to speculators.

This uncoupling of changes in the value of the underlying security from the economy and the shifting of price changes mostly to speculators have reinforced the perception that investing and gambling are equivalent, no matter what the investment horizon. This stance is most clearly seen in the common practice of actuaries to model the liabilities of pension funds by taking short-term returns (annual returns) and risk (the standard deviation of monthly returns), and extrapolating them out over 30-year horizons. It is also reflected in the tendency of individuals and the media to focus on short-term trends and values.

If markets do not follow a random walk, it is possible that we may be over- or understating our risk and return potential from investing versus speculating. In the next section, we will examine the statistical characteristics of markets more closely.

STATISTICAL CHARACTERISTICS OF MARKETS

In general, statistical analysis requires the normal distribution, or the familiar bell-shaped curve. It is well known that market returns are not normally distributed, but this information has been downplayed or rationalized away over the years to maintain the crucial assumption that market returns follow a random walk.

Figure 2.1 shows the frequency distribution of 5-day and 90-day Dow Jones Industrials returns from January 2, 1888, through December 31, 1991, some 103 years. The normal distribution is also shown for comparison. Both return distributions are characterized by a high peak at the mean and fatter tails than the normal distribution, and the two Dow distributions are virtually the same shape. The kink upward at four standard deviations is the total greater than (less than) four (−4) standard deviations above (below) the mean. Figure 2.2 shows the total probability contained within intervals of standard deviation for

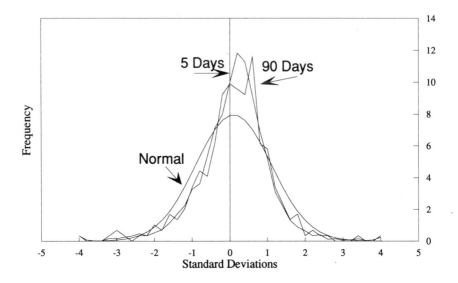

FIGURE 2.1   Dow Jones Industrials, frequency distribution of returns: 1888–1991.

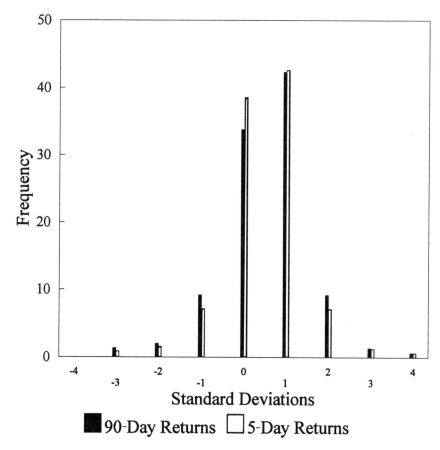

FIGURE 2.2   Dow Jones Industrials, frequency within intervals.

the two Dow investment horizons. Again, the two distributions are very similar, and they are not "normal." Figure 2.3 shows the difference between the 5-day return distribution and the normal distribution. The tails are not only fatter than the normal distribution, they are *uniformly* fatter. Up to four standard deviations away from the mean, we have as many observations as we did two standard deviations away from the mean. Even at four sigmas, the tails are not converging to zero.

Figure 2.4 shows similar difference curves for (a)1-day, (b)10-day, (c)20-day, (d)30-day, and (e)90-day returns. In all cases, the tails are fatter, and the peaks are higher than in the normal distribution. In fact, they all look similar to one another.

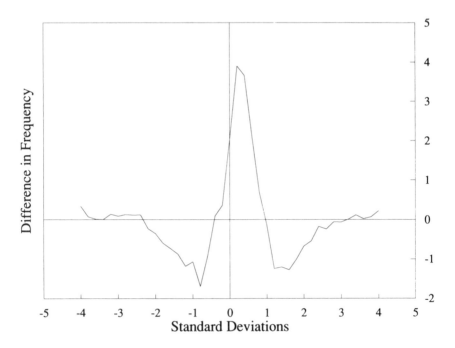

FIGURE 2.3   Dow Jones Industrials, 5-day returns — normal frequency.

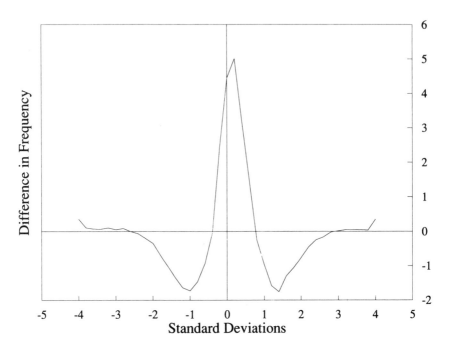

FIGURE 2.4a   Dow Jones Industrials, 1-day returns — normal frequency.

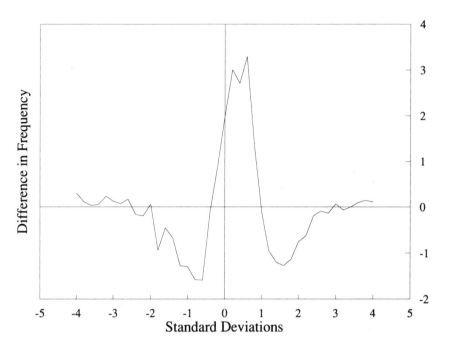

FIGURE 2.4b Dow Jones Industrials, 10-day returns − normal frequency.

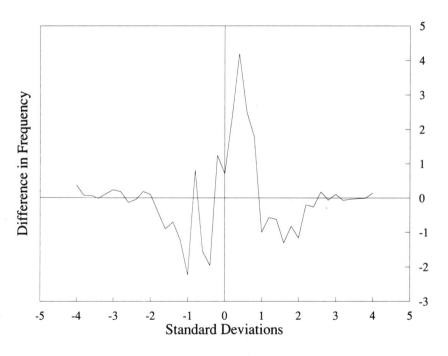

FIGURE 2.4c Dow Jones Industrials, 20-day returns − normal frequency.

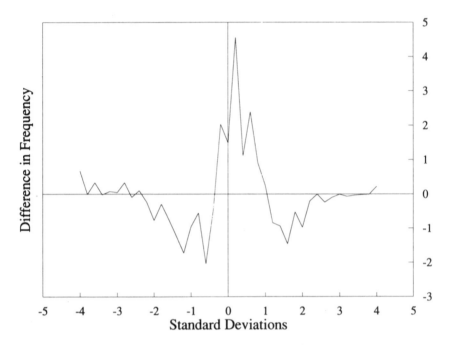

FIGURE 2.4d   Dow Jones Industrials, 30-day returns − normal frequency.

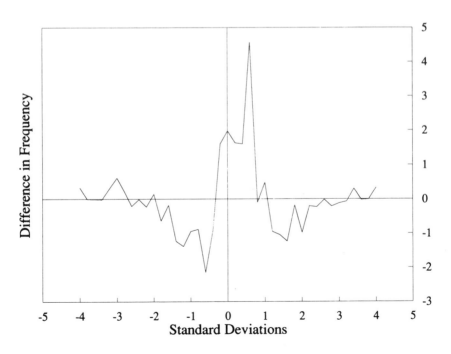

FIGURE 2.4e   Dow Jones Industrials, 90-day returns − normal frequency.

What does this mean? The risk of a large event's occurring is much higher than the normal distribution implies. The normal distribution says that the probability of a greater-than-three standard deviation event's occurring is 0.5 percent, or 5 in 1,000. Yet, Figure 2.2 shows us that the actual probability is 2.4 percent, or 24 in 1,000. Thus, the probability of a large event is almost five times greater than the normal distribution implies. As we measure still larger events, the gap between theory and reality becomes even more pronounced. The probability of a four standard deviation event is actually 1 percent instead of 0.01 percent, or 100 times greater. In addition, this risk is virtually identical in all the investment horizons shown here. Therefore, daily traders face the same number of six-sigma events in their time frame as 90-day investors face in theirs. This statistical self-similarity, which should sound familiar to those who have read Chapter 1, will be discussed in detail in Chapter 7.

Figures 2.5 and 2.6 show similar distributions for the yen/dollar exchange rate (1971–1990), and 20-year U.S. T-Bond yields (1979–1992), respectively. Fat tails are not just a stock market phenomenon. Other capital markets show similar characteristics. These fat-tailed distributions are often evidence of a

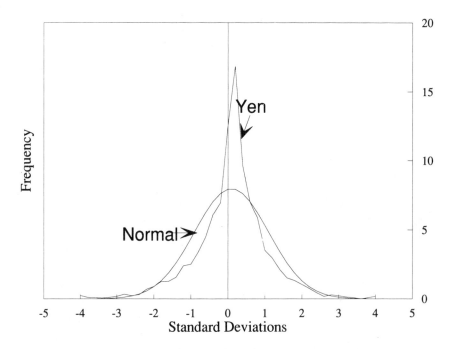

FIGURE 2.5 Yen/Dollar exchange rate, frequency distribution of returns: 1971–1990.

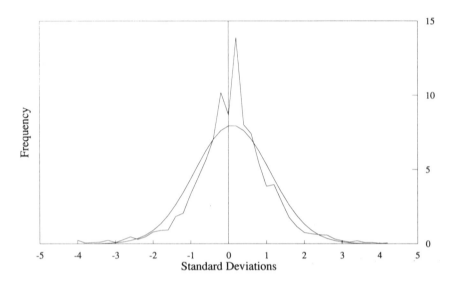

FIGURE 2.6   Twenty-year U.S. T-Bond yields, frequency distribution of returns: 1979–1992.

long-memory system generated by a nonlinear stochastic process. This nonlinear process can be caused by time-varying variance (ARCH), or a long-memory process called Pareto–Levy. In due course, we will discuss both. At this point, we can simply say that fat-tailed distributions are often symptomatic of a nonlinear stochastic process.

THE TERM STRUCTURE OF VOLATILITY

Another basic assumption needed to apply the normal distribution involves the term structure of volatility. Typically, we use standard deviation to measure volatility, and we assume that it scales according to the square root of time. For instance, we "annualize" the standard deviation of monthly returns by multiplying it by the square root of 12. This practice is derived from Einstein's (1905) observation that the *distance* that a particle in brownian motion covers increases with the square root of time used to measure it.

However, despite this widespread method for "annualizing risk," it has been well known for some time that standard deviation scales at a faster rate than the square root of time. Turner and Weigel (1990), Shiller (1989), and Peters (1991b) are recent empirical studies confirming this scale rate. Lagged white noise, ARCH disturbances, and other causes have been investigated to account for this property, which goes so contrary to random walk theory and the Efficient Market Hypothesis (EMH).

Stocks

The term structure of volatility is even stranger than these researchers thought. Figure 2.7 is a plot of the log of standard deviation versus the log of time for the 103-year daily Dow Jones Industrials data. This graph was done by evenly dividing the full 103-year period into all subintervals that included both the beginning and end points. Because the number of usable subperiods depends on the total number of points, an interval of 25,000 days was used. Returns were calculated for contiguous periods, and the standard deviations of these returns were calculated. Table 2.1 lists the results. Thus, we have subperiods ranging from 25,000 one-day returns, to four 6,250-day returns, or about 28 years.

The square root of time is shown by the solid 45-degree line in Figure 2.7. Volatility does indeed grow at a faster rate than the square root of time. Table 2.2 first shows the regression results up to 1,000 days ($N = {<}1{,}000$ days). Up to this point, standard deviation grows at the 0.53 root of time. Compared to the regression results after 1,000 days ($N = {>}1{,}000$ days), the slope has dropped dramatically to 0.25. If we think of risk as standard deviation,

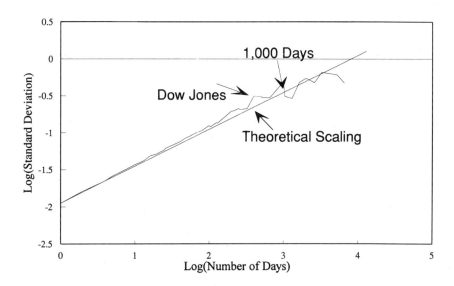

FIGURE 2.7   Dow Jones Industrials, volatility term structure: 1888–1990.

Table 2.1   Dow Jones Industrials, Term Structure of
Volatility: 1888–1990

Number of Days	Standard Deviation	Number of Days	Standard Deviation
1	0.011176	130	0.135876
2	0.016265	200	0.196948
4	0.022354	208	0.196882
5	0.025838	250	0.213792
8	0.032904	260	0.20688
10	0.037065	325	0.213301
13	0.041749	400	0.314616
16	0.048712	500	0.309865
20	0.052278	520	0.301762
25	0.058831	650	0.298672
26	0.061999	1,000	0.493198
40	0.075393	1,040	0.314733
50	0.087089	1,300	0.293109
52	0.087857	1,625	0.482494
65	0.0989	2,000	0.548611
80	0.107542	2,600	0.479879
100	0.125939	3,250	0.660229
104	0.120654	5,200	0.612204
125	0.137525	6,500	0.475797

Table 2.2   Dow Jones Industrials, Regression Results,
Term Structure of Volatility: 1888–1990

	N = <1,000 Days	N = >1,000 Days
Regression output:		
Constant	−1.96757	−1.47897
Standard error of Y (estimated)	0.026881	0.10798
R squared	0.996032	0.612613
Number of observations	30	10
Degrees of freedom	28	8
X coefficient(s)	0.534713	0.347383
Standard error of coefficient	0.006378	0.097666

investors incur more risk than is implied by the normal distribution for investment horizons of less than four years. However, investors incur increasingly less risk for investment horizons greater than four years. As we have always known, long-term investors incur less risk than short-term investors.

Another approach is to examine the ratio of return to risk, or, as it is better known, the "Sharpe ratio," named after its creator, Nobel Laureate William Sharpe. The Sharpe ratio shows how much return is received per unit of risk, or standard deviation. (See Table 2.3.) For periods of less than 1,000 days, or four years, the Sharpe ratio steadily declines; at 1,200 days, it increases dramatically. This means that long-term investors are rewarded more, per unit of risk, than are short-term investors.

Statistically speaking, the term structure of volatility shows that the stock market is not a random walk. At best, it is a stochastic "bounded" set. This means that there are limits to how far the random walker will wander before he or she heads back home.

The most popular explanation for boundedness is that returns are mean reverting. A mean-reverting stochastic process can produce a bounded set, but not

Table 2.3   Dow Jones Industrials: 1888–1990

Number of Days	Sharpe Ratio	Number of Days	Sharpe Ratio
1	1.28959	130	1.13416
2	1.217665	200	0.830513
4	1.289289	208	0.864306
5	1.206357	250	0.881
8	1.190143	260	0.978488
10	1.172428	325	1.150581
13	1.201372	400	0.650904
16	1.086107	500	0.838771
20	1.178697	520	0.919799
25	1.163449	650	1.173662
26	1.0895	1,000	0.66218
40	1.133486	1,040	1.691087
50	1.061851	1,300	2.437258
52	1.085109	1,625	1.124315
65	1.070387	2,000	1.070333
80	1.114178	2,600	1.818561
100	1.015541	3,250	1.200915
104	1.150716	5,200	2.234748
125	1.064553	6,500	4.624744

an increasing Sharpe ratio. A mean reverting process implies a zero sum game. Exceptionally high returns in one period are offset by lower than average returns later. The Sharpe ratio would remain constant because returns would also be bounded. Thus, mean reversion in returns is not a completely satisfying explanation for the boundedness of volatility. Regardless, the process that produces the observed term structure of volatility is clearly not Gaussian, nor is it described well by the normal distribution.

Finally, we can see that short-term investors face different risks than long-term investors in U.S. stocks. "Short-term" now means investment horizons of less than four years. At this level, we have seen that the frequency distribution of returns is self-similar up to 90 days. We can speculate that this self-similar statistical structure will continue up to approximately four-year horizons, although we will all be long gone before we can obtain enough empirical evidence. In the longer term, something else happens. The difference in standard deviation between the long term and short term affects how we analyze markets. The tools we use depend on our investment horizon. This certainly applies to stocks, but what about other markets?

Bonds

Despite the fact that the U.S. bond market is large and deep, there is an absence of "high-frequency" information; that is, trading information is hard to come by at intervals shorter than monthly. Bonds are traded over-the-counter, and no exchange exists to record the trades. The longest time series I could obtain was daily 20-year T-Bond yields maintained by the Fed from January 1, 1979, through September 30, 1992, a mere 14 years of data. (See Figure 2.8.) However, we can see—less convincingly, to be sure—a term structure of bond volatility that is similar to the one we saw for stocks. Table 2.4 summarizes the results.

Currencies

For currencies, we face similar data problems. Until the Bretton Woods agreement of 1972, exchange rates did not float; they were fixed by the respective governments. From 1973 onward, however, we have plenty of information on many different, actively traded exchange rates.

In Figure 2.5, we saw that the yen/dollar exchange rate had the now familiar fat-tailed distribution. Figure 2.9(a)–(c) shows similar frequency distributions for the mark/dollar, pound/dollar, and yen/pound exchange rates. In all cases,

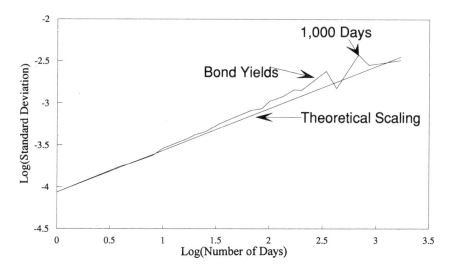

FIGURE 2.8 Daily bond yields, volatility term structure: January 1, 1979–September 30, 1992.

we have a similarly shaped distribution. In fact, the frequency distribution of currency returns has a higher peak and fatter tails than U.S. stocks or bonds.

Figure 2.10(a)–(c) shows the term structure of volatility for the three exchange rates, and Table 2.5 shows the log/log regression results. In all cases, the slope—and hence, the scaling of standard deviation—increases at a faster rate than U.S. stocks or bonds, and *they are not bounded.*

Table 2.4 Long T-Bonds, Term Structure of Volatility:
January 1, 1978–June 30, 1990

	N = <1,000 Days	N = >1,000 Days
Regression output:		
Constant	−4.0891	−2.26015
Standard error		
of Y (estimated)	0.053874	0.085519
R squared	0.985035	0.062858
Number of		
observations	21	3
Degrees of		
freedom	19	1
X coefficient(s)	0.548102	−0.07547
Standard error		
of coefficient	0.015499	0.29141

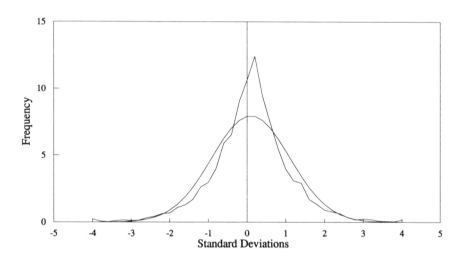

FIGURE 2.9a   Mark/Dollar, frequency distribution of returns.

To examine whether U.S. stocks remain a bounded set over this period, we check the term structure of volatility in Figure 2.7. It remains bounded. Table 2.5 includes these results as well. Therefore, either currencies have a longer "bounded" interval than stocks, or they have no bounds. The latter would imply that exchange rate risk grows at a faster rate than the normal distribution but never stops growing. Therefore, long-term holders of currency face ever-increasing

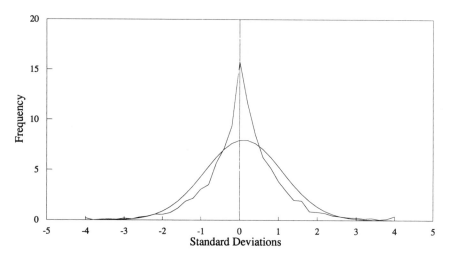

FIGURE 2.9b   Pound/Dollar, frequency distribution of returns.

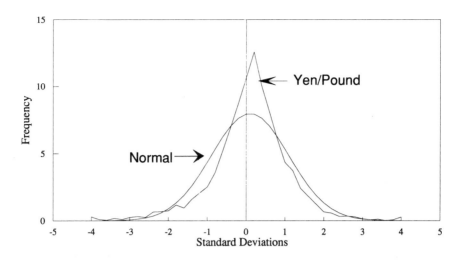

FIGURE 2.9c   Yen/Pound, frequency distribution of returns.

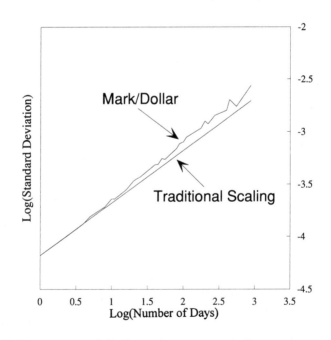

FIGURE 2.10a   Mark/Dollar exchange rate, volatility term structure.

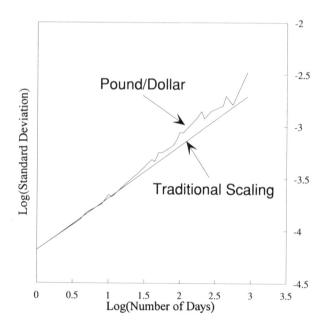

FIGURE 2.10b   Pound/Dollar exchange rate, volatility term structure.

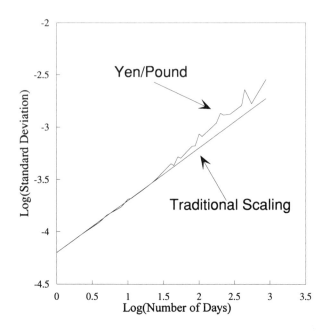

FIGURE 2.10c   Yen/Pound exchange rate, volatility term structure.

Table 2.5 Currency Exchange Rates, Term Structure of Volatility

	Mark/Dollar	Pound/Dollar	Yen/Pound
Regression output:			
Constant	−4.19741	−4.22978	−4.25958
Standard error of Y (estimated)	0.023194	0.040975	0.042455
R squared	0.99712	0.991569	0.991174
Number of observations	27	27	27
Degrees of freedom	25	25	25
X coefficient(s)	0.548986	0.565224	0.572267
Standard error of coefficient	0.0059	0.010424	0.0108

levels of risk as their investment horizon widens. Unlike stocks and bonds, currencies offer no investment incentive to a buy-and-hold strategy.

In the short term, stock, bond, and currency speculators face similar risks, but in the long term, stock and bond investors face reduced risk.

THE BOUNDED SET

The appearance of bounds for stocks and bonds, but not for currencies, seems puzzling at first. Why should currencies be a different type of security than stocks and bonds? That question contains its own answer.

In mathematics, paradoxes occur when an assumption is inadvertently forgotten. A common mistake is to divide by a variable that may take zero as a value. In the above paragraph, the question called a currency a "security." Currencies are traded entities, but they are not securities. They have no investment value. The only return one can get from a currency is by *speculating* on its value versus that of another currency. Currencies are, thus, equivalent to the purely speculative vehicles that are commonly equated with stocks and bonds.

Stocks and bonds are different. They do have investment value. Bonds earn interest, and a stock's value is tied to the growth in its earnings through economic activity. The aggregate stock market is tied to the aggregate economy. Currencies are not tied to the economic cycle. In the 1950s and 1960s, we had an expanding economy and a strong dollar. In the 1980s, we had an expanding economy and a falling dollar. Currencies do not have a "fundamental" value that is necessarily related to economic activity, though it may be tied to economic variables like interest rates.

Why are stocks and bonds bounded sets? A mean-reverting stochastic process is a possible explanation of boundedness, but it does not explain the faster-growing standard deviation. Bounds and fast-growing standard deviations are usually caused by deterministic systems with periodic or nonperiodic cycles.

Figure 2.11 shows the term structure of volatility for a simple sine wave. We can clearly see the bounds of the system and the faster-growing standard deviation. But we know that the stock and bond markets are not periodic. Granger (1964) and others have performed extensive spectral analysis and have found no evidence of periodic cycles.

However, Peters (1991b) and Cheng and Tong (1992) have found evidence of nonperiodic cycles typically generated by nonlinear dynamical systems, or "chaos."

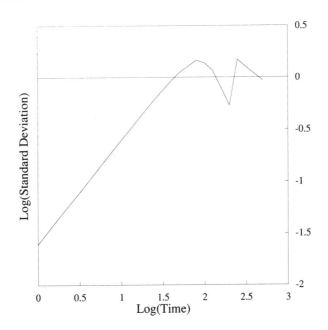

FIGURE 2.11   Sine wave, volatility term structure.

At this point, we can see evidence that stocks, bonds, and currencies are possible nonlinear stochastic processes in the short term, as evidenced by their frequency distributions and their term structures of volatility. However, stocks and bonds show evidence of long-term determinism. Again, we see local randomness and global determinism.

SUMMARY

In this book, we will examine techniques for distinguishing among an independent process, a nonlinear stochastic process, and a nonlinear deterministic process, and will probe how these distinctions influence our investment strategies and our modeling capabilities. These strategies and modeling capabilities are closely tied to the asset type and to our investment horizon.

We have seen evidence that stocks and bonds are nonlinear stochastic in the short term and deterministic in the long term. Currencies appear to be nonlinear stochastic at all investment horizons. Investors would be more interested in the former; traders can work with all three vehicles in the short term.

3
A Fractal Market Hypothesis

We have seen in the previous chapter that the capital markets are not well-described by the normal distribution and random walk theory. Yet, the Efficient Market Hypothesis continues to be the dominant paradigm for how the markets work. Myron Scholes (coauthor of the Black–Scholes option pricing formula) said in *The New York Observer,* "It's not enough just to criticize." So, in this chapter, I offer an alternative theory of market structure.

The Efficient Market Hypothesis (EMH) was covered in detail in my earlier book (Peters, 1991b). However, a brief review of the EMH is necessary in order to offer an alternative. After that review, we shall go back to basics: Why do markets exist? What do participants expect and require from markets? From there, we shall formulate the Fractal Market Hypothesis. The Fractal Market Hypothesis is an alternative to the EMH, not to the Capital Asset Pricing Model (CAPM). But, because it is based on efficient markets, the CAPM also needs a replacement. Undoubtedly, such a replacement will be developed—perhaps, but not necessarily, based on the Fractal Market Hypothesis.

The Fractal Market Hypothesis gives an economic and mathematical structure to fractal market analysis. Through the Fractal Market Hypothesis, we can understand why self-similar statistical structures exist, as well as how risk is shared distributed among investors.

EFFICIENT MARKETS REVISITED

The EMH attempts to explain the statistical structure of the markets. In the case of the EMH, however, the theory came after the imposition of a statistical structure. Bachelier (1900) first proposed that markets follow a random walk and can be modeled by standard probability calculus. However, he offered little empirical proof that such was the case. Afterward, a number of mathematicians realized that stock market prices were a time series, and as long as the markets fulfilled certain restrictive requirements, they could be modeled by probability calculus. This approach had the advantage of offering a large body of tools for research. However, there was a division in the mathematical community about whether statistics (which dealt primarily with sampling and quality control) could be applied to time series.

The most stringent requirement was that the observations had to be independent or, at best, had to have a short-term memory; that is, the current change in prices could not be inferred from previous changes. This could occur only if price changes were a random walk and if the best estimate of the future price was the current price. The process would be a "martingale," or fair game. (A detailed history of the development of the EMH can be found in Peters (1991a).) The random walk model said that future price changes could not be inferred from past price changes. It said nothing about exogenous information—economic or fundamental information. Thus, random walk theory was primarily an attack on technical analysis. The EMH took this a step further by saying, in its "semistrong" form, that current prices reflected all public information—all past prices, published reports, and economic news—because of fundamental analysis. The current prices reflected this information because all investors had equal access to it, and, being "rational," they would, in their collective wisdom, value the security accordingly. Thus investors, in aggregate, could not profit from the market because the market "efficiently" valued securities at a price that reflected all known information.

If there had been sufficient empirical evidence to justify the EMH, then its development would have followed normal scientific reasoning, in which:

- A certain behavior and structure are first observed in a system or process.
- A theory is then developed to fit the known facts.
- The theory is modified or revised as new facts become known.

In the case of the EMH, the theory was developed to justify the use of statistical tools that require independence or, at best, a very short-term memory. The theory was often at variance with observed behavior. For instance, according to the EMH, the frequency of price changes should be well-represented by the normal distribution. We have seen in Chapter 2 that this is not the case. There are far too many large up-and-down changes at all frequencies for the normal curve to be fitted to these distributions. However, the large changes were labeled special events, or "anomalies," and were left out of the frequency distribution. When one leaves out the large changes and renormalizes, the normal distribution is the result. Price changes were labeled "approximately normal." Alternatives to the normal distribution, like the stable Paretian distribution, were rejected even though they fit the observed values without modification. Why? Standard statistical analysis could not be applied using those distributions.

The EMH, developed to make the mathematical environment easier, was truly a scientific case of putting the cart before the horse. Instead, we need to develop a market hypothesis that fits the observed facts and takes into account why markets exist to begin with.

STABLE MARKETS VERSUS EFFICIENT MARKETS

The New York Stock Exchange was started by a group of traders who gathered beneath that famous buttonwood tree in New York City. They shared one basic need: liquidity. They envisioned one place where they could all meet and find a buyer if one of them wanted to sell, and a seller if one of them wanted to buy. They wanted these transactions to bring a good price, but sometimes one takes what one can get. They needed sufficient liquidity to allow investors with different investment horizons to invest indifferently and anonymously with one another. In the past two centuries, technological advances have made trading of large volumes of stock easier; no matter what their investment horizon, buyers and sellers are matched up in a quick, efficient manner. Thus, day traders with a 15-minute investment horizon could trade efficiently with institutional investors with a monthly or longer investment horizon. Except for securities regulation to protect investors from fraud, there has been no attempt to make the trades "fair." A buyer who wants to buy a large block of a thinly traded stock must pay a premium for it. Investors who want to sell into a market with low demand will sell at a lower price than they would like. The technology is in place to ensure that a trader will find a buyer (or seller, as the case may be), but there is no agreed-on mechanism for determining what the "fair price" should be. The capitalist system of supply and demand is strictly adhered to.

Investors require liquidity from a market. Liquidity will ensure that:

1. The price investors get is *close* to what the market considers fair;
2. Investors with different investment horizons can trade efficiently with one another;

3. There are no panics or stampedes, which occur when supply and demand become imbalanced.

Liquidity is not the same as trading volume. The largest crashes have occurred when there has been low liquidity but high trading volume. Another name for low liquidity could be imbalanced trading volume.

The EMH says nothing about liquidity. It says that prices are always fair whether liquidity exists or not, or, alternatively, that there is always enough liquidity. Thus, the EMH cannot explain crashes and stampedes; when liquidity vanishes, getting a "fair" price may not be as important as completing the trade at any cost.

A stable market is not the same as an "efficient" market, as defined by the EMH. A stable market is a liquid market. If the market is liquid, then the price can be considered close to "fair." However, markets are not always liquid. When lack of liquidity strikes, participating investors are willing to take any price they can, fair or not.

THE SOURCE OF LIQUIDITY

If all information had the same impact on all investors, there would be no liquidity. When they received information, all investors would be executing the same trade, trying to get the same price. However, investors are not homogeneous. Some traders must trade and generate profits every day. Some are trading to meet liabilities that will not be realized until years in the future. Some are highly leveraged. Some are highly capitalized. In fact, the importance of information can be considered largely dependent on the investment horizon of the investor.

Take a typical day trader who has an investment horizon of five minutes and is currently long in the market. The average five-minute price change in 1992 was $-.000284$ percent, with a standard deviation of 0.05976 percent. If, for technical reasons, a six standard deviation drop occurred for a five-minute horizon, or 0.359 percent, our day trader could be wiped out if the fall continued. However, an institutional trader—a pension fund, for example—with a weekly trading horizon, would probably consider that drop a buying opportunity because weekly returns over the past ten years have averaged 0.22 percent with a standard deviation of 2.37 percent. In addition, the technical drop has not changed the outlook of the weekly trader, who looks at either longer technical or fundamental information. Thus, the day trader's six-sigma event is a 0.15-sigma event to the weekly trader, or no big deal. The weekly trader steps in, buys, and creates liquidity. This liquidity, in turn, stabilizes the market.

All of the investors trading in the market simultaneously have different investment horizons. We can also say that the information that is important at each investment horizon is different. Thus, the source of liquidity is investors with different investment horizons, different information sets, and consequently, different concepts of "fair price."

INFORMATION SETS AND INVESTMENT HORIZONS

In any trading room, virtually all of the tools of the day trader are technical. Although there are likely to be news services that offer earnings announcements, and reports from securities analysts may be lying about, the charts are the most important tool. A portfolio manager is likely to have both technical and fundamental information, but the proportions will be reversed. The buy-and-sell decision, in normal circumstances, will depend on fundamental information, although technical analysis may be used in the course of trading.

There are exceptions to these two simplified portraits, but I believe that most practitioners will find them close to experience. Short-term investors primarily follow technical analysis. Longer-term investors are more likely to follow fundamentals. (There are, of course, many portfolio managers with short investment horizons.) As long as this pattern holds true, the "fair" value of a stock is identified in two different ways:

1. For day traders, the bogey is the high for the day if they are selling, or the low for the day if they are buying. Whether this price has anything to do with intrinsic value is a moot point.
2. For long-term investors, the actual buying or selling price becomes less important, relative to the high or low of the day. It is not unimportant, but if the stock has been held for six months, a +31 percent return is still considered as acceptable as +32 percent. However, that 1 percent difference can be very significant for a day trader.

Liquidity also depends on the type of information that is circulating through the market, and on which investment horizon finds it important.

STATISTICAL CHARACTERISTICS OF MARKETS, REVISITED

In Chapter 2, we discussed some of the statistical characteristics of markets. For stocks, bonds, and currencies we found that the frequency distribution of returns is a fat-tailed, high-peaked distribution that exists at many different investment horizons. Table 3.1 shows data for 5-minute, 30-minute, and 60-minute returns for 1989 through 1990. Compare them to the frequency distributions shown in Chapter 2. There is little difference between them, and they are definitely not normally distributed. A new market hypothesis would have to account for this observed property of the markets.

A second property we observed in Chapter 2 involved the term structure of volatility. The standard deviation of returns increased at a faster rate than the square root of time. For stocks and bonds, the term structure of volatility was bounded; for currencies, there were no bounds. Again, these are important properties that must be accounted for. We must also account for why standard Gaussian statistics seems to work so well at some times, and so poorly at others. It is well known that correlations come and go and that volatility is highly unstable. In addition, the betas of CAPM are usually stable, but not always. Confusing the debate over the EMH is the fact that time periods can be found to support both sides of the argument. When markets are considered "stable," the EMH and CAPM seem to work fine. However, during panics and stampedes, those models break down, like "singularities" in physics. This is not unexpected, because the EMH and the CAPM are equilibrium models. They cannot handle the transition to turbulence. The new market hypothesis would need the ability to explain this singular characteristic of traded markets.

THE FRACTAL MARKET HYPOTHESIS

The Fractal Market Hypothesis emphasizes the impact of liquidity and investment horizons on the behavior of investors. To make the hypothesis as general as possible, it will place no statistical requirements on the process. We will leave that to later chapters. The purpose of the Fractal Market Hypothesis is to give a model of investor behavior and market price movements that fits our observations.

Markets exist to provide a stable, liquid environment for trading. Investors wish to get a good price, but that would not necessarily be a "fair" price in the economic sense. For instance, short covering rarely occurs at a fair price. Markets remain stable when many investors participate and have many different investment horizons. When a five-minute trader experiences a six-sigma event, an investor with a longer investment horizon must step in and stabilize the market. The investor will do so because, within his or her investment horizon, the five-minute trader's six-sigma event is not unusual. As long as another investor

Table 3.1 Frequency distributions (%) of intraday returns

Standard Deviations		1989–1990 60-Minute	1989–1990 30-Minute	1989 5-Minute	1990 5-Minute
Less than	−4.00	0.40%	0.37%	0.52%	0.47%
	−3.80	0.05	0.11	0.08	0.08
	−3.60	0.00	0.05	0.11	0.08
	−3.40	0.05	0.15	0.15	0.09
	−3.20	0.10	0.12	0.12	0.15
	−3.00	0.07	0.16	0.17	0.13
	−2.80	0.10	0.27	0.18	0.20
	−2.60	0.25	0.13	0.23	0.23
	−2.40	0.50	0.30	0.35	0.28
	−2.20	0.69	0.41	0.48	0.35
	−2.00	0.79	0.46	0.51	0.41
	−1.80	0.89	0.66	0.65	0.58
	−1.60	0.87	0.94	0.76	0.67
	−1.40	1.46	1.18	0.89	0.78
	−1.20	1.61	1.75	1.21	0.99
	−1.00	2.70	2.27	1.34	1.62
	−0.80	3.05	3.21	2.27	2.16
	−0.60	4.61	4.30	3.60	3.85
	−0.40	6.49	7.19	6.71˙	7.15
	−0.20	8.45	9.18	11.75	13.77
	0.00	16.11	15.22	16.44	19.58
	0.20	13.28	15.14	19.92	16.26
	0.40	9.52	9.57	10.80	10.60
	0.60	7.78	8.37	6.28	6.04
	0.80	5.63	5.25	3.65	3.00
	1.00	4.61	4.08	2.52	2.13
	1.20	3.02	2.48	1.86	1.42
	1.40	1.81	1.63	1.25	1.43
	1.60	1.16	1.39	1.00	1.18
	1.80	0.99	0.86	0.82	0.95
	2.00	0.82	0.73	0.67	0.65
	2.20	0.57	0.58	0.50	0.47
	2.40	0.55	0.36	0.43	0.45
	2.60	0.35	0.27	0.26	0.32
	2.80	0.12	0.20	0.31	0.28
	3.00	0.17	0.17	0.20	0.22
	3.20	0.05	0.12	0.15	0.24
	3.40	0.07	0.07	0.13	0.15
	3.60	0.05	0.08	0.12	0.14
	3.80	0.05	0.01	0.06	0.08
Greater than	4.00	0.15	0.20	0.53	0.47

has a longer trading horizon than the investor in crisis, the market will stabilize itself. For this reason, investors must share the same risk levels (once an adjustment is made for the scale of the investment horizon), and the shared risk explains why the frequency distribution of returns looks the same at different investment horizons. We call this proposal the *Fractal* Market Hypothesis because of this self-similar statistical structure.

Markets become unstable when the fractal structure breaks down. A breakdown occurs when investors with long investment horizons either stop participating in the market or become short-term investors themselves. Investment horizons are shortened when investors feel that longer-term fundamental information, which is the basis of their market valuations, is no longer important or is unreliable. Periods of economic or political crisis, when the long-term outlook becomes highly uncertain, probably account for most of these events.

This type of instability is not the same as bear markets. Bear markets are based on declining fundamental valuation. Instability is characterized by extremely high levels of short-term volatility. The end result can be a substantial fall, a substantial rise, or a price equivalent to the start—all in a very short time. However, the former two outcomes seem to be more common than the latter.

An example was market reaction when President Kennedy was assassinated on November 22, 1963. The sudden death of the nation's leader sent the market into a tail spin; the impact his death would have on the long-term prospects for the country was uncertain. My proposition is that long-term investors either did not participate on that day, or they panicked and became short-term investors. Once fundamental information lost its value, these long-term investors shortened their investment horizon and began trading on overwhelmingly negative technical dynamics. The market was closed until after the President's funeral. By the time the market reopened, investors were better able to judge the impact of the President's death on the economy, long-term assessment returned, and the market stabilized.

Prior to the crash of October 19, 1987, long-term investors had begun focusing on the long-term prospects of the market, based on high valuation and a tightening monetary policy of the Fed. As a result, they began selling their equity holdings. The crash was dominated entirely by traders with extremely short investment horizons. Either long-term investors did nothing (which meant that they needed lower prices to justify action), or they themselves became short-term traders, as they did on the day of the Kennedy assassination. Both behaviors probably occurred. Short-term information (or technical information) dominated in the crash of October 19, 1987. As a result, the market reached new heights of instability and did not stabilize until long-term investors stepped in to buy during the following days.

More recently, the impending Gulf War caused a classic market roller coaster on January 19, 1990. James Baker, then Secretary of State, met with the Iraqi Foreign Minister, Tarik Aziz, to discuss the Iraqi response to the ultimatum delivered by the Allies. The pending war caused investors to concentrate on the short term; they had evidently decided that fundamental information was useless in such an uncertain environment. As a result, the market traded on rumors and idle speculation. When the two statesmen met for longer than expected, the Dow Jones Industrials soared 40 points on expectation that a negotiated solution was at hand. When the meeting finally broke and no progress was reported, the market plummeted 39 points. There was no fundamental reason for such a wide swing in the market. Investors had, evidently, become short-term-oriented, or the long-term investors did not participate. In either case, the market lost liquidity and became unstable.

The fractal statistical structure exists because it is a stable structure, much like the fractal structure of the lung, discussed in Chapter 1. In the lung, the diameter of each branching generation decreases according to a power law. However, within each generation, there is actually a range of diameters. These exist because each generation depends on previous ones. If one generation was malformed, and each branch was the same diameter, then the entire lung could become malformed. If one branch is malformed in a fractal structure, the overall statistical distribution of diameters makes up for the malformed branch. In the markets, the range of statistical distributions over different investment horizons fulfills the same function. As long as investors with different investment horizons are participating, a panic at one horizon can be absorbed by the other investment horizons as a buying (or selling) opportunity. However, if the entire market has the same investment horizon, then the market becomes unstable. The lack of liquidity turns into panic.

When the investment horizon becomes uniform, the market goes into "free fall"; that is, discontinuities appear in the pricing sequence. In a Gaussian environment, a large change is the sum of many small changes. However, during panics and stampedes, the market often skips over prices. The discontinuities cause large changes, and fat tails appear in the frequency distribution of returns. Again, these discontinuities are the result of a lack of liquidity caused by the appearance of a uniform investment horizon for market participants.

Another explanation for some large events exists. If the information received by the market is important to both the short- and long-term horizons, then liquidity can also be affected. For instance, on April 1, 1993, Phillip Morris announced price cuts on Marlboro cigarettes. This, of course, reduced the long-term prospects for the company, and the stock was marked down accordingly. The stock opened at $48, 17⅛ lower than its previous close of $55⅛. However, before the stock opened, technical analysts on CNBC, the cable financial news network, said that the stock's next resistance level was 50. Phillip Morris closed at 49½. It is possible that 49½ was Phillip Morris' "fair" value, but it is just as likely that technicians stabilized the market this time.

Even when the market has achieved a stable statistical structure, market dynamics and motivations change as the investment horizon widens. The shorter the term of the investment horizon, the more important technical factors, trading activity, and liquidity become. Investors follow trends and one another. Crowd behavior can dominate. As the investment horizon grows, technical analysis gradually gives way to fundamental and economic factors. Prices, as a result, reflect this relationship and rise and fall as earnings expectations rise and fall. Earnings expectations rise gradually over time. If the perception is a change in economic direction, earnings expectations can rapidly reverse. If the market has no relationship with the economic cycle, or if that relationship is very weak, then trading activity and liquidity continue their importance, even at long horizons.

If the market is tied to economic growth over the long term, then risk will decrease over time because the economic cycle dominates. The economic cycle is less volatile than trading activity, which makes long-term stock returns less volatile as well. This relationship would cause variance to become bounded.

Economic capital markets, like stocks and bonds, have a short-term fractal statistical structure superimposed over a long-term economic cycle, which may be deterministic. Currencies, being a trading market only, have only the fractal statistical structure.

Finally, information itself would not have a uniform impact on prices; instead, information would be assimilated differently by the different investment horizons. A technical rally would only slowly become apparent or important to investors with long-term horizons. Likewise, economic factors would change expectations. As long-term investors change their valuation and begin trading, a technical trend appears and influences short-term investors. In the short term, price changes can be expected to be noisier because general agreement on fair price, and hence the acceptable band around fair price, is a larger component of total return. At longer investment horizons, there is more time to digest the information, and hence more consensus as to the proper price. As a result, the longer the investment horizon, the smoother the time series.

SUMMARY

The Fractal Market Hypothesis proposes the following:

1. The market is stable when it consists of investors covering a large number of investment horizons. This ensures that there is ample liquidity for traders.
2. The information set is more related to market sentiment and technical factors in the short term than in the longer term. As investment horizons increase, longer-term fundamental information dominates. Thus, price changes may reflect information important only to that investment horizon.
3. If an event occurs that makes the validity of fundamental information questionable, long-term investors either stop participating in the market or begin trading based on the short-term information set. When the overall investment horizon of the market shrinks to a uniform level, the market becomes unstable. There are no long-term investors to stabilize the market by offering liquidity to short-term investors.
4. Prices reflect a combination of short-term technical trading and long-term fundamental valuation. Thus, short-term price changes are likely to be more volatile, or "noisier," than long-term trades. The underlying trend in the market is reflective of changes in expected earnings, based on the changing economic environment. Short-term trends are more likely the result of crowd behavior. There is no reason to believe that the length of the short-term trends is related to the long-term economic trend.
5. If a security has no tie to the economic cycle, then there will be no long-term trend. Trading, liquidity, and short-term information will dominate.

Unlike the EMH, the Fractal Market Hypothesis (FMH) says that information is valued according to the investment horizon of the investor. Because the different investment horizons value information differently, the diffusion of information will also be uneven. At any one time, prices may not reflect all available information, but only the information important to that investment horizon.

The FMH owes much to the Coherent Market Hypothesis (CMH) of Vaga (1991) and the K-Z model of Larrain (1991). I discussed those models extensively in my previous book. Like the CMH, the FMH is based on the premise that the market assumes different states and can shift between stable and unstable regimes. Like the K-Z model, the FMH finds that the chaotic regime occurs when investors lose faith in long-term fundamental information. In many ways, the FMH combines these two models through the use of investment horizons; it specifies when the regime changes and why markets become unstable when fundamental information loses its value. The key is that the FMH says the market is stable when it has no characteristic time scale or investment horizon. Instability occurs when the market loses its fractal structure and assumes a fairly uniform investment horizon.

In this chapter, I have outlined a new view on the structure of markets. Unfortunately, most standard market analysis assumes that the market process is, essentially, stochastic. For testing the Efficient Market Hypothesis (EMH), this assumption causes few problems. However, for the FMH, many of the standard tests lose their power. That is not to say that they are useless. Much research using standard methodologies has pointed to inconsistencies between the EMH and observed market behavior; however, new methodologies are also needed to take advantage of the market structure outlined in the FMH. Many methodologies have already been developed to accomplish these ends. In Part Two, we will examine one such methodology: R/S analysis. My emphasis on R/S analysis does not assume that it will supplant other methodologies. My purpose is to show that it is a robust form of time-series analysis and should be one of any analyst's tools.

PART TWO
FRACTAL (R/S) ANALYSIS

4
Measuring Memory—
The Hurst Process and
R/S Analysis

Standard statistical analysis begins by assuming that the system under study is primarily random; that is, the causal process that created the time series has many component parts, or degrees of freedom, and the interaction of those components is so complex that a deterministic explanation is not possible. Only probabilities can help us understand and take advantage of the process. The underlying philosophy implies that randomness and determinism cannot coexist. In Chapter 1, we discussed nonlinear stochastic and deterministic systems that were combinations of randomness and determinism, such as the Chaos Game. Unfortunately, as we saw in Chapter 2, these systems are not well-described by standard Gaussian statistics. So far, we have examined these nonlinear processes using numerical experiments on a case-by-case basis. In order to study the statistics of these systems and create a more general analytical framework, we need a probability theory that is nonparametric. That is, we need a statistics that makes no prior assumptions about the shape of the probability distribution we are studying.

Standard Gaussian statistics works best under very restrictive assumptions. The *Central Limit Theorem* (or the Law of Large Numbers) states that, as we have more and more trials, the limiting distribution of a random system will be the normal distribution, or bell-shaped curve. Events measured must be "independent and identically distributed" (IID). That is, the events must not influence one another, and they must all be equally likely to occur. It has long been assumed that most large, complex systems should be modeled in this manner. The assumption of normality, or near-normality, was usually made when examining a large, complex system so that standard statistical analysis could be applied.

But what if a system is not IID? Then adjustments are made to create statistical structures which, while not IID, are close enough so standard methods can still be applied, with some modifications. There certainly are instances where that logic is justified, but it amounted to a rationalization process in the case of capital markets and economic theory, and the process has led us to our current dead end. In *Chaos and Order in the Capital Markets,* I discussed this at some length. I do not intend to repeat those arguments here, but it is worth mentioning that statistical analysis of markets came first and the Efficient Market Hypothesis followed.

If the system under study is not IID, or close, then what are we to do? We need a nonparametric method. Luckily, a very robust, nonparametric methodology was discovered by H. E. Hurst, the celebrated British hydrologist, who in 1951 published a paper titled "The Long-Term Storage Capacity of Reservoirs." Superficially, the paper dealt with modeling reservoir design, but Hurst extended his study to many natural systems and gave us a new statistical methodology for distinguishing random and nonrandom systems, the persistence of trends, and the duration of cycles, if any. In short, he gave us a method, called rescaled range, or R/S analysis, for distinguishing random time series from fractal time series. We now turn to his methodology.

This chapter gives a brief background of Hurst's reasoning and examples of his early work. In Chapter 5, we will look at the significance of the results. Chapter 6 will show how R/S analysis can be used to analyze periodic and nonperiodic cycles.

BACKGROUND: DEVELOPMENT OF R/S ANALYSIS

H. E. Hurst (1900–1978) built dams. In the early 20th century, he worked on the Nile River Dam Project. He studied the Nile so extensively that some Egyptians reportedly nicknamed him "the Father of the Nile." The Nile River posed an interesting problem for Hurst as a hydrologist. When designing a dam, hydrologists are concerned with the storage capacity of the resulting reservoir. An influx of water occurs from a number of natural elements (rainfall, river overflows, and so on), and a regulated amount is released for crops. The storage capacity of the reservoir is based on an estimate of the water inflow and of the need for water outflow. Most hydrologists begin by assuming that the water inflow is a random process—a perfectly reasonable assumption when dealing with a complex ecosystem. Hurst, however, had studied the 847-year record that the Egyptians had kept of the Nile River's overflows, from 622 A.D. to 1469 A.D. To him, the record did not appear random. Larger-than-average overflows were more likely to be followed by more large overflows. Abruptly, the process would change to a lower-than-average overflow, which was followed by other lower-than-average overflows. In short, there appeared to be cycles, but their length was nonperiodic. Standard analysis revealed no statistically significant correlations between observations, so Hurst developed his own methodology.

Hurst was aware of Einstein's (1908) work on brownian motion (the erratic path followed by a particle suspended in a fluid). Brownian motion became the primary model for a random walk process. Einstein found that the distance that a random particle covers increases with the square root of time used to measure it, or:

$$R = T^{0.50} \tag{4.1}$$

where R = the distance covered
  T = a time index

Equation (4.1) is called the *T to the one-half rule,* and is commonly used in statistics. We use it in financial economics to annualize volatility or standard deviation. We take the standard deviation of monthly returns and multiply it by the square root of 12. We are assuming that the dispersion of returns increases with the square root of time. Hurst felt that, using this property, he could test the Nile River's overflows for randomness.

We begin with a time series, $x = x_1, \ldots, x_n$, to represent n consecutive values. (In this book, we will refer to the time series x to mean all x_r, where r = 1 to n. A specific element of x will include its subscript. This notation will apply to all time series.) The time index is unimportant in general. In Hurst's case, it was annual discharges of the Nile River. For markets, it can be the daily changes in price of a stock index. The mean value, x_m, of the time series x is defined as:

$$x_m = (x_1 + \ldots + x_n)/n \tag{4.2}$$

The standard deviation, s_n, is estimated as:

$$s_n = n^{-1/2} * \sqrt{(x_r - x_m)^2} \tag{4.3}$$

which is merely the standard normal formula for standard deviation. The rescaled range was calculated by first rescaling or "normalizing" the data by subtracting the sample mean:

$$Z_r = (x_r - x_m); \quad r = 1, \ldots, n \tag{4.4}$$

The resulting series, Z, now has a mean of zero. The next step creates a cumulative time series Y:

$$Y_1 = (Z_1 + Z_r) \quad r = 2, \ldots, n \tag{4.5}$$

Note that, by definition, the last value of Y (Y_n) will always be zero because Z has a mean of zero. The adjusted range, R_n, is the maximum minus the minimum value of the Y_r:

$$R_n = \max(Y_1, \ldots, Y_n) - \min(Y_1, \ldots, Y_n) \tag{4.6}$$

The subscript, n, for R_n now signifies that this is the adjusted range for $x_1, \ldots, x_n$. Because Y has been adjusted to a mean of zero, the maximum value of Y will always be greater than or equal to zero, and the minimum will always be less than or equal to zero. Hence, the adjusted range, R_n, will always be nonnegative.

This adjusted range, R_n, is the distance that the system travels for time index n. If we set n = T, we can apply equation (4.1), provided that the time series, x, is independent for increasing values of n. However, equation (4.1) applies only to time series that are in brownian motion: they have zero mean, and variance equal to one. To apply this concept to time series that are not in brownian motion, we need to generalize equation (4.1) and take into account systems that are not independent. Hurst found that the following was a more general form of equation (4.1):

$$(R/S)_n = c*n^H \tag{4.7}$$

The subscript, n, for $(R/S)_n$ refers to the R/S value for $x_1, \ldots, x_n$; c = a constant.

The R/S value of equation (4.7) is referred to as the *rescaled range* because it has zero mean and is expressed in terms of local standard deviation. In general, the R/S value scales as we increase the time increment, n, by a power-law value equal to H, generally called the *Hurst exponent.* This is the first connection of the Hurst phenomena with the fractal geometry of Chapter 1. Remember, all fractals scale according to a power law. In the mammalian lung, the diameter of each branch decreased in scale according to an inverse power-law value. This inverse power-law value was equal to the fractal dimension of the structure. However, in the case of time series, we go from smaller to larger increments of time, rather than from larger to smaller branching generations, as in the lung. The range increases according to a power. This is called *power-law scaling.* Again, it is a characteristic of fractals, though not an exclusive one. We need other characteristics before we can call the Hurst phenomena "fractal." Those will come in due course.

Rescaling the adjusted range, by dividing by the standard deviation, turned out to be a master stroke. Hurst originally performed this operation so he could compare diverse phenomena. As we shall see, rescaling also allows us to compare periods of time that may be many years apart. In comparing stock returns of the 1920s with those of the 1980s, prices present a problem because of inflationary growth. Rescaling minimizes this problem. By rescaling the data to zero mean and standard deviation of one, to allow diverse phenomena and time periods to be compared, Hurst anticipated renormalization group theory in physics. Renormalization group theory performs similar transformations to study phase transitions, where characteristic scales cease to exist. Rescaled range analysis can also describe time series that have no characteristic scale. Again, this is a characteristic of fractals.

The Hurst exponent can be approximated by plotting the log (R/S_n) versus the log (n) and solving for the slope through an ordinary least squares regression. In particular, we are working from the following equation:

$$\log(R/S_n) = \log(c) + H*\log(n) \tag{4.8}$$

If a system were independently distributed, then H = 0.50. Hurst first investigated the Nile River. He found H = 0.91! The rescaled range was increasing at a faster rate than the square root of time. It was increasing at the 0.91 root of time, which meant that the system (in this case, the range of the height of the Nile River) was covering more distance than a random process would. In order to cover more distance, the changes in annual Nile River overflows had to be influencing each other. They had to be correlated. Although there are autoregressive (AR) processes that can cause short-term correlations, these river overflows were one year apart. It seemed unlikely that a simple AR(1) or AR(2) process was causing these anomalous results.

Table 4.1 Hurst (1951) R/S Analysis

| Phenomenon | Range of N Years | Number | | K | | | Coeff. of Autocorrelation |
		Phenomena	Sets	Mean	Std. Devn.	Range	
Properties of K from Natural Phenomena							
River discharges	10–100	39	94	0.72	0.091	0.50–0.94	
Roda Gauge	80–1,080	1	66	0.77	0.055	0.58–0.86	0.025 ± 0.26 $n = 15$
River and lake levels	44–176	4	13	0.71	0.082	0.59–0.85	0.07 ± 0.08* $n = 65$
Rainfall	24–211	39	173	0.70	0.088	0.46–0.91	
Varves							
Lake Saki	50–2,000	1	114	0.69	0.064	0.56–0.87	-0.07 ± 0.11 $n = 39$
Moen and Tamiskaming	50–1,200	2	90	0.77	0.094	0.50–0.95	
Corintos and Haileybury	50–650	2	54	0.77	0.098	0.51–0.91	
Temperatures	29–60	18	120	0.68	0.087	0.46–0.92	
Pressures	29–96	8	28	0.63	0.070	0.51–0.76	
Sunspot numbers	38–190	1	15	0.75	0.056	0.65–0.85	
Tree-rings and spruce index	50–900	5	105	0.79	0.076	0.56–0.94	
Totals and means of sections							
Water statistics		83	346	0.72	0.08	0.46–0.94	
Varves		5	258	0.74	0.09	0.50–0.95	
Meteorology and trees		32	268	0.72	0.08	0.46–0.94	
Grand totals and means	10–2,000	120	872	0.726	0.082	0.46–0.95	

*Includes also river discharges.

From H. E. Hurst, "The Long-Term Storage Capacity of Reservoirs," *Transactions of the American Society of Civil Engineers*, 116 (1951). Reproduced with permission.

When Hurst decided to check other rivers, he found that the records were not as extensive as for the Nile. He then branched out to more diverse natural phenomena—rainfall, sunspots, mud sentiments, tree rings, anything with a long time series. His results are reprinted in Table 4.1 and Figure 4.1. Both are reproduced from Hurst (1951).

Figure 4.1 is the first in a series of log/log plots that we will be investigating. Hurst originally labeled the scaling factor "K." Mandelbrot renamed it "H" in Hurst's honor, and we continue that tradition. Therefore, in Figure 4.1 and Table 4.1, K = H. The slope of these log/log plots is the Hurst exponent H.

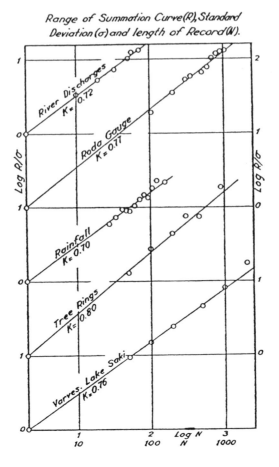

FIGURE 4.1 Hurst (1951) R/S analysis. (Reproduced with permission of the American Society of Civil Engineers.)

In all cases, Hurst found H greater than 0.50. He was intrigued that H often took a value of approximately 0.70. Could there be some sort of universal phenomenon taking place? Hurst decided to find out.

THE JOKER EFFECT

Before the age of computers, it took fortitude to be an applied mathematician. The numerical experiments, which we conduct so easily on personal computers or at workstations, were especially time-consuming and prone to error. Hurst felt that a *biased* random walk was causing his results, but he needed a simulation method. He devised an elegant process that serves as an excellent metaphor for the Hurst process. This process has been described in Feder (1988), Mandelbrot (1982), and Peters (1989, 1991a), but because I feel that understanding the Hurst phenomena is fundamentally bound up in the simulation method, I am repeating it here in abbreviated form. Although I am introducing additional insights, readers familiar with my earlier work may wish to skip to the next section. For readers who are new to the Hurst phenomena, this section is essential.

Hurst simulated a random process by using a probability pack of cards, that is, a deck of 52 cards that contained ± 1, ± 3, ± 5, ± 7, and ± 9, to approximate a normal distribution. He would shuffle this deck and, by noting the number of repeated cuttings, generate a random time series. Performing R/S analysis on the resulting series generated a Hurst exponent of approximately 0.50. It was close enough to meet the standards of the day. Hurst performed 1,000 trials and found that the slope varied little.

To simulate a biased random walk, he would first shuffle the deck and cut it once, noting the number. For this example, we will use $+3$ as the initial cut. He would replace this card and reshuffle the deck. Then he would deal out two hands of 26 cards, which we will name decks A and B. Because the initial cut was $+3$, he would take the three highest cards from deck A and place them in deck B. He would then remove the three lowest cards in deck B. Deck B was then biased to a level of $+3$. Finally, he would place a joker in deck B and reshuffle it. He would use the now biased deck B as his time series generator, until he cut the joker. Then Hurst would create a new biased hand.

Hurst did 1,000 trials of 100 hands. He calculated H = 0.72, much as he had done in nature. Think of the process involved: first, the bias of each hand, which is determined by a random cut of the deck; then, the generation of the time series itself, which is another series of random cuts; and finally, the appearance of the joker, which again occurs at random. Despite the use of all these random events, H = 0.72 would always appear. Again, we have local randomness and a global structure, much like the Chaos Game in Chapter 1. In this case, it is a global statistical structure rather than a geometric one.

If markets are Hurst processes, they exhibit trends that persist until an economic equivalent of the joker arises to change that bias in magnitude, or direction, or both.

RANDOMNESS AND PERSISTENCE: INTERPRETING THE HURST EXPONENT

According to the original theory, H = 0.50 would imply an independent process. It is important to realize that R/S analysis does not require that the underlying process be Gaussian, just independent. This, of course, would include the normal distribution, but it would also include non-Gaussian independent processes like the Student-t, or gamma, or any other shape. R/S analysis is nonparametric, so there is no requirement for the shape of the underlying distribution.

0.50 < H ≤ 1.00 implies a *persistent* time series, and a persistent time series is characterized by long memory effects. Theoretically, what happens today impacts the future forever. In terms of chaotic dynamics, there is sensitive dependence on initial conditions. This long memory occurs regardless of time scale. All daily changes are correlated with all future daily changes; all weekly changes are correlated with all future weekly changes. *There is no characteristic time scale,* the key characteristic of fractal time series.

0 ≤ H < 0.50 signifies *antipersistence*. An antipersistent system covers *less* distance than a random one. For the system to cover less distance, it must reverse itself more frequently than a random process. Theorists with a standard background would equate this behavior with a mean-reverting process. However, that assumes that the system under study has a stable mean. We cannot make this assumption.

As we have seen, persistent time series are the most common type found in nature. We will also see that they are the most common type in the capital markets and in economics. To assess that statement, we must turn to more practical matters, such as calculating numbers.

R/S ANALYSIS: A STEP-BY-STEP GUIDE

R/S analysis is a simple process that is highly data-intensive. This section breaks equations (4.2) through (4.8) into a series of executable steps. A program in the GAUSS language is supplied in Appendix 2. These are the sequential steps:

1. Begin with a time series of length M. Convert this into a time series of length $N = M - 1$ of logarithmic ratios:

    $$N_i = \log(M_{(i+1)}/M_i), \ i = 1, 2, 3, \ldots, (M-1) \tag{4.9}$$

2. Divide this time period into A contiguous subperiods of length n, such that $A*n = N$. Label each subperiod I_a, with $a = 1, 2, 3, \ldots, A$. Each element in I_a is labeled $N_{k,a}$ such that $k = 1, 2, 3, \ldots, n$. For each I_a of length n, the average value is defined as:

    $$e_a = (1/n)* \sum_{k=1}^{n} N_{k,a} \tag{4.10}$$

    where e_a = average value of the N_i contained in subperiod I_a of length n

3. The time series of accumulated departures $(X_{k,a})$ from the mean value for each subperiod I_a is defined as:

    $$X_{k,a} = \sum_{i=1}^{k} (N_{i,a} - e_a) \tag{4.11}$$
    $$k = 1, 2, 3, \ldots, n$$

4. The range is defined as the maximum minus the minimum value of $X_{k,a}$ within each subperiod I_a:

    $$R_{I_a} = \max(X_{k,a}) - \min(X_{k,a}) \tag{4.12}$$

    where $1 \leq k \leq n$.

5. The sample standard deviation calculated for each subperiod I_a:

    $$S_{I_a} = ((1/n)* \sum_{k=1}^{n} (N_{k,a} - e_a^2))^{0.50}$$

6. Each range, R_{I_a}, is now normalized by dividing by the S_{I_a} corresponding to it. Therefore, the rescaled range for each I_a subperiod is equal to

R_{1_a}/S_{1_a}. From step 2 above, we had A contiguous subperiods of length n. Therefore, the average R/S value for length n is defined as:

$$(R/S)_n = (1/A) * \sum_{a=1}^{A} (R_{1_a}/S_{1_a}) \tag{4.13}$$

7. The length n is increased to the next higher value, and $(M - 1)/n$ is an integer value. We use values of n that include the beginning and ending points of the time series, and steps 1 through 6 are repeated until $n = (M - 1)/2$. We can now apply equations (4.7) and (4.8) by performing an ordinary least squares regression on log(n) as the independent variable and $\log(R/S)_n$ as the dependent variable. The intercept is the estimate for log(c), the constant. The slope of the equation is the estimate of the Hurst exponent, H.

In subsequent chapters, we will elaborate more on other practical matters. For now, we add one other rule of thumb: In general, run the regression over values of $n \geq 10$. Small values of n produce unstable estimates when sample sizes are small. In Chapter 5, when we go over significance tests, we will see other rules of thumb.

AN EXAMPLE: THE YEN/DOLLAR EXCHANGE RATE

As an initial example, R/S analysis has been applied to the daily yen/dollar exchange rate from January 1972 to December 1990. Unfortunately, an autoregressive (AR) process can bias the Hurst exponent, H, for reasons given in Chapter 5. Therefore, we have used AR(1) residuals of the change in exchange rate; that is, we have transformed the raw data series in the following manner:

$$A_t = Y_t - (a + b * Y_{(t-1)})$$

where A_t = new value at time t
$\quad Y_t$ = change in the yen/dollar exchange rate at time t
$\quad a, b$ = constants

Beginning with the A_t, we used step 2 above and calculated the R/S values for various N. The results are shown in Table 4.2, and the log/log plot is shown

Table 4.2   R/S Analysis

Regression output, Daily yen:		
Constant		−0.187
Standard error of Y (estimated)		0.012
R squared		0.999
Hurst exponent	0.642	
Standard error of coefficient	0.004	
Significance	5.848	

as Figure 4.2. Note that the yen/dollar exchange rate produces the anomalous value, H = 0.64.

Because the Hurst exponent is different from 0.50, we are tempted to say that the yen/dollar exchange rate exhibits the Hurst phenomena of persistence. But, how significant is this result? Without some type of asymptotic theory, it would be difficult to assess significance. Luckily, we have developed significance tests, and they are the subject of Chapter 5.

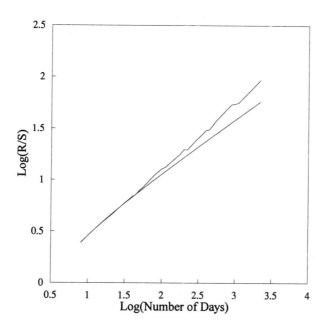

FIGURE 4.2   R/S analysis, daily yen: January 1972 through December 1990.

5
Testing R/S Analysis

We are always faced with one major question when analyzing any process: How do we know that our results did not happen by chance? We know from experience, or anecdotally from others, that "freak" things happen—highly improbable events do occur. Random events, even those that are highly unlikely, are labeled *trivial*. In statistics, we check our results against the probability that they could be trivial. If they occur only 5 percent of the time or less, we say that we are 95 percent sure that they did not occur at random and are *significant*. We say that there is still a 5 percent chance that this event did happen by accident, but we are highly *confident* that the results are significant and tell us something important about the process under study. Significance testing around probabilistic confidence intervals has become one of the main foci of statistics.

Therefore, to evaluate the significance of R/S analysis, we also need confidence tests of our findings, much like the "t-statistics" of linear regression. R/S analysis has been around for some years, but a full statistical evaluation of the results has been elusive. Using powerful personal computers, we can now do simulations to calculate the expected value of the R/S statistic and the Hurst exponent. When these simulations are combined with previously developed asymptotic theory, it is now possible to assess the significance of our findings. We do so by first investigating the behavior of R/S analysis when the system under study is an independent, random system. Once we have fully investigated the expected results for a random system, we can compare other processes to the random null hypothesis and gauge their significance.

This chapter traces the historical development of the random null hypothesis, proceeds with the development of full tests, and concludes with a guide to application.

THE RANDOM NULL HYPOTHESIS

Hypothesis testing postulates the most likely result as the probable answer. If we do not understand the mechanics behind a particular process, such as the stock market, then a statistical structure that is independent and identically distributed (IID), and is characterized by a random walk, is our best first guess. The structure is Gaussian, and its probability density function is the normal distribution, or bell-shaped curve. This initial guess is called the *null hypothesis*. We chose the Gaussian case as the null hypothesis because it is easier, mathematically speaking, to test whether a process is a random walk and be able to say it is not one, than it is to prove the existence of fractional brownian motion (or some other long memory process). Why? The Gaussian case lends itself to optimal solutions and is easily simulated. In addition, the Efficient Market Hypothesis (EMH) is based on the Gaussian case, making it the null hypothesis by default.

Hurst (1951) based his null hypothesis on the binomial distribution and the tossing of coins. His result for a random walk is a special case of equation (4.7):

$$(R/S)_n = (n*\pi/2)^{0.50} \tag{5.1}$$

where n = the number of observations

Feller (1951) found a similar result, but he worked strictly with the adjusted range, R'. Hurst postulated equation (5.1) for the rescaled range, but it was not really proven in the formal sense. Feller worked with the adjusted range (that is, the cumulative deviations with the sample mean deleted), and developed the expected value of R' and its variance. The rescaled range, R/S, was considered intractable because of the behavior of the sample standard deviation, especially for small values of N. It was felt that, because the adjusted range could be solved and should asymptotically (that is, at infinity) be equivalent to the rescaled range, that result was close enough.

Feller (1951) found the following formulas, which were essentially identical to Hurst's equation (5.1) for the expected value of the adjusted range, and also calculated its variance:

$$E(R'(n)) = (n*\pi/2)^{0.50} \tag{5.2}$$

$$Var(E(R'(n))) = (\pi^2/6 - \pi/2)*n \tag{5.3}$$

The variance formula, equation (5.3), supplies the variance for one value of R'(n). Because we can expect that the R/S values of a random number will be normally distributed (we will show this later through simulations), the variance of R'(n) will decrease, the more samples we have. For instance, if we have a time series that consists of N = 5,000 observations, we have 100 independent samples of R'(50) if we use nonoverlapping time periods. Therefore, the expected variance of our sample will be Var(E(R'(n)))/100, as shown in elementary statistics.

Equations (5.1) and (5.2) are standard assumptions under the null hypothesis of brownian motion. The range increases with the square root of time. Hurst went a bit further and suggested that the rescaled range also increases with the square root of time. Feller also said that the variance of the range increases linearly with time. Neither result is particularly surprising, given our discussions in Chapter 4. However, we now have access to tools that Hurst, in particular, would have found very useful.

Monte Carlo Simulations

The tool that has eased the way is the personal computer. With random number generators, we can use the process outlined in Chapter 4, especially equations (4.7) and (4.8), and simulate many samplings of R/S values. We can calculate the means and variances empirically, and see whether they conform to equations (5.1), (5.2), and (5.3). This process is the well-known "Monte Carlo" method of simulation, which is particularly appropriate for testing the Gaussian Hypothesis.

Before we begin, we must deal with the myth of "random numbers." No random number generator produces true random numbers. Instead, an algorithm produces *pseudo-random* numbers—numbers that are statistically independent according to most Gaussian tests. These pseudo-random numbers actually have a long cycle, or memory, after which they begin repeating. Typically, the cycles are long enough for the repetition to be undetectable. Recently, however, it was found that pseudo-random numbers can corrupt results when large amounts of data are used in Monte Carlo simulations. We usually do not have this problem in financial economics. However, many of the algorithms used as random number generators are versions of chaotic systems. R/S analysis is particularly adept at uncovering deterministic chaos and long memory processes. Therefore, to ensure the randomness of our tests, all random number series in this book are scrambled according to two other pseudo-random number series before they are used. This technique does not eliminate all dependence, but it reduces it to virtually unmeasurable levels, even for R/S analysis.

We begin with a pseudo-random number series of 5,000 values (normally distributed with mean zero and standard deviation of one), scrambled twice. We calculate R/S values for all n that are evenly divisible into 5,000; that is, each R/S_n value will always include the beginning and ending value of the complete time series. We then repeat this process 300 times, so that we have 300 R/S_n values for each n. The average of these R/S_n is the expected value, $E(R/S_n)$, for a system of Gaussian random numbers. Variances are calculated, and the final values are compared to those obtained by using equations (5.1), (5.2), and (5.3). The results are shown in Table 5.1 and graphed in Figure 5.1.

The simulated R/S_n values converge to those in equations (5.1) and (5.2) when n is greater than 20. However, for smaller values of n, there is a consistent deviation. The R/S_n values created by the simulation are systematically lower than those from Feller's and Hurst's equations. The variances of the R/S_n were also systematically lower than Feller's equation (5.3). Hurst, however, knew that he was calculating an asymptotic relationship, one that would hold only for large n. Feller also knew this. Rescaling was another problem.

Table 5.1 Log (R/S) Value Estimates

Number of Observations	Monte Carlo	Hurst	Anis and Lloyd (1976)	Empirical Correction
10	0.4577	0.5981	0.4805	0.4582
20	0.6530	0.7486	0.6638	0.6528
25	0.7123	0.7970	0.7208	0.7120
40	0.8332	0.8991	0.8382	0.8327
50	0.8891	0.9475	0.8928	0.8885
100	1.0577	1.0981	1.0589	1.0568
125	1.1097	1.1465	1.1114	1.1097
200	1.2190	1.2486	1.2207	1.2196
250	1.2710	1.2970	1.2720	1.2711
500	1.4292	1.4475	1.4291	1.4287
625	1.4801	1.4960	1.4795	1.4792
1,000	1.5869	1.5981	1.5851	1.5849
1,250	1.6351	1.6465	1.6349	1.6348
2,500	1.7839	1.7970	1.7889	1.7888
Mean square error:		0.0035	0.0001	0.0000

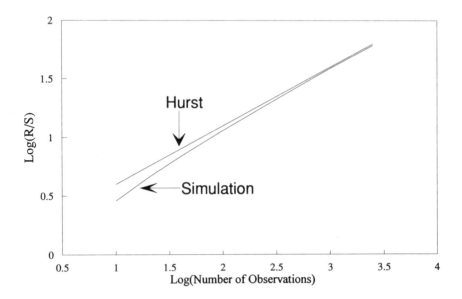

FIGURE 5.1   R/S values, Monte Carlo simulation versus Hurst's equation.

Feller was working with the adjusted range, not the rescaled range. Was the scaling behavior of the standard deviation relative to the range for small values of n causing this deviation? The fact remains that the mean value of the R/S statistic is quite different from the value predicted by Feller's theory.

Many years later, Anis and Lloyd (1976) developed the following equation to circumvent the systematic deviation of the R/S statistic for small n:

$$E(R/S_n) = [\Gamma\{0.5*(n-1)\} / (\sqrt{\pi}*\Gamma(0.5*n))] * \sum_{r=1}^{n-1} \sqrt{(n-r)/r} \qquad (5.4)$$

The derivation of this equation is beyond the scope of this book. Those interested in the derivation should consult Anis and Lloyd (1976). For large values of n, equation (5.4) becomes less useful because the gamma values become too large for most personal computer memories. However, using Sterling's Function, the equation can be simplified to the following:

$$E(R/S_n) = (n*\pi/2)^{-0.50} * \sum_{r=1}^{n-1} \sqrt{(n-r)/r} \qquad (5.5)$$

Equation (5.5) can be used when n > 300. As n becomes larger, equation (5.5) approaches equation (5.2). Equations (5.4) and (5.5) adjust for the distribution of the variance of the normal distribution to follow the gamma distribution; that is, the standard deviation will scale at a slower rate than the range for small values of n. Hence, the rescaled range will scale at a faster rate (H will be greater than 0.50) when n is small. Mandelbrot and Wallis (1969a,b,c) referred to the region of small n as "transient" because n was not large enough for the proper behavior to be seen. However, in economics, we rarely have enough data points to throw out the smaller n: that may be all that we have. Mandelbrot and Wallis would not start investigating scaling behavior until H = 20. Theoretically, Anis and Lloyd's formula was expected to explain the behavior seen from the Monte Carlo experiments.

Table 5.1 and Figure 5.2 show the results. There is some progress, but equations (5.4) and (5.5) still generate R/S values for small n that are higher than the sampled values.

There is a possibility that the results are caused by a bias, originating in the pseudo-random number generator, that double scrambling does not reduce. Perhaps a sample size of 300 is still not enough. To test for sample bias, an independent series of numbers was used. This series was 500 monthly S&P 500 changes, normalized to mean zero and unit variance. These numbers were scrambled 10 times before starting. Then they were randomly scrambled 300

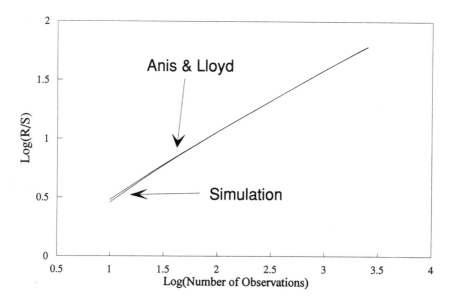

FIGURE 5.2   R/S values, Monte Carlo simulation versus Anis and Lloyd's equation.

Table 5.2 Log (R/S) Value Estimates

Number of Observations	Scrambled S&P 500	Monte Carlo
10	0.4551	0.4577
20	0.6474	0.6530
25	0.7055	0.7123
50	0.8812	0.8891
100	1.0472	1.0577
125	1.1012	1.1097
250	1.2591	1.2710

times, and R/S values were calculated as before. Table 5.2 shows the results. They are virtually indistinguishable from the Gaussian generated series. The results are even more remarkable when we consider that market returns are not normally distributed; they are fat-tailed with a high peak at the mean, even after scrambling. From these results, we can say that the Anis and Lloyd formula is missing something for values of n less than 20. What they are missing is unknown. However, empirically, I was able to derive a correction to the Anis and Lloyd formula. This correction multiplies (5.4) and (5.5) with a correction factor and yields:

$$E(R/S_n) = ((n - 0.5)/n)*(n*\pi/2)^{-0.50}* \sum_{r=1}^{n-1} \sqrt{(n - r)/r} \qquad (5.6)$$

The results of this empirically derived correction are shown in Table 5.1 and Figure 5.3. The correction comes very close to the simulated R/S values. From this point forward, all expected R/S values under the random null hypothesis will be generated using equation (5.6).

The Expected Value of the Hurst Exponent

Using the results of equation (5.6), we can now generate expected values of the Hurst exponent. Judging from Table 5.1 and Figure 5.3, we can expect that the Hurst exponent will be significantly higher than 0.50 for values less than 500—showing, again, that H = 0.50 for an independent process is an asymptotic limit. The expected Hurst exponent will, of course, vary, depending on the values of n we use to run the regression. In theory, any range will be appropriate as long as the system under study and the E(R/S) series cover the same values of n. In keeping with the primary focus of this book, which is financial

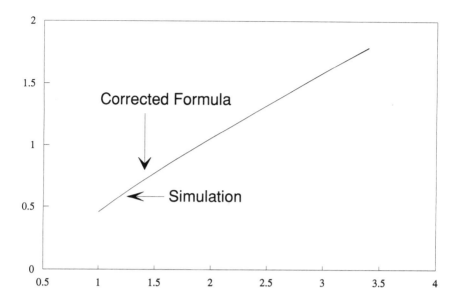

FIGURE 5.3   R/S values, Monte Carlo simulation versus corrected Anis and Lloyd equation.

economics, we will begin with n = 10. The final value of n will depend on the system under study. In Peters (1991a), the monthly returns of the S&P 500 were found to have persistent scaling for n < 50 months, with H = 0.78. As shown in Figure 5.4, the E(H) is equal to 0.613 for $10 \leq n \leq 50$, a significantly lower value—at least it looks significantly lower. But is it?

Because the R/S values are random variables, normally distributed, we would expect that the values of H would also be normally distributed. In that case, the expected variance of the Hurst exponent would be:

$$\text{Var}(H)n = 1/T \tag{5.7}$$

where T = the total number of observations in the sample

This would be the variance around the $E(H)_n$, as calculated from $E(R/S)_n$. Note that the Var(H)n does not depend on n or H, but, instead, depends on the total sample size, T.

Once again, Monte Carlo experiments were performed to test the validity of equation (5.7). For a normally distributed random variable scrambled twice,

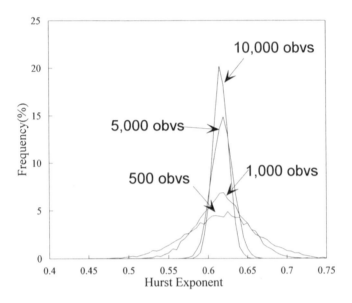

FIGURE 5.4   E(H) for $10 < n < 50$, nonnormalized frequency in percent.

7,000 values of H were calculated for $10 \leq n \leq 50$. The simulations were done for $T = 200$, 500, 1,000, and 5,000. Table 5.3 shows the results:

1. The mean values of H conform to E(H) using the E(R/S) values from equation (5.6), showing that the empirical correction to Anis and Lloyd's formula is valid.
2. The variance in each case is very close to 1/T.

The simulations were repeated for $10 \leq n \leq 500$, $10 \leq n \leq 1,000$, and $10 \leq n \leq 5,000$. In each case, the E(H) conformed to the value predicted by equation (5.6), and the variance is approximately equal to 1/T. Based on the results in Table 5.1, we can say that E(H) for IID random variables can be calculated from equation (5.6), with variance 1/T. Figure 5.5 shows the "normalized" distributions for various values of T. As expected, they appear normally distributed.

What if the independent process is other than Gaussian? As we saw in Table 5.2, a fat-tailed, high-peaked independent distribution does exhibit mean values as predicted in equation (5.6). However, the variance does differ. Unfortunately, the variance for distributions that are not normally distributed differs

Table 5.3   Standard Deviation of E(H): $10 < n < 50$

Number of Observations	Simulated Hurst Exponent	Theoretical Hurst Exponent	Simulated Standard Deviation	Theoretical Standard Deviation
200	0.613	0.613	0.0704	0.0704
500	0.615	0.613	0.0451	0.0446
1,000	0.615	0.613	0.0319	0.0315
5,000	0.616	0.613	0.0138	0.0141
10,000	0.614	0.613	0.0101	0.0100

on an individual basis. Therefore, our confidence interval is only valid for IID random variables. There are, of course, ways of filtering out short-term dependence, and we will use those methods below.

The following section examines R/S analysis of different types of time series that are often used in modeling financial economics, as well as other types of stochastic processes. Particular attention will be given to the possibility of a Type II error (classification of a process as long-memory when it is, in reality, a short-memory process).

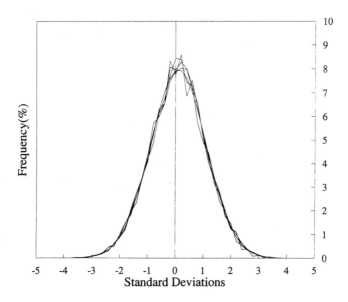

FIGURE 5.5   E(H) for $10 < n < 50$, normalized frequency: T = 500, 1,000, 5,000, 10,000.

STOCHASTIC MODELS

Five basic types of short-memory processes have been proposed for financial time series:

1. Autoregressive (AR);
2. Moving average (MA);
3. Autoregressive moving average (ARMA);
4. Autoregressive integrated moving average (ARIMA);
5. Autoregressive conditional heteroskedastic (ARCH).

Each of these has a number of variants, which are refinements of the basic models. These refinements attempt to bring the characteristics of the time series closer to actual data. We will examine each of these processes in turn, but we will focus on the basic models. Variants of the basic models will be left to future research. In addition, a long-memory process called fractional brownian motion has been proposed by Mandelbrot (1964, 1972, 1982). The study of fractional brownian motion will be deferred to Chapter 13. Table 5.4 summarizes the following section.

Autoregressive Processes

An autoregressive process is one in which the change in a variable at a point in time is linearly correlated with the previous change. In general, the correlation declines exponentially with time and is gone in a relatively short period. A general form follows:

$$C_n = e_n + a*C_{n-1} + b*C_{n-2} \tag{5.8}$$

where C_n = change in C at time n, $0 \le C \le 1$
$\quad$ a,b = constants with $|a| \le 1$, $|b| \le 1$
$\quad$ e = a white noise series with mean 0, and variance σ_e^2

Equation (5.8) is an autoregressive process of order 2, or AR(2), because the change in time n is related to the change in the last two periods. It is possible to have an AR(q) process where the change in C at time n is dependent on the previous q periods. To test for the possibility of an AR process, a regression is run where the change at time n is the dependent variable, and the changes in the previous q periods (the lags) are used as the independent variables. The

Table 5.4 R/S Analysis of Stochastic Processes

	H = Original Series	Significance	H = AR(1) Residual	Significance	E(H)	T	n	Trials
AR(1)	0.669	6.59	0.574	− 0.11	0.576	5,000	250	300
MA(1)	0.615	2.76	0.541	− 2.49	0.576	5,000	250	300
ARMA(1,1)	0.669	6.59	0.568	− 0.51	0.576	5,000	250	300
ARCH	0.618	0.38	0.618	0.38	0.614	8,000	50	1
*GARCH	0.633	1.67	0.635	1.85	0.614	8,000	50	1

*Generalized autoregressive conditional heteroskedastic.

t-statistic for each lag is evaluated. If any t-statistics are significant at the 5 percent level, then we can form a hypothesis that an AR process is at work. The restrictions on the range of values for the coefficients ensure that the process is *stationary,* meaning that there is no long-term trend, up or down, in the mean or variance.

Financial time series of high frequency (changes occur daily or more than once daily) generally exhibit significant autoregressive tendencies. We would expect this trait, because high-frequency data are primarily trading data, and traders do influence one another. Hourly data, for instance, can show significance at lags up to ten hours. However, once the frequency is taken at weekly or monthly intervals, the process generally reduces to an AR(1) or AR(2) process. As the time interval lengthens, the correlation effect from trading reduces. Therefore, in this simulation, we will concentrate on AR(1) processes, as defined in equation (5.8).

We have used a strong AR(1) process, with a = 0.50. The change at time n also contains 50 percent of the previous change. For the e values, 5,000 random variables were generated, and R/S analysis was performed. Figure 5.6 shows the results using the V statistic. The V statistic plot shows a significant Hurst exponent, as would be expected for an infinite memory process such as an AR(1).

We can correct for the AR process by taking AR(1) residuals. We do so by regressing C_n as the dependent variable against $C_{(n-1)}$ as the independent variable. The resulting equation will give a slope (a) and an intercept (c). We calculate the AR(1) residual in the following manner:

$$r_n = C_n - (c + a*C_{n-1}) \tag{5.9}$$

where r_n is the AR(1) residual of C at time n. In equation (5.9), we have subtracted out the linear dependence of C_n on $C_{(n-1)}$. Figure 5.6 also shows the V statistic plot of the AR(1) residual time series. The persistence has been reduced to insignificant levels.

If, however, a longer AR process is in effect, then residuals for longer lags would also have to be taken. Such a longer lag structure can be found by regressing lagged values and testing for significant relationships, such as with t-statistics. However, how long a lag is equivalent to "long" memory? Is four years of monthly returns a "long" memory? I postulate that an AR(48) relationship for monthly data is long memory, and an AR(48) for daily data is not. This reasoning is arbitrary but can be justified as follows. For most investors, a four-year memory will be the equivalent of a long memory because it is far

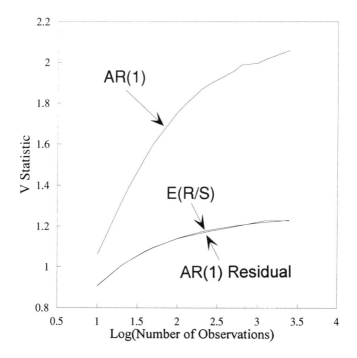

FIGURE 5.6 V statistic, AR(1) process.

beyond their own investment horizon. A four-year memory and an "infinite" memory have no practical difference, and knowing one or the other will not change these investors' outlook. However, because a 48-day memory does change the way an investor perceives market activity, it is "short-term." Once again, length of time is more important than number of observations.

Moving Average Processes

In a moving average (MA) process, the time series is the result of the moving average of an unobserved time series:

$$C_n = c*e_{n-1} + e_n \tag{5.10}$$

where e = an IID random variable
c = a constant, with $|c| < 1$

The restriction on the moving average parameter, c, ensures that the process is *invertible*. c > 1 would imply that (1) future events affect the present, which would be somewhat unrealistic, and (2) the process is stationary. Restrictions on e, the random shock, are that, like the AR process, it is an IID random variable with mean zero and variance σ_e^2.

The observed time series, C, is the result of the moving average of an unobserved random time series, e. Again, because of the moving average process, there is a linear dependence on the past and a short-term memory effect. However, unlike an AR(1) process, a random shock has only a one-period memory. Figure 5.7 shows that this can, once again, bias the log/log plot and result in a significant value of H. We can also see that taking AR(1) residuals by applying equation (5.9) overcorrects for the short-term memory problem, and now gives a significant antipersistent value of H. This appears to be a clue to moving average behavior; that is, the Hurst exponent flips from strongly persistent to strongly antipersistent.

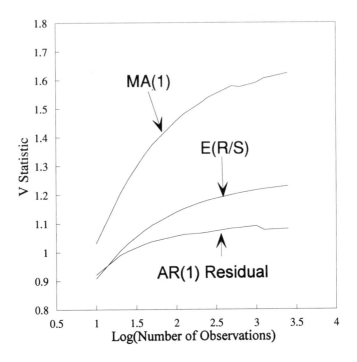

FIGURE 5.7   V statistic, MA(1) process.

ARMA Models

In this type of model, we have both an autoregressive and a moving average term. The moving average term is, once again, an unobserved random series:

$$C_n = a*C_{n-1} + e_t - b*e_{t-1} \qquad (5.11)$$

Models of this type are called *mixed models* and are typically denoted as ARMA(p,q) models. p is the number of autoregressive terms, and q represents the number of moving average terms; that is, an ARMA(2,0) process is the same as an AR(2) process because it has no moving average terms. An ARMA(0,2) process is the same as an MA(2) process because it has no autoregressive terms.

Figure 5.8 shows that the ARMA(1,1) model can bias R/S analysis because it is an infinite memory process, like the AR(1) process, although it includes an MA(1) term. However, the graph also shows that taking AR(1) residuals minimizes this problem.

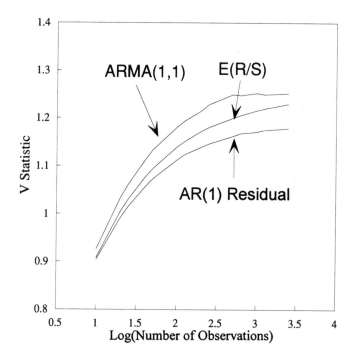

FIGURE 5.8   V statistic, ARMA(1,1) process.

ARIMA Models

Both AR and ARMA models can be absorbed into a more general class of processes. Autoregressive integrated moving average models (ARIMA) are specifically applied to time series that are *nonstationary*—these processes have an underlying trend in their mean and variance. However, by taking successive differences of the data, the result is stationary.

For instance, a price series is not stationary merely because it has a long-term growth component. It can grow without bound, so the price itself will not tend toward an average value. However, it is generally accepted by the Efficient Market Hypothesis (EMH) that the changes in price (or returns) are stationary. Typically, price changes are specified as percent changes or, in this case, log differences. However, this is just the first difference. In some series, higher-order differences may be needed to make the data stationary. For instance, the difference of the differences is a second-order ARIMA process. It could go to higher differences.

Therefore, we can say that C_t is a *homogeneous nonstationary process of order d* if:

$$w_t = \Delta^d C_t \tag{5.12}$$

is stationary. Δ represents differencing, and d represents how much differencing is needed. For example:

$$\Delta C_t = C_t - C_{t-1}$$
$$\Delta^2 C_t = \Delta C_t - \Delta C_{t-1}$$

and so forth.

If w_t is an ARMA(p,q) process, then C_t is considered an *integrated autoregressive moving average process of order (p,d,q)*, or an ARIMA(p,d,q) process. Once again, p is the number of autoregressive terms, and q is the number of moving average terms. The parameter, d, refers to the number of differencing operations needed. The process does not have to be mixed. If C_t is an ARIMA(p,d,0) process, then w_t is an AR(p) process. Likewise, if C_t is an ARIMA(0,d,q) process, then w_t is an MA(0,q).

For prices, taking AR(1) residuals is an accepted method for making the process stationary. Therefore, no additional simulations are needed here. However, the classic ARIMA(p,d,q) model assumes integer differencing. By relaxing the integer assumption, fractional differencing allows for a wide range of processes, including the persistence and antipersistence of the Hurst process (more fully discussed in Chapter 13). The ARIMA class is discussed here for completeness and as preparation for the fractional differencing method, or ARFIMA models.

ARCH Models

Models that exhibit autoregressive conditional heteroskedasticity (ARCH) have become popular in the past few years, for a number of reasons:

1. They are a family of nonlinear stochastic processes, as opposed to the linear-dependent AR and MA processes;
2. Their frequency distribution is a high-peaked, fat-tailed one;
3. Empirical studies have shown that financial time series exhibit statistically significant ARCH.

But what is ARCH?

The basic ARCH model was developed by Engle (1982). Engle considered time series that were defined by normal probability distributions but time-dependent variances; the expected variance of a process was conditional on what it was previously. Variance, although stable for the individual distributions, would appear to be "time varying," hence the *conditional heteroskedasticity* of the process name. The process is also autoregressive in that it has a time dependence. A sample frequency distribution would be an average of these expanding and contracting normal distributions. As such, it would appear as a fat-tailed, high-peaked distribution at any point in time. The basic ARCH model was defined as follows:

$$C_n = s_n * e_n$$
$$S_n^2 = f_o + f * e_{n-1}^2 \qquad\qquad (5.13)$$

Where e = a standard normal random variable
   f = a constant

For matters of convenience, $f_0 = 1$ and $f = 0.50$ are typical values. We can see that the ARCH model has a similarity to the AR models discussed previously: the observed value, C, is once again the result of an unobserved series, e, which is dependent on past realizations of itself. However, the ARCH model is nonlinear. Small changes will likely be followed by other small changes, and large changes by other large changes, but the sign will be unpredictable. Also, because ARCH is nonlinear, large changes will amplify and small changes will contract. This results in the fat-tailed, high-peaked distribution.

The ARCH model was modified to make the s variable dependent on the past as well. Bollerslev (1986) formalized the generalized ARCH (or GARCH) model in the following manner:

$$C_n = s_n * e_n$$

$$s_n^2 = f_o + f * e_{n-1}^2 + g * s_{n-1}^2 \qquad\qquad (5.14)$$

For GARCH, it is typical to set $f_0 = 1$, $f = 0.10$, and $g = 0.80$, although all three variables can range from 0 to 1. GARCH also creates a fat-tailed, high-peaked frequency distribution. Equations (5.13) and (5.14) are the basic ARCH and GARCH models; there are many variations. (Readers wishing a more complete picture are encouraged to consult Bollerslev, Chou, and Kroner (1990), who did an excellent survey.) The extended ARCH and GARCH models fine-tune the characteristics so that the models better conform to empirical observations. However, for our purposes here, there will be little change in the scaling properties of an ARCH or GARCH process, although the changes improve the theoretical aspects of the models. We will examine these other "improvements" in Chapter 14.

Because the basic ARCH and GARCH models have many characteristics that conform to empirical data, simulated ARCH and GARCH values are an excellent test for R/S analysis.

Figure 5.9 shows the V-statistic plot for the ARCH model, as described above. The model has a distinctive R/S spectrum, with higher-than-expected values for short time period, and lower-than-expected values for longer time periods. This implies that ARCH processes have short-term randomness and long-term antipersistence. Taking AR(1) residuals does not appear to affect the graph. This characteristic reflects the "mean reverting" behavior often associated with basic ARCH models.

GARCH, on the other hand, has marginally persistent values, as shown in Figure 5.10. However, they are not significant at the 5 percent level. Again, the AR(1) residual does not affect the scaling process. Unfortunately, these plots do not match the yen/dollar R/S graph in Figure 4.2, even though GARCH is often postulated as the appropriate model for currencies. We will examine this discrepancy further in the coming chapters.

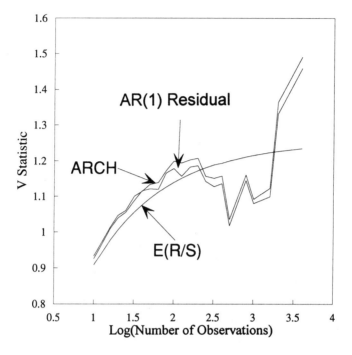

FIGURE 5.9   V statistic, ARCH process.

Problems with Stochastic Models

The four models briefly summarized above are the most popular alternative
models to the Hurst process for markets. Each seems to capture certain empirical findings of markets, but none has been completely satisfying. The problem
seems to be that each addresses a *local* property of markets. Many of these
local properties seem to be tied to some investment horizons, but not all. AR
processes, for instance, are characteristic of very high-frequency data, such as
intraday trades. They are less of a problem with longer-term horizons, such
as monthly returns. GARCH has a fat-tailed, high-peaked distribution, but it is
not self-similar; the GARCH parameters appear to be period-dependent, and
are not constant once an adjustment is made for scale. In general, these models
do not fit with the Fractal Market Hypothesis, but they must be considered
when investigating period-specific data. An exception is the fractional version
of the ARIMA family of models, but discussion of this important class must
wait until Chapter 13. Another exception is the IGARCH model, which has

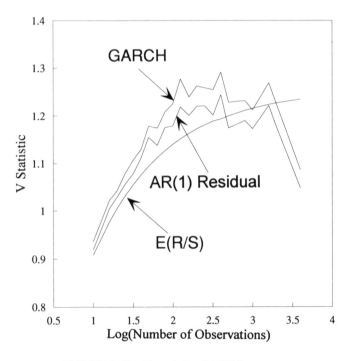

FIGURE 5.10 V statistic, GARCH process.

finite conditional variance but infinite unconditional variance. This model
will be discussed in Chapter 14.

SUMMARY

In this chapter, we have developed significance tests for R/S analysis. We have
found that an empirical correction to an earlier formula developed by Anis and
Lloyd (1976) will calculate the expected value of the R/S statistic for independent random variables. From this, we have been able to calculate the expected
value of the Hurst exponent, H. The variance was found, again through Monte
Carlo simulations, to be 1/T, where T is the number of observations. When we
tested a number of popular stochastic models for the capital markets, we found
that none of them exhibited the Hurst effect of persistence, once short-term
memory processes were filtered out. ARCH and GARCH series could not be
filtered, but did not exhibit long-term memory effects in raw form either.

6
Finding Cycles:
Periodic and Nonperiodic

For some technical analysts, finding cycles is synonymous with market analysis. There is something comforting in the idea that markets, like many natural phenomena, have a regular ebb and flow. These technicians believe that there are regular market cycles, hidden by noise or irregular perturbations, that drive the market's underlying clockwork mechanism. Such "cycles" have proven fickle to unwary investors. Sometimes they work, sometimes they do not. Statistical tests, such as spectral analysis, find only correlated noise. The search for cycles in the market and in the economy has proven frustrating for all concerned.

Unfortunately, Western science has typically searched for regular or *periodic* cycles—those that have a predictable schedule of occurrence. This tradition probably goes back to the beginnings of science. Originally, there was the change in the seasons, and the planning that was required for hunting and agriculture. Then there was astronomy, which revealed the regular lunar and solar cycles. Primitive constructs, such as Stonehenge, are based on the regularity of the vernal and autumnal equinox. Because they are smooth and symmetrical, regular cycles also appealed to the ancient Greeks. They even believed that nature preferred the perfect circle, and Aristotle created a model of the universe based on the heavenly bodies' moving in perfect circles. Later, machines, such as the pendulum, were based on regular, periodic movements. From this tradition developed Newtonian mechanics and the analysis of periodic cycles mathematically.

Early on, problems arose. The calendar caused conflict for centuries; even now, the problems have not been satisfactorily resolved. The lunar and solar calendars do not coincide. Our day is based on the rotation of the earth on its axis, and our year, on the rotation of the earth around the sun. We would like every solar year to contain the same number of lunar days, but, unfortunately, this is not so. To compensate for this lack of regularity, we add an extra day to the solar year every four years. In this way, we impose regularity on an irregular system.

Western music is based on a 12-note scale that fits within an octave. Unfortunately, perfectly tuning the half-steps (so that they are pure, and without beats) results in a 12-note scale that is less than an octave. The most popular fix to this problem spreads the error out over all the notes. This "equal tempered tuning" works in most cases, but it is, again, an attempt to fit regularity into an irregular system.

In astronomy, it was observed that wandering stars, the planets, did not follow a regular path, but often reversed direction, briefly. The Greeks continued to believe that nature would abhor any planetary system that would not consist of perfect circles, as outlined earlier by Aristotle. As a result, Ptolemy and his followers developed elaborate schemes to show that observed irregularity could result from unobserved regularity. For instance, the planetary reversal phenomenon was explained in the following manner. Planets, while orbiting the earth (in a perfect circle), also followed a smaller orbital circle, much as our moon orbits the earth as both orbit the sun. The two regular movements, occurring in conjunction, result in an observed irregular motion. This method explained the irregularity of planetary movements, while preserving the idea that nature's underlying structure was still regular. The Ptolemaic model worked well for explaining observations and predicting planetary movements far in the future. Unfortunately, its underlying theory was wrong.

In time series analysis, the focus has also been on regular, periodic cycles. In Fourier analysis, we assume that irregularly shaped time series are the sum of a number of periodic sine waves, each with differing frequencies and amplitudes. Spectral analysis attempts to break an observed irregular time series, with no obvious cycle, into these sine waves. Peaks in the power spectrum are considered evidence of cyclical behavior. Like the Ptolemaic model of the universe, spectral analysis imposes an unobserved periodic structure on the observed nonperiodic time series. Instead of a circle, it is a sine or cosine wave.

Granger (1964) was the first to suggest that spectral analysis could be applied to market time series. His results were inconclusive. Over the years, various transformations of the data were performed to find evidence of cycles that, intuitively, were felt to be there; but they could not be found. Finally, most of the field gave up and decided that the cycles were like the lucky runs of gamblers—an illusion.

Unfortunately, there is no intuitive reason for believing that the underlying basis of market or economic cycles has anything to do with sine waves or any other periodic cycle. Spectral analysis would be an inappropriate tool for market cycle analysis. In chaos theory, nonperiodic cycles exist. These cycles have an average duration, but the exact duration of a future cycle is unknown. Is that where we should look? If so, we need a more robust tool for cycle analysis, a tool that can detect both periodic and nonperiodic cycles. Luckily, R/S analysis can perform that function.

We begin this chapter by examining the effectiveness of R/S analysis in uncovering periodic cycles, even when the cycles are superimposed on one another. We will then turn to nonperiodic cycles and chaotic systems. The chapter concludes by examining some natural systems that are known to exhibit nonperiodic cycles. We will turn to analyzing markets in Chapter 7.

PERIODIC CYCLES

Hurst (1951) was the first to realize that an underlying periodic component could be detected with R/S analysis. A periodic system corresponds to a limit cycle or a similar type of attractor. As such, its phase space portrait would be a bounded set. In the case of a sine wave, the time series would be bounded by the amplitude of the wave. Because the range could never grow beyond the amplitude, the R/S values would reach a maximum value after one cycle. Mandelbrot and Wallis (1969a–1969d) did an extensive series of computer simulations, especially considering the technology available at the time. We will repeat and augment some of those experiments here, to show the behavior of R/S analysis in the presence of periodic components.

We begin with a simple sine wave:

$$Y_t = \sin(t) \tag{6.1}$$

where t = a time index

Figure 6.1 shows the log/log plot for a sine wave with a cycle length of 100 iterations. The break at t = 100 is readily apparent. Other methods, such as spectral analysis, can easily find such simple periodic components. It is the

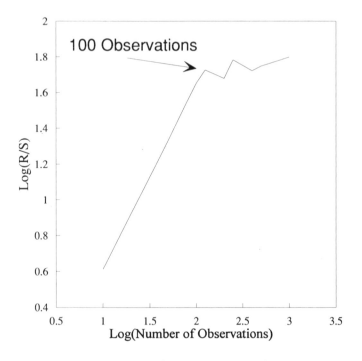

FIGURE 6.1 R/S analysis, sine wave: cycle = 100.

manner in which R/S analysis captures this process that is important. Essentially, once the sine wave has covered a full cycle, its range stops growing, because it has reached its maximum amplitude. Its maximum range, from peak to trough, is no larger for 500 observations than it was for 100. The average R/S stops growing after 100 observations.

Karl Weirstrass, a German mathematician, created the first fractal function. This function was continuous everywhere, but nowhere differentiable. The function is an infinite sum of a series of sine (or cosine) waves in which the amplitude decreases, while the frequency increases according to different factors. West (1990) has used this function extensively as an introduction to fractal time series. Here, we will see how R/S analysis can determine not only the primary cycle, but the underlying cycles as well, as long as the number of subcycles is a small, finite number.

The Weirstrass function superimposes an infinite number of sine waves. We begin with the major, or fundamental frequency, w, with an amplitude of 1. A second harmonic term is added, with frequency bw and amplitude 1/a, with a and b greater than 1. The third harmonic term has frequency b^2w and amplitude $1/a^2$. The fourth term has frequency b^3w and amplitude $1/a^3$. As usual with a continuous function, the progression goes on indefinitely. Each term has frequency that is a power of b greater than the previous one, and amplitude that is a power of a smaller. Drawing upon equation (1.5) in Chapter 1, the fractal dimension, D, of this curve would be $\ln(a)/\ln(b)$. The formal equation of the Weirstrass function is as follows, written as a Fourier series:

$$F(t) = \sum_{n=0}^{\infty} (1/a^n)*\cos(b^n*w*t) \qquad (6.2)$$

Figure 6.2 shows the Weirstrass function using the first four terms (n = 1 to 4). Figure 6.3 shows the first four terms broken out, to reveal the superimposition of the cycles. The final graph is the sum of four sine waves, each with its own frequency and amplitude. For small time increments, the range will steadily increase until it crosses the cycle length of the smallest frequency. It will begin to grow again with the next longer frequency, but it will also have

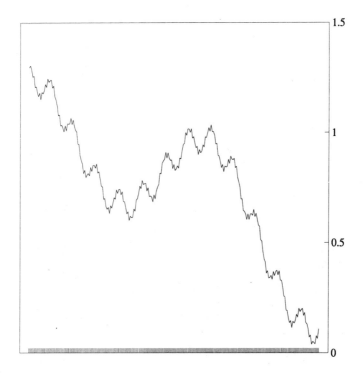

FIGURE 6.2 The Weirstrass function.

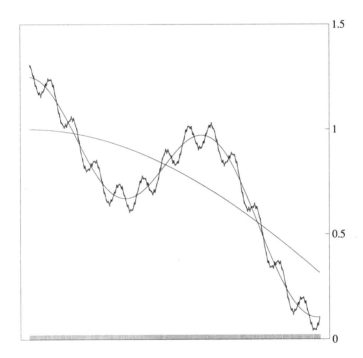

FIGURE 6.3 The Weirstrass function, the first four frequencies.

the shorter frequency superimposed, resulting in a "noisier" cycle. This range will continue to grow until it reaches the end of its cycle; the range will then stop growing until it picks up the next, longer frequency. The range for this frequency will again grow, but it will have the other two shorter frequencies superimposed. As a result, it will appear noisier still. The final, longest frequency will react as the others.

The log/log plot for R/S analysis is shown as Figure 6.4. The end of each frequency cycle, and the beginning of the next, can be seen clearly as "breaks" or flattening in the R/S plot. Notice that the slope for each frequency drops as well. For the shortest frequency, $H = 0.95$; for the longest frequency, $H = 0.72$. The portion of the R/S plot for the second shortest frequency includes a "bump" at its start. This bump is the appearance of the shorter, previous frequency. In the third shortest frequency, two bumps are vaguely visible. However, by the third frequency, the superimposition of the self-affine structure is too jagged to discern smaller structures. This leads us to the conclusion that R/S analysis can discern cycles within cycles, if the number of cycles is

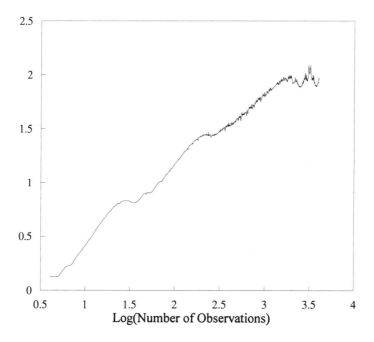

FIGURE 6.4   R/S analysis, Weirstrass function.

less than four. At greater numbers, the cycles become smeared over. If there were an infinite number of cycles, as in the complete Weirstrass function, then the log/log plot would be a straight line with H ≈ 0.70.

There is an easier way to see when the breaks in the log/log plot occur, and to make a better estimate of the cycle length. The following simple statistic was originally used by Hurst (1951) to test for stability. I have also found that it gives a more precise measure of the cycle length, which works particularly well in the presence of noise. The statistic, which is called V, is defined as follows:

$$V_n = (R/S)_n / \sqrt{n}$$ (6.3)

This ratio would result in a horizontal line if the R/S statistic was scaling with the square root of time. In other words, a plot of V versus log(n) would be flat if the process was an independent, random process. On the other hand, if the process was persistent and R/S was scaling at a faster rate than the square root of time (H > 0.50), then the graph would be upwardly sloping. Conversely, if the process was antipersistent (H < 0.50), the graph would be downward sloping. By plotting V on the y axis and log(n) on the x axis, the "breaks" would occur when the V chart flattens out. At those points, the long-memory process has dissipated.

Figure 6.5 shows the V statistic for the Weirstrass equation. Note the flattening in the slope at the end of each periodic cycle. By examining the maximum value of V at each interval, we can estimate the cycle length for each frequency.

From Figure 6.5, we can see that R/S analysis is capable of determining periodic cycles, even when they are superimposed. But we have other tools for that. The real power of R/S analysis is in finding nonperiodic cycles.

NONPERIODIC CYCLES

A nonperiodic cycle has no absolute frequency. Instead, it has an average frequency. We are familiar with many processes that have absolute frequencies, and they tend to be big, very important systems. These include the time needed for

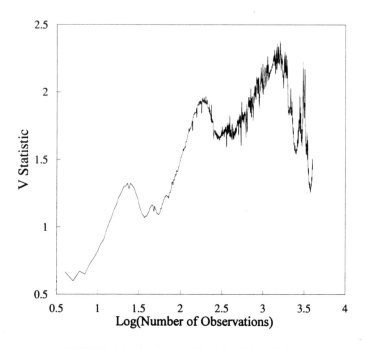

FIGURE 6.5   Weirstrass function, V statistic.

one revolution of the Earth around the sun, and the time it takes for our planet to rotate once on its axis. We have developed clocks and calendars that precisely divide these frequencies into increments called years, days, or minutes. The seasonal pattern seems absolutely periodic. Spring is followed by Summer, Autumn, and Winter, in that order. We have become accustomed to implying the word *periodic* every time we use the word *cycle*. Yet, we know that some things have cycles, but we cannot be sure exactly how long each cycle lasts. The seasonal pattern of the Earth's weather is perfectly predictable, but we know that exceptionally high temperatures can be followed by more of the same, causing a "heat wave." We also know that the longer the heat wave lasts, the more likely that it will come to an end. But we don't know exactly when.

We now know that these nonperiodic cycles can have two sources:

1. They can be statistical cycles, exemplified by the Hurst phenomena of persistence (long-run correlations) and abrupt changes in direction;
2. They can be the result of a nonlinear dynamic system, or deterministic chaos.

We will now briefly discuss the differences between these two systems.

Statistical Cycles

The Hurst process, examined closely in Chapter 4, is a process that can be described as a biased random walk, but the bias can change abruptly, in direction or magnitude. These abrupt changes in bias, modeled by Hurst as the joker in his probability pack of cards, give the appearance of cycles. Unfortunately, despite the robustness of the statistical structure, the appearance of the joker is a random event. Because the cutting of the probability deck occurs with replacement, there is no way to predict when the joker will arrive. When Mandelbrot (1982) said that "the cycles mean nothing" if economic cycles are a Hurst process, he meant that the duration of the cycle had no meaning and was not a product of the time series alone. Instead, the arrival of the joker was due to some exogenous event that may or may not be predictable. In light of this, Hurst "cycles" have no average length, and the log/log plot continues to scale indefinitely. Figure 6.6(a) shows a simulated time series with H = 0.72. The time series "looks like" a stock market chart, with positive and negative runs and the usual amount of "noise." Figure 6.6(b) is an R/S plot for the same series. Although the series is over 8,000 observations in length, there is no tendency to deviate from the trend line. There is no average cycle length.

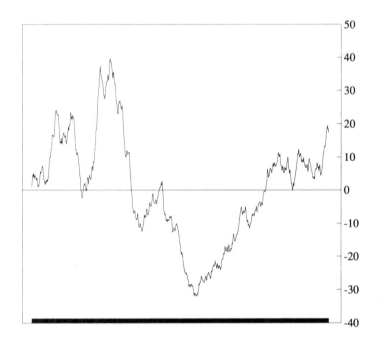

FIGURE 6.6a   Fractal time series: H = 0.72.

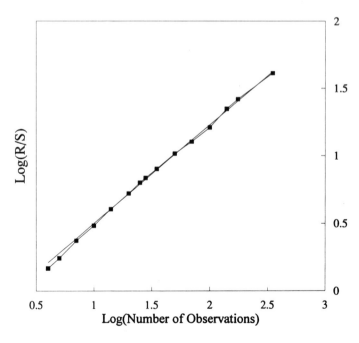

FIGURE 6.6b   R/S analysis, fractal time series: H = 0.72.

Chaotic Cycles

Nonlinear dynamical systems are deterministic systems that can exhibit erratic behavior. When discussing chaos, it is common to refer to *chaotic maps.* Maps are usually systems of iterated difference equations, such as the famous Logistic Equation:

$$X_t = a*X_{t-1}*(1 - X_{t-1}), \; 0 < X < 1$$

This type of equation is a wonderful teaching tool because it generates statistically random numbers, deterministically. However, as a tool for market or economic analysis, the equation is not really useful. Iterative maps, like the Logistic Equation, exhibit once-per-iteration chaos; that is, their memory length is extremely short. They do not exhibit the types of cycles that we see in economics or investments.

Instead, we will study *chaotic flows,* continuous systems of interdependent differential equations. Such systems are used to model large ecosystems (like weather, for example) and thermodynamic systems. The best known system of this type is the celebrated attractor of Lorenz (1963), which is well-documented in many chaos articles and is extensively discussed in Gleick (1987).

A simpler system is the Mackey–Glass (1977) equation, which was developed to model red blood cell production. Its basic premise is that current production is based on past production and current measurement. A delay between production and the measurement of current levels produces a "cycle" related to that delay. Because the system is nonlinear, over- and underproduction tend to be amplified, resulting in nonperiodic cycles. The average length of the nonperiodic cycles, however, is very close to the delay time. An additional characteristic of the Mackey–Glass equation is that it is a delay differential equation: it has an infinite number of degrees of freedom, much like the markets. This trait, of course, makes it a good candidate for simulation. The delay differential equation can be turned into a difference equation, as follows:

$$X_t = 0.9*X_{t-1} + 0.2*X_{t-n} \tag{6.4}$$

The degree of irregularity and, therefore, the underlying fractal dimension depend on the time lag, n. However, the equation offers the convenience of varying the lag and, hence, the cycle used. We can use the Mackey–Glass equation to test our hypothesis that R/S analysis can estimate the average length of a nonperiodic cycle.

The version of the Mackey–Glass equation shown in equation (6.4) is the original delay differential equation converted into a difference equation. In this form, it can be easily simulated in a spreadsheet. Beginning with lag n = 50, the steps are:

1. Insert 0.10 in cell A1. Copy 0.10 down for the first 50 cells in column A.
2. In cell A51, type: 0.9*A50 + .2*a1.
3. Copy Cell A51 down for 8,000 cells.

When varying the lag, n, enter 0.10 for the first n cells in column A. Proceed as above, starting step 2 at cell A(n + 1).

Figure 6.7 shows the first 500 observations of the 8,000 used for this test. Note the irregular cycle lengths, typical of a nonlinear dynamic system. Figure 6.8 shows the R/S plot for the full 8,000 values, with apparent H = 0.93 for n < 50. However, at H > 50, the slope is practically zero, showing that the maximum range has been reached. The Mackey–Glass equation, being a smooth, deterministic system, has a Hurst exponent close to 1. Figure 6.9 shows the

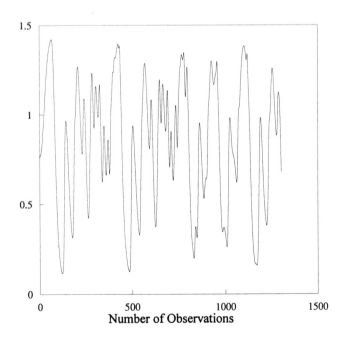

FIGURE 6.7 Mackey–Glass equation: observation lag = 50.

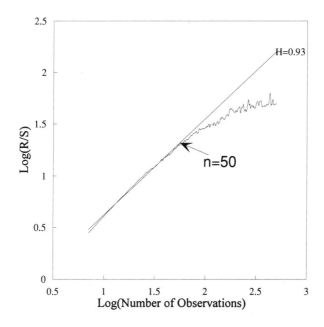

FIGURE 6.8   R/S analysis, Mackey–Glass equation: observation lag = 50.

V-statistic plot for the same values. The cycle length at approximately 50 observations is readily apparent. In Figure 6.10, the lag was changed to 100 observations. The break in the R/S graph now occurs at n = 100, confirming that R/S analysis can detect different cycle lengths. The reader is encouraged to vary the lag of the Mackey–Glass equation in order to test this conclusion.

Adding Noise

Figure 6.8 shows that R/S analysis can determine the average length of nonperiodic cycles for a large value of H. However, many tests work very well in the absence of noise, but once a small amount of noise is added, the process fails. Examples include Poincaré sections and phase space reconstruction. However, because R/S analysis was made to measure the amount of noise in a system, we might expect that R/S analysis would be more robust with respect to noise.

There are two types of noise in dynamical systems. The first is called *observational* or *additive noise*. The system is unaffected by this noise; instead, the noise is a measurement problem. The observer has trouble precisely measuring the output of the system, so the recorded value has a noise increment added.

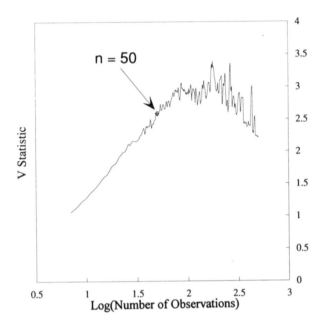

FIGURE 6.9   V statistic, Mackey–Glass equation: observation lag = 50.

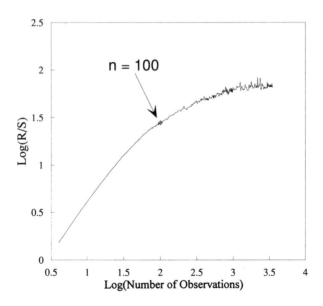

FIGURE 6.10   R/S analysis, Mackey–Glass equation: observation lag = 100.

For example, suppose you are studying a dripping faucet by measuring the time between drips. You have set up a measuring device on a table and have placed a microphone under the spot where the water drips, to record the exact instant the water drop hits bottom. Unfortunately, you are in a busy lab filled with other people who are also performing experiments. Every time someone walks by, your table jiggles a little, and this changes the time when the drip hits the microphone. Additive noise is external to the process. It is the observer's problem, not the system's.

Unfortunately, when most people think of noise, they think of additive noise. However, a second type of noise, called *dynamical noise,* may be even more common and is much more of a problem. When the system interprets the noisy output as an input, we have dynamical noise, because the noise invades the system. We will examine dynamical noise more closely in Chapter 17.

For now, we will deal with additive noise. Figure 6.11 shows the same points as Figure 6.7, with one standard deviation of noise added. The time series looks much more like a natural time series. Figure 6.12 shows the R/S plot, with H = 0.76. Adding one standard deviation of noise has reduced the

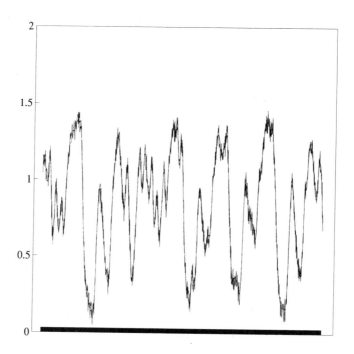

FIGURE 6.11   Mackey–Glass equation, observational noise added.

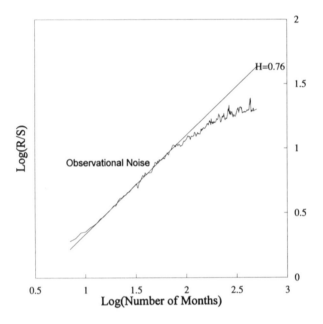

FIGURE 6.12   R/S analysis, Mackey–Glass equation with observational noise.

Hurst exponent, as would be expected, because the time series is now more jagged. The V statistic in Figure 6.13 is also unaffected by the addition of a large amount of noise. The cycle length at n = 50 can still be estimated.

R/S analysis is particularly robust with respect to noise—indeed, it seems to thrive on it.

An Empirical Example: Sunspots

In *Chaos and Order in the Capital Markets,* I examined sunspots. I repeat that study here, using some of the new techniques outlined in this chapter.

The sunspot series was obtained from Harlan True Stetson's *Sunspots and Their Effects* (1938). The time series contains monthly sunspot numbers from January, 1749, through December, 1937. The series was recorded by people who looked at the sun daily and counted the number of sunspots. Interestingly, if a large number of sunspots were closely clustered, they were counted as one large sunspot. As you can see, there would be a problem with observational noise in this series, even for the monthly average. In addition, the sunspot system is well-known for having a nonperiodic cycle of about 11 years. The 11-year cycle has

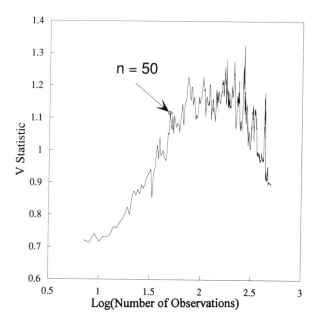

FIGURE 6.13   V statistic, Mackey–Glass equation: observation lag = 50.

been obtained from observation. Figure 6.14 shows the R/S plot of the sunspot numbers. The small values of n have a flattened slope, which shows the effects of the observational noise at short frequencies. Once the slope begins increasing, we obtain H = 0.72, for n < 11 years. At approximately 11 years, the slope flattens out, showing that the length of the nonperiodic cycle is, indeed, approximately 11 years. The V-statistic plot in Figure 6.15 confirms that the cycle is approximately 11 years.

SUMMARY

In this chapter, we have seen that R/S analysis can not only find persistence, or long memory, in a time series, but can also estimate the length of periodic or nonperiodic cycles. It is also robust with respect to noise. This makes R/S analysis particularly attractive for studying natural time series and, in particular, market time series. In the next chapter, we will examine some market and economic time series for persistence and cycles.

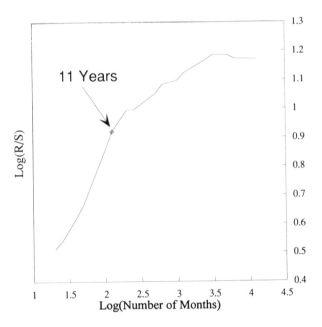

FIGURE 6.14 R/S analysis, sunspots: January 1749–December 1937.

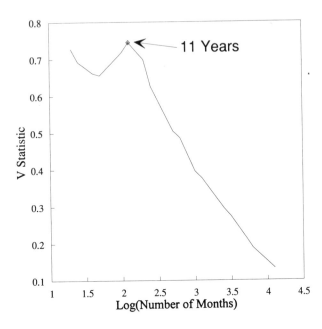

FIGURE 6.15 V statistic, sunspots: January 1749–December 1937.

103

PART THREE
APPLYING FRACTAL ANALYSIS

7
Case Study Methodology

In this part of the book, we will analyze a number of market time series using the tools from Chapters 4 through 6. Readers familiar with *Chaos and Order in the Capital Markets* will recall such an analysis in that earlier work. However, there are some important differences between my earlier study and the one in these chapters.

The primary purpose of my earlier study was to show evidence that the Efficient Market Hypothesis (EMH) is flawed, and that markets are Hurst processes, or biased random walks. That point was effectively made. My purpose here is to illustrate technique, which can be applied to readers' own area of interest. Therefore, the study done here is more a step-by-step process. Each example has been chosen to study a particular element, or a problem in applying R/S analysis, and how to compensate for it. The studies are interesting in themselves, for understanding markets. They have been chosen as illustrations so that reader's can apply R/S analysis to their own areas of interest.

This study will use the significance tests and data preparation methods outlined in the previous chapters. In my earlier book, those methods had not been worked out; indeed, my 1991 book has been criticized because the "power" of R/S analysis was unknown. Using significance tests, we can now analyze the type of system we are dealing with. As already suggested in Chapter 2, the different markets may actually have different structures, once the investment horizon is extended.

The chapter begins with a discussion of the methodology used in the analysis. We will then analyze different markets on a case-by-case basis. R/S analysis will be used on different time series, and the results will be contrasted for the various possible stochastic models investigated in Chapter 5. Analysis of the markets will be followed by analysis of some economic data.

METHODOLOGY

We will analyze AR(1) residuals of logarithmic returns for the capital markets. The AR(1) residuals are used to eliminate—or, at least, to minimize—linear dependency. As we saw in Chapter 5, linear dependency can bias the Hurst exponent (and may make it look significant when no long-memory process exists) or a Type I error. By taking AR(1) residuals, we minimize the bias, and, we hope, reduce the results to insignificance. The process is often called *prewhitening,* or *detrending.* The latter term will be used here. Detrending is not appropriate for all statistical tests, although it seems to be used in an almost willy-nilly fashion. For some tests, detrending may mask significant information. However, in the case of R/S analysis, detrending will eliminate serial correlation, or short memory, as well as inflationary growth. The former is a problem with very high-frequency data, such as five-minute returns. The latter is a problem with low-frequency data, such as 60 years of monthly returns. However, for R/S analysis, the short-memory process is much more of a problem than the inflationary growth problem, as we will see.

We begin with a series of logarithmic returns:

$$S_t = \log(P_t/P_{t-1}) \tag{7.1}$$

where S_t = logarithmic return at time t
      P_t = price at time t

We then regress S_t as the dependent variable against $S_{(t-1)}$ as the independent variable, and obtain the intercept, a, and the slope, b. The AR(1) residual of S_t subtracts out the dependence of S_t on $S_{(t-1)}$:

$$X_t = S_t - (a + b*S_{t-1}) \tag{7.2}$$

where X_t = the AR(1) residual of S at time t

The AR(1) residual method does not eliminate all linear dependence. However, Brock, Dechert, and Sheinkman (1987) felt that it eliminated enough dependence to reduce the effect to insignificant levels, even if the AR process is level 2 or 3.

R/S analysis is then performed, starting with step 2 of the step-by-step guide provided in Chapter 4. We begin with step 2 because step 1 has already been outlined above.

Even in this early phase, there are important differences between this methodology and the one used in Peters (1991b, 1992). The differences hark back to Peters (1989). We now use only time increments that include both the beginning and ending points; that is, we use even increments of time. Previously, all time increments, n, were used. If there were fewer than n data points left at the end, they were not used. This had little impact on R/S values for small values of n, because there are many R/S samples, and the number of "leftover points" is small. For example, a time series of T = 500 observations has 12 R/S values for n = 40, with 20 unused observations, or 4 percent of the sample. The average of the 12 samples would be a good estimate of the true value of $R/S_{50,}$ and the impact of the unused 20 observations would be minimal. However, for n = 200, there would be only two values, and 100 unused observations, or 20 percent of the sample. The R/S_{200} value will be unstable for 500 observations; that is, the value of R/S can be influenced by the starting point. This makes a small number of R/S_{200} values for a time series of 500 observations misleading. Using values of n that use both beginning and ending points (step 2 in Chapter 4) significantly reduces this bias.

Even as this method is eliminating a bias, it is presenting another problem. Because we are using even increments of time, we need a value of T that offers the most divisors, in order to have a reasonable number of R/S values. Therefore, odd values of T, such as 499, should not be used. It would be better to use 450 data points, which has 9 divisors, rather than 499, which has two, even though 499 has more data points. Having more R/S values is certainly more desirable than having more data points, when we are interested in the scaling of R/S.

DATA

We begin in Chapter 8 with a series of cases taken from a file of daily prices of the Dow Jones Industrials. This price file, which covers the period from January 1888 to December 1990, or 102 years of daily data, contains 26,520 data points. As we have discussed above, a large number of data points is not all that is required. A long time interval is also needed. This file appears to fulfill both requirements. We will be calculating returns for different time horizons, to see whether the R/S behavior varies depending on the time increment used. This amounts to sampling the time series at different intervals. With such a long series, we can investigate whether "oversampling" the system can result in biases.

We can expect a number of things to happen as we change the sampling interval:

1. The Hurst exponent can be expected to increase as we increase the sampling interval. At shorter intervals, or higher frequencies, there is bound to be more noise in the data. Less frequent sampling should minimize the impact of noise and eliminate the impact of any fractional noise that may exist at the higher frequency. As we saw in the Weirstrass function, the addition of higher-frequency cycles makes the time series more jagged, and so decreases the Hurst exponent (or increases the fractal dimension). Less frequent sampling "skips" over the higher frequencies.

2. Any "cycles" that exist at the longer intervals should remain. If a cycle appears at 1,000 one-day intervals, it should still be apparent at 100 ten-day intervals.

3. The first two points will not hold if the process is a Gaussian random walk. White noise appears the same at all frequencies (like the "hiss" we hear on recording tapes, which sounds the same at all speeds). And, there are no cycles. If a break in the R/S graph appears at the daily interval but not at the ten-day interval, the break in the daily graph was an artifact, not a true cycle.

STABILITY ANALYSIS

With a long time series, we will be able to study the stability of the R/S analysis. Greene and Fielitz (1977, 1979) suggested that R/S analysis should ideally be run over all starting points. This would mean that an R/S value can be the average of overlapping time periods. There is no reason to believe that this approach is valid, although, at first glance, it would appear to help when there is a short data set. However, using overlapping periods means that the estimate of R/S_n is not a result of independent sampling from the time series *without replacement*. Instead, the sampling is done *with* replacement. All of the confidence tests presented in previous chapters require independent samples (without replacement). Every time we calculate an R/S value for n values, we are taking a sample. If these samples are independent, we can average them and estimate the significance of the average R/S for n values, R/S_n, using the methods previously outlined. If we use overlapping intervals for the average, we no longer have tools to judge the significance of the R/S estimate.

A more acceptable approach would redo the R/S analysis with a different starting date. The resulting R/S_n and Hurst exponent estimates would be compared to the previous run to see whether the results are significantly different. The statistics previously defined can be used to judge significance. A long time series, like the Dow Jones Industrials data, will allow us to run R/S analysis for intervals that begin as long as ten years apart. Using this methodology, we can test whether the market's underlying statistical characteristics have significantly changed, and test once and for all whether the market does undergo the type of "structural change" long used as an excuse by econometricians.

"Tick data" for the S&P 500, from January 2, 1989, through December 31, 1992, or four years' worth of data, are analyzed in Chapter 9. This information is of most interest to traders and can yield tens of thousands of data points. However, the important problems of oversampling and short memory must be considered. This series of high-frequency data offers an opportunity to see how serious those problems are when analyzing "trading" data.

Chapter 10 examines volatility, both realized and implied. Unlike other series, volatility is antipersistent. We will examine the two measures of volatility and compare them.

Inflation and gold are the subjects of Chapter 11. Unlike the tick data, these time series show possible problems with undersampling.

Chapter 12 examines currencies, which are known as strongly trending markets. We will find that they are somewhat different from the other investment vehicles we have studied.

Part Three is concerned primarily with performing R/S analysis and with the pitfalls of doing so; it does not address the cause of long memory, just its measurement. The possible causes are the subject of Parts Four and Five. There are many potential sources for long memory, and the latter parts of the book present arguments for all of them, in the context of the Fractal Market Hypothesis.

8

Dow Jones Industrials, 1888–1990: An Ideal Data Set

NUMBER OF OBSERVATIONS VERSUS LENGTH OF TIME

In this chapter, we will do an extensive analysis of the Dow Jones Industrial Average (DJIA). This widely followed index has been published daily in *The Wall Street Journal* since 1888. The file we will work from contains daily closing prices for the Dow Jones Industrials (which we will call "the Dow," for convenience) from January 2, 1888, through December 31, 1991, or 104 years of data. We used this file in Chapter 2 when examining the term structure of volatility. This data file is the most complete file that we will study. It has a large number of observations and covers a long time period. The tick trading data for the S&P 500, used in Chapter 9, will include many more observations, but having more observations is not necessarily better.

Suppose we have a system, like the sunspot cycle, that lasts for 11 years. Having a year's worth of one-minute observations, or 518,400 observations, will not help us find the 11-year cycle. However, having 188 years of monthly numbers, or 2,256 observations, was enough for the 11-year cycle to be clearly seen in Chapter 6.

In the Dow data file, we have both length and number of observations, we can learn much from this time series. All holidays are removed from the time series. Therefore, five-day returns are composed of five trading days. They will *not* necessarily be a Monday-to-Friday calendar week. In this chapter, because we will not be using calendar increments larger than one day, there will be no "weekly," "monthly," or "quarterly" data. Instead, we will have five-day returns, 20-day returns, and 60-day returns.

TWENTY-DAY RETURNS

Figure 8.1 shows the log R/S plot for 20-day return data for $T = 1,320$ observations. The 20-day returns are approximately one calendar month in length. Also plotted is $E(R/S_n)$ (calculated using equation (5.6)) as a comparison against the null hypothesis that the system is an independent process. There is clearly a systematic deviation from the expected values. However, a break in the R/S graph appears to be at 52 observations ($\log(52)) \approx 1.8$). To estimate precisely where this break occurs, we calculate the V statistic using equation

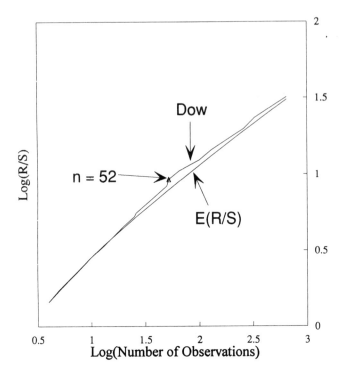

FIGURE 8.1   R/S analysis, Dow Jones Industrials: 20-day returns.

(6.3), and plot it versus log(n) in Figure 8.2. Remember, the V statistic is the ratio of R/S_n to $\sqrt{\{n\}}$. If the series exhibits persistence ($H > 0.50$), then the ratio will be increasing. When the slope crosses over to a random walk ($H = 0.50$) or to antipersistence ($H < 0.50$), the ratio will go sideways or will decline, respectively. In Figure 8.2, the V statistic clearly stops growing at $n = 52$ observations, or 1,040 trading days. Table 8.1 shows both the R/S_n values and the V_n. A peak occurs at $n = 52$. Therefore, we will run our regression to estimate H for R/S_n values, $10 \leq n \leq 50$. Table 8.2 shows the results.

The regression yielded $H = 0.72$ and $E(H) = 0.62$. The variance of $E(H)$, as shown in equation (5.7), is $1/T$ or $1/1,323$, for Gaussian random variables. The standard deviation of $E(H)$ is 0.028. The H value for Dow 20-day returns is 3.6 standard deviations above its expected value, a highly significant result.

The regression results for $n > 50$ are also shown in Table 8.2. $H = 0.49$, showing that the "break" in the R/S graph may signal a periodic or nonperiodic component in the time series, with frequency of approximately 50 20-day periods. Spectral analysis through a plot of frequency versus power in Figure 8.3 shows a featureless spectrum. No periodic components exist. Therefore, the 50-period, or 1,000-day cycle appears to be nonperiodic.

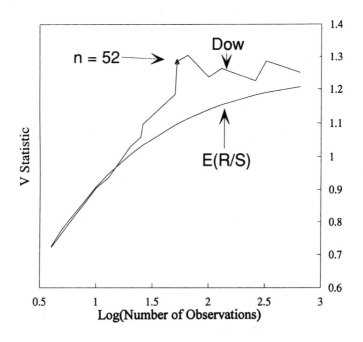

FIGURE 8.2 V statistic, Dow Jones Industrials: 20-day returns.

Table 8.1   Dow Jones Industrials, 20-Day Returns

n	Log(n)	R/S, Dow Jones	E(R/S)	V Statistic Dow Jones	E(R/S)
4	0.6021	0.1589	0.1607	0.7209	0.7239
5	0.6990	0.2331	0.2392	0.7648	0.7757
10	1.0000	0.4564	0.4582	0.9045	0.9083
13	1.1139	0.5288	0.5341	0.9371	0.9486
20	1.3010	0.6627	0.6528	1.0283	1.0053
25	1.3979	0.7239	0.7120	1.0592	1.0305
26	1.4150	0.7477	0.7223	1.0971	1.0347
50	1.6990	0.9227	0.8885	1.1837	1.0939
52	1.7160	0.9668	0.8982	1.2847	1.0969
65	1.8129	1.0218	0.9530	1.3043	1.1130
100	2.0000	1.0922	1.0568	1.2366	1.1396
130	2.1139	1.1585	1.1189	1.2634	1.1533
260	2.4150	1.2956	1.2802	1.2250	1.1822
325	2.5119	1.3652	1.3313	1.2862	1.1896
650	2.8129	1.5037	1.4880	1.2509	1.2067

Table 8.2   Regression Results: Dow Jones Industrials, 20-Day Returns

	Dow Jones Industrials, $10 < n < 52$		E(R/S) $10 < n < 52$		Dow Jones Industrials, $52 < n < 650$
Regression output:					
Constant		−0.2606		−0.1344	0.1252
Standard error of Y (estimated)		0.0096		0.0088	0.0098
R squared		0.9991		0.9990	0.9979
Number of observations		10.0000		10.0000	7.0000
Degrees of freedom		8.0000		8.0000	5.0000
Hurst exponent	0.7077		0.6072		0.4893
Standard error of coefficient	0.0076		0.0072		0.0101
Significance	3.6262				

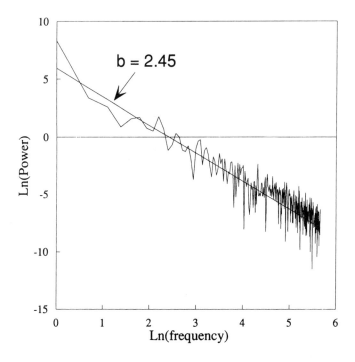

FIGURE 8.3   Spectral analysis, Dow Jones Industrials, 20-day returns.

From the above analysis, 20-day changes in the price of the Dow are characterized as a persistent Hurst process, with H = 0.72. This is significantly different from the result for a random walk. Because the series consists of AR(1) residuals, we know that a true long-memory process is at work. The characteristics of this series have little in common with other stochastic processes, examined in Chapter 4. They are particularly separate from ARCH and GARCH series (see Chapter 4), which have so often been used as models of market processes. However, the persistent scaling does have a time limit. It occurs only for periods shorter than 1,000 trading days. Therefore, the process is not an infinite memory process, but is instead a long, but finite memory with a nonperiodic cycle of approximately four years. The four-year cycle may be tied to the economic cycle. It also seems related to the term structure of volatility studied in Chapter 2. Volatility also stopped scaling after four years.

However, if this four-year cycle is a true nonperiodic cycle and not simply a stochastic boundary due to data size, it should be independent of the time period. That is, five-day returns should also have a nonperiodic cycle of 1,000 trading days, or 200 five-day periods.

FIVE-DAY RETURNS

With five-day returns, we have maintained our 104-year time series, but now we have 5,280 observations for examination. Many people feel that there are shorter cycles than the four-year cycle. Perhaps R/S analysis can uncover these values.

Figure 8.4 shows the R/S graph for five-day returns. Once again, we see a systematic deviation from the E(R/S) line. There is also a break in the log/log plot, this time at n = 208 observations. Again, this is approximately four years, showing that the break in the 20-day R/S plot was not a stochastic boundary. Figure 8.5 shows the V-statistic plot. Once again, the peak is clearly seen at approximately four years.

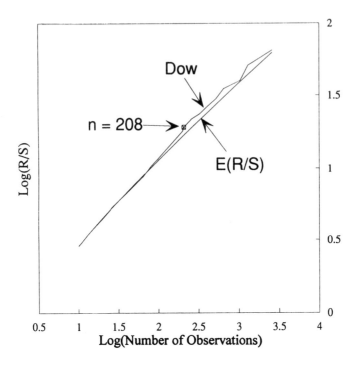

FIGURE 8.4   R/S analysis, Dow Jones Industrials, five-day returns.

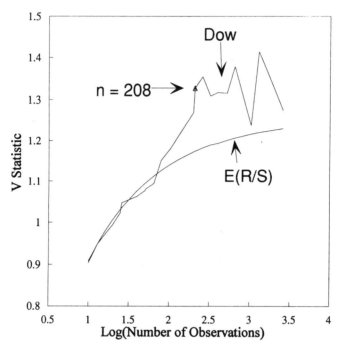

FIGURE 8.5   V statistic, Dow Jones Industrials, five-day returns.

Table 8.3 summarizes the values used in these plots. There is no conclusive evidence of a cycle shorter than four years. Values of H were again estimated from the R/S plot and the E(R/S). The results of the regression are shown in Table 8.4. Regressions were run for $10 \leq n \leq 208$. Five-day returns have a lower value of H than the 20-day returns. This reflects the increased level of detail, and "noise" in the data. Because the time series is more jagged, the Hurst exponent is lower. Five-day returns have $H = 0.61$, and $E(H) = 0.58$. This difference does not appear large, but the variance of E(H) is now 1/5,240, or a standard deviation of 0.014. Thus, five-day Dow returns have a Hurst exponent that is 2.44 standard deviations away from the mean. Again, the five-day returns have a highly significant value of H.

Most encouraging is that, even though the time increment has changed, the four-year cycle again appears. This provides additional evidence that the cycle is not a statistical artifact or an illusion.

Table 8.3   Dow Jones Industrials, Five-Day Returns

n	Log(n)	R/S, Dow Jones Industrials	E(R/S)	V Statistic Dow Jones Industrials
10	1.0000	0.4563	0.4582	0.9043
13	1.1139	0.5340	0.5341	0.9485
16	1.2041	0.5891	0.5921	0.9706
20	1.3010	0.6476	0.6528	0.9934
25	1.3979	0.7086	0.7120	1.0224
26	1.4150	0.7274	0.7223	1.0468
40	1.6021	0.8272	0.8327	1.0622
50	1.6990	0.8812	0.8885	1.0758
52	1.7160	0.8921	0.8982	1.0817
65	1.8129	0.9457	0.9530	1.0947
80	1.9031	1.0128	1.0033	1.1515
100	2.0000	1.0705	1.0568	1.1764
104	2.0170	1.0805	1.0661	1.1804
130	2.1139	1.1404	1.1189	1.2117
200	2.3010	1.2541	1.2196	1.2693
208	2.3181	1.2819	1.2287	1.3270
260	2.4150	1.3391	1.2802	1.3540
325	2.5119	1.3727	1.3313	1.3084
400	2.6021	1.4206	1.3779	1.3169
520	2.7160	1.4770	1.4376	1.3151
650	2.8129	1.5458	1.4880	1.3783
1,040	3.0170	1.6014	1.5937	1.2384
1,300	3.1139	1.7076	1.6435	1.4145
2,600	3.4150	1.8129	1.7975	1.2748

However, we have failed to find any nonperiodic cycles with frequencies of less than four years. Once again, we will increase our level of detail and analyze daily data.

DAILY RETURNS

With daily returns, we find once again that the Hurst exponent has declined. However, E(H) has also declined, as has the variance of E(H). The daily data have 24,900 observations, and the standard deviation of E(H) is now 0.006. Figure 8.6 shows the results of the R/S analysis.

Table 8.4   Regression Results

	Dow Jones Industrials, $10 < n < 208$	E(R/S), $10 < n < 208$
Regression output:		
Constant	−0.1537	−0.1045
Standard error		
of Y (estimated)	0.0076	0.0081
R squared	0.9993	0.9989
Number of observations	17.0000	16.0000
Degrees of freedom	15.0000	14.0000
Hurst exponent	0.6137	0.5799
Standard error		
of coefficient	0.0043	0.0050
Significance	2.4390	

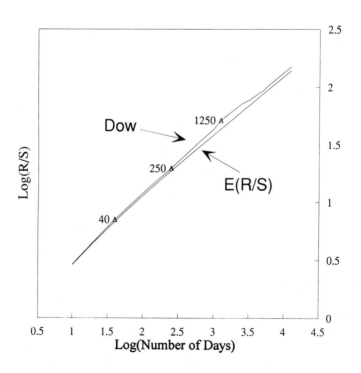

FIGURE 8.6   R/S analysis, Dow Jones Industrials, one-day returns.

For daily data, we again see a persistent deviation in observed R/S values from the expected R/S values under the null hypothesis of independence. We also see a break in the R/S plot at about 1,000 days. The V-statistic plot in Figure 8.6 shows the peak to be 1,250 days, or roughly four years. This corresponds almost exactly to the cycle of 1,040 days found with the five-day and 20-day returns. Looking at the V-statistic plot, it appears that the slope is higher for the smaller values of n (n < 50), becomes parallel for a period, and then begins growing again at approximately 350 days. We can see whether this is indeed the case by examining the difference between the R/S plots for daily Dow returns and the Gaussian null.

Figure 8.7 confirms that the slope does increase at a faster rate for n ≤ 40. The difference becomes flat for values between 40 and 250, meaning that the local slope in this region looks the same as a random walk. The slope increases dramatically between 250 and 1,250 days, after which it again goes flat. Table 8.5 shows these values. A similar graph, with multiple cycles and frequencies, was seen for the Weirstrass function in Chapter 5. We can now run regressions to assess the significance of these visual clues.

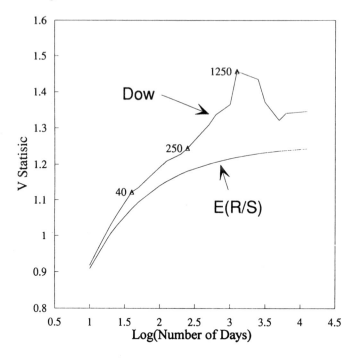

FIGURE 8.7 V statistic, Dow Jones Industrials, one-day returns.

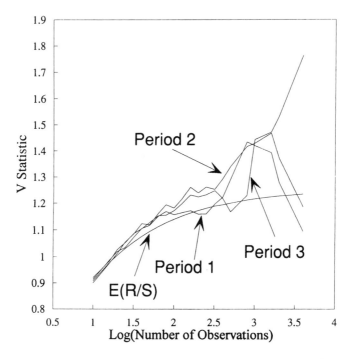

FIGURE 8.8 V statistic, Dow Jones Industrials, contiguous 8,300-day periods.

First, we calculate H for the longer 1,250-day cycle. Table 8.6 shows the results. The daily Dow has H = 0.58 and E(H) = 0.553. Again, this does not look significant, but the standard deviation of E(H) is 0.0060 for 24,900 observations. The Hurst exponent for the daily Dow is 4.13 standard deviations away from its expected value. Again, this is a highly significant result.

Table 8.6 also shows regression results for the subperiods. For 10 ≤ n ≤ 40, H = 0.65, which at first looks highly significant. However, the short end of the log/log plot has a high slope as well, with E(H) = 0.62. However, this value of H = 0.65 is still 3.65 standard deviations above the expected value, and is significant at the 99 percent level.

The next subperiod is 40 ≤ n ≤ 250, where the slope appeared to follow the E(R/S) line. Sure enough, H = 0.558 in this region, where E(H) = 0.551. Therefore, H is only 1.04 standard deviations away from its expected value, and is insignificant.

As n increases, the expected value of H (particularly the "local" value) approaches its asymptotic limit, 0.50. In the next subperiod, 250 ≤ n ≤ 1,250,

Table 8.5 Dow Jones Industrials, One-Day Returns

n	Log(n)	R/S, Dow Jones Industrials	E(R/S)	V Statistic Dow Jones Industrials	E(R/S)
10	1.0000	0.4626	0.4582	0.9174	0.9083
20	1.3010	0.6632	0.6528	1.0296	1.0053
25	1.3979	0.7249	0.7120	1.0614	1.0305
40	1.6021	0.8511	0.8327	1.1222	1.0757
50	1.6990	0.9043	0.8885	1.1345	1.0939
100	2.0000	1.0759	1.0568	1.1911	1.1396
125	2.0969	1.1308	1.1097	1.2088	1.1514
200	2.3010	1.2399	1.2196	1.2284	1.1724
250	2.3979	1.2941	1.2711	1.2450	1.1808
500	2.6990	1.4662	1.4287	1.3084	1.2000
625	2.7959	1.5239	1.4792	1.3366	1.2057
1,000	3.0000	1.6351	1.5849	1.3649	1.2159
1,250	3.0969	1.7119	1.6348	1.4570	1.2199
2,500	3.3979	1.8557	1.7888	1.4344	1.2298
3,125	3.4949	1.8845	1.8381	1.3710	1.2323
5,000	3.6990	1.9705	1.9418	1.3215	1.2367
6,250	3.7959	2.0254	1.9908	1.3409	1.2385
12,500	4.0969	2.1775	2.1429	1.3459	1.2428

$E(H) = 0.52$. For the daily Dow, $H = 0.59$, which is 10.65 standard deviations away from the mean. This highly significant value is virtually the same as the earlier subperiod.

In the final subperiod, $1,250 < n < 12,500$, the local Hurst exponent drops significantly again. In this range, $H = 0.46$, and $E(H) = 0.51$. This Hurst exponent is also significant, at the 95 percent level, because it is 7.77 standard deviations below its mean. Therefore, after the four-year cycle, the process becomes antipersistent. This conforms to Fama and French's (1992) finding that returns are "mean reverting" in the long term. We have already said that antipersistent is not the same as mean reverting (there is no mean to revert to), but, semantics aside, we are referring to a similar process.

We have found that the Dow has two nonperiodic cycles. The longest is a 1,250-day cycle, or about four years. The second is 40 days, or about two months. This information can be used in any number of ways. The most obvious is as the basis of momentum analysis and other forms of technical analysis. The second use is in choosing periods for model development, particularly for backtesting.

Table 8.6 Regression Results

	Dow Jones Industrials, 0 < n < 1,250		E(R/S), 0 < n < 1,250
Regression output:			
Constant		−0.09126	−0.0635
Standard error			
of Y (estimated)		0.011428	0.013988
R squared		0.999228	0.998732
Number of observations		13	13
Degrees of freedom		11	11
Hurst exponent	0.579		0.553331
Standard error			
of coefficient	0.005		0.005945
Significance	4.133		

	Dow Jones Industrials, 10 < n < 40		E(R/S), 10 < n < 40
Regression output:			
Constant		−0.18149	−0.1624
Standard error			
of Y (estimated)		0.004195	0.00482
R squared		0.999553	0.999366
Number of observations		4	4
Degrees of freedom		2	2
Hurst exponent	0.647		0.623532
Standard error			
of coefficient	0.01		0.011109
Significance	3.648		

	Dow Jones Industrials, 40 < n < 250		E(R/S), 40 < n < 250
Regression output:			
Constant		−0.0414	−0.04773
Standard error			
of Y (estimated)		0.002365	0.002309
R squared		0.999858	0.999861
Number of observations		6	6
Degrees of freedom		4	4
Hurst exponent	0.558		0.550943
Standard error			
of coefficient	0.003		0.003247
Significance	1.043		

Table 8.6   *(Continued)*

	Dow Jones Industrials, $250 < n < 1{,}250$		E(R/S), $250 < n < 1{,}250$
Regression output:			
Constant		−0.11788	0.024022
Standard error			
of Y (estimated)		0.008376	0.000564
R squared		0.997972	0.999988
Number of observations		5	5
Degrees of freedom		3	3
Hurst exponent	0.588		0.520278
Standard error			
of coefficient	0.015		0.00103
Significance	10.65		

	Dow Jones Industrials, $1{,}250 < n < 12{,}500$		E(R/S), $1{,}250 < n < 12{,}500$
Regression output:			
Constant		0.287021	0.062167
Standard error			
of Y (estimated)		0.010672	0.000617
R squared		0.996407	0.99999
Number of observations		6	6
Degrees of freedom		4	4
Hurst exponent	0.459		0.508035
Standard error			
of coefficient	0.014		0.000796
Significance	−7.77		

STABILITY ANALYSIS

Some questions remain: How stable are these findings? Are they period-specific? These questions are particularly important when dealing with economic and market data. There is an underlying feeling that, as the structure of the economy changes, its dynamics will change as well. For markets, this is an extremely important consideration because the technology and the predominant type of investor are quite different now than they were 40 years ago. Because of these reservations, there is doubt that examining data that predate the recent period will be useful. It would be like trying to forecast the current weather based on data collected during the Ice Age. But there are counterarguments to this line of thought. In particular, the market reacts to information, and the way it reacts is not very different from the way it reacted in the 1930s, even though the type of information is different. Therefore the underlying dynamics and, in particular, the statistics of the market have not changed. This would be especially true of fractal statistics.

Point Sensitivity

A question that often arises about R/S analysis concerns the rescaling of the range by the local standard deviation. The variance of fractal processes is undefined; therefore, aren't we scaling by an unstable variable?

Luckily, the answer is No. Because R/S analysis uses the average of many R/S values, it becomes more stable the more points we have, as long as the sampling frequency is higher than the "noise level" of the data.

To test this point sensitivity, we reran the daily R/S analysis with three different starting points, each 1,000 days apart, using 24,000 days. The results are in Table 8.7. There is little change in the value or significance of the Hurst exponent, which indicates remarkable stability.

Time Sensitivity

An appropriate test would be to take two or more independent periods, analyze them separately, and compare the results. With market data, we are limited by the cycle limit. A rule of thumb implies that ten cycles of information should be used for nonlinear analysis, as discussed in Peters (1991a, 1991b). We have 104 years of data, and an implied four-year cycle. For this analysis, we will divide the period into three segments of 36 years, using daily returns, or 8,300 observations. While using only nine cycles rather than ten, we can hope that the time periods will be sufficient.

Table 8.8 shows the results of the three equations. There is good news and bad news. The good news is that the Hurst exponent shows remarkable stability. H was 0.585 for the first period (roughly, 1880–1916), 0.565 for the second period (roughly, 1917–1953), and 0.574 for the last period (roughly, 1954–1990). The bad news is that, although E(H) still equals 0.555, the standard deviation has risen to the square root of 1/8,300, or 0.011. This means that the first and last periods are still significant at the 5 percent level or greater, but the middle period is not. In addition, neither the 42-day nor the four-year cycle existed for the second period, as shown in the V-statistic plot (Figure 8.8).

Table 8.7   Stability Analysis, Dow Jones Industrials

	First 24,000		Second 24,000
Regression output:			
Constant	−0.08651		−0.08107
Standard error			
of Y (estimated)	0.011205		0.012098
R squared	0.998942		0.998749
Number of observations	37		37
Degrees of freedom	35		35
Hurst Exponent	0.584898		0.580705
Standard error			
of coefficient	0.003218		0.003474
Significance	4.543908		3.894397

	Third 24,000		E(R/S)
Regression output:			
Constant	−0.07909		−0.06525
Standard error			
of Y (estimated)	0.013315		0.011181
R squared	0.998472		0.998832
Number of observations	37		37
Degrees of freedom	35		35
Hurst exponent	0.578292	0.555567	0.006455
Standard error			
of coefficient	0.003824	0.003211	
Significance	3.520619		

There is scant evidence for the 42-day cycle in period 3, but it is much stronger in period 1.

Period 2 was the most tumultuous period of the 20th century. It included World Wars I and II, the great boom of the 1920s, the depression of the 1930s, and the Korean War. The level of persistence in the market, as measured by the Hurst exponent, is stable, but cycle lengths are not. They can be influenced by political events, wars, and price controls. Technicians, beware!

RAW DATA AND SERIAL CORRELATION

As we saw in Chapter 5, various short-memory processes can cause a bias in R/S analysis. AR(1) processes, which are, technically, infinite memory

Table 8.8   Time Sensitivity, Dow Jones Industrials

		Period 1		Period 2
Regression output:				
Constant		−0.106		−0.074
Standard error				
of Y (estimated)		0.012		0.019
R squared		0.999		0.997
Number of observations		19.000		19.000
Degrees of freedom		17.000		17.000
Hurst exponent	0.585		0.565	
Standard error				
of coefficient	0.005		0.008	
Significance	2.683		0.894	

		Period 3		E(R/S)
Regression output:				
Constant		−0.096		−0.077
Standard error				
of Y (estimated)		0.016		0.014
R squared		0.998		0.999
Number of observations		19.000		10.000
Degrees of freedom		17.000		8.000
Hurst exponent	0.574		0.555	
Standard error				
of coefficient	0.006		0.007	
Significance	1.699			

processes as well, can give results that look significant. In this section, we will compare the log first differences of the prices with the AR(1) residuals, to see whether a significant serial correlation problem is present in the raw data.

Figure 8.9 shows the V-statistic plot for the raw data versus AR(1) residuals for the 20-day return. Table 8.9 shows the R/S values for the two series, as well as the Hurst exponent calculation. A small AR(1) bias in the raw data causes the R/S values to be a little higher than when using residuals. The Hurst exponent calculation is also slightly biased. However, the 20 sampling frequency seems to reduce the impact of serial correlation, as we have always known.

Figure 8.10 shows a similar V-statistic plot for the daily returns. The impact is more obvious here, but it is still uniform. All of the R/S values are biased upward, so the scaling feature, the Hurst exponent, is little affected by the

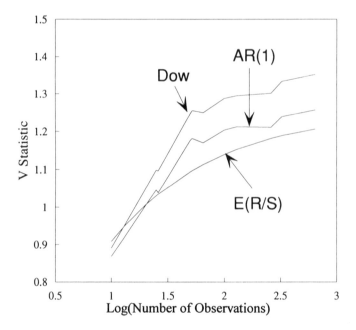

FIGURE 8.9   V statistic, Dow Jones Industrials, 20-day returns.

Table 8.9   R/S Values, Dow Jones
Industrials, 20-Day Returns

Dow	AR(1)	n
2.82	2.75	10
3.42	3.31	13
4.69	4.49	20
5.49	5.23	25
5.59	5.30	26
8.82	8.32	50
9.06	8.52	52
10.08	9.44	65
12.88	12.04	100
14.77	13.83	130
20.99	19.53	260
24.04	22.35	325
34.48	32.07	650

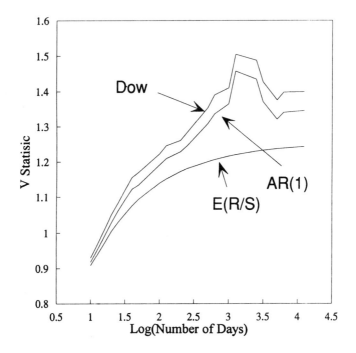

FIGURE 8.10   V statistic, Dow Jones Industrials, one-day returns.

bias, although the bias is definitely present. Table 8.10 summarizes the values. These results show that infrequent sampling does minimize the impact of a short-term memory process on R/S analysis.

SUMMARY

We have seen strong evidence that the Dow Jones Industrials are characterized by a persistent Hurst process for periods up to four years. The four-year cycle was found independent of the time increment used for the R/S analysis. There was weaker evidence of a 40-day cycle as well. The Hurst exponent was most significant for 20-day returns and much less so, although not insignificant, for daily returns. The "noise" in higher-frequency data makes the time series more jagged and random-looking.

This time series is an example of the "ideal" time series for R/S analysis. It covers a long time period and has many observations. This combination allows

Table 8.10 R/S Values Dow Jones
Industrials, One-Day Returns

n	R/S Dow Jones Industrials	AR(1)
10	2.901206	2.939259
20	4.604629	4.701588
25	5.307216	5.413394
40	7.097245	7.307622
50	8.02196	8.274441
100	11.91072	12.22428
125	13.51477	13.92784
200	17.37277	17.83037
250	19.68504	20.28953
500	29.25644	30.27235
625	33.41443	34.75578
1,000	43.16259	44.57676
1,250	51.51228	53.19354
2,500	71.72203	74.38682
3,125	76.64355	79.7547
5,000	93.44286	97.25385
6,250	106.0108	110.5032
12,500	150.4796	156.4324

the problem of overfrequent sampling (and the serial correlation bias) to be minimized. In the next chapter, that will not be the case.

In addition, we found that the Hurst exponent was remarkably stable and lacks significant sensitivity to point or time changes in the Dow time series. The question now is: Does the level of "noise" increase for even higher-frequency data? In the next chapter, we will examine tick data for the S&P 500 and the trade-off between a large number of high-frequency data points and a shortened time span for total analysis.

9

S&P 500 Tick Data, 1989–1992: Problems with Oversampling

In this chapter, we will analyze a large number of data points that cover a short period of time. We will look at intraday prices for the S&P 500, covering a four-year time span. For much of the general public, the march of stock prices and unintelligible symbols passing in a continuous line at the bottom of a television screen is quintessential Wall Street. In previous generations, the image was a banker looking at a piece of ticker tape. In either case, investors "play" the stock market by reading meaning into the rapid change of prices. No wonder the general public confuses investing with gambling.

When data are referred to as high-frequency data, it means that they cover very short time horizons and occur frequently. High-frequency data are known to have significant statistical problems. Foremost among these problems is high levels of serial correlation, which can distort both standard methods of analysis and R/S analysis. Using AR(1) residuals compensates for much of this problem, but it makes any analysis questionable, no matter what significance tests are used.

The great advantage of high-frequency data is that there is so much of it. In standard probability calculus, the more observations one has, the more significance one finds. With tick data, we can have over 100,000 one-minute observations per year, or enough observations to make any statistician happy.

However, a large number of observations covering a short time period may not be as useful as a few points covering a longer time period. Why? Suppose that we wished to test whether the earth was round or flat. We decided to do so by measuring the curvature of a distance of 500,000 feet, sampling once every six inches for 1 million observations. If we were to do so, we would have to smooth out the regular variations that occur over the earth's surface. Even so, we would probably not get a reading that was significantly different from that of a flat surface. Thus, we would conclude that the earth was flat, even though we would have a large number of observations. The problem is that we are examining the problem from too close a vantage point.

Similarly, for a nonlinear dynamical system, the number of observations may not be as important as the time period we study. For instance, take the well-known Lorenz (1963) attractor, which was well described conceptually and graphically in Gleick (1987). The Lorenz attractor is a dynamical system of three interdependent nonlinear differential equations. When the parameters are set at certain levels, the system becomes chaotic; its pattern becomes nonrepeating. However, there is a global structure, which can be easily seen in Figure 9.1, where two of the three values are graphed against one another. The result is a famous "owl eyes" image. The nonperiodic cycle of this system is about 0.50 second. Because the system is continuous, one can generate as many points as are desired. However, when analyzing a chaotic system, 1 billion points filling one orbit (or 0.50 second) will not be as useful as 1,000 points covering ten orbits, or five seconds. Why? The existence of nonperiodic cycles can be inferred only if we average enough cycles together. Therefore, data sufficiency cannot be judged unless we have an idea of the length of one cycle.

In Peters (1991), the S&P 500 was found to have a cycle of about four years. In Chapter 8, we saw that the cycle of the Dow Jones Industrials is also approximately four years. Therefore, our tick data time series may have over 400,000 one-minute observations, but it still covers only one orbit. What can we learn from such a time series? What are the dangers and the advantages?

THE UNADJUSTED DATA

The unadjusted data are merely the log difference in price. We will examine the difference at three frequencies: three-minute, five-minute, and 30-minute.

The period from 1989 to 1992 was an interesting time. The 1980s were taking their last gasp. Despite the Fed's tightening of monetary policy and the rise of inflation, 1989 began as a strong up-year. There was a high level of optimism

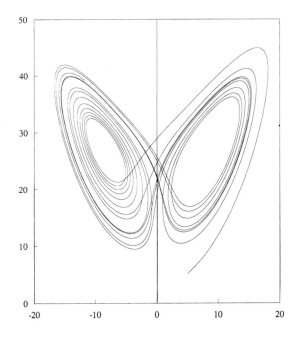

FIGURE 9.1   The Lorenz attractor.

that the Fed could engineer a "soft landing" scenario: gradually raise interest rates, ease inflation pressures, and leave the economy relatively unaffected. In fact, there was speculation that the traditional business cycle had been replaced by a series of rolling recessions, which made broad economic declines a thing of the past. Leveraged buy-outs (LBOs) and takeovers reached new extremes with the RJR/Nabisco deal. The early part of 1989 was dominated by the proposed buy-out of United Airlines, at a highly inflated value. There was sentiment that any company could be taken over and that stocks should be valued at their "liquidation value" rather than their book value. This concept came to a halt in October 1992, with the "mini-crash" that accompanied the collapse of the United Airlines deal.

The recession began in 1990. Iraqi invaded Kuwait at a time when the United States was facing a serious economic slowdown. A rise in oil prices, in August 1990, brought a significant decline in the stock market. The possibility of a Gulf War brought a high level of uncertainty, causing high volatility in the market. In October 1990, a bull market began and has continued through the early part of 1993.

The swift and successful conclusion of the Gulf War made 1991 a very positive year for stocks. However, most of the gains were concentrated in the first and fourth quarters, as the markets tried to decide whether the recession of 1990 was over yet or not.

The presidential election year, 1992, resulted in mediocre returns.

Figure 9.2(a) shows the R/S graph for unadjusted three-minute returns. The log/log plot shows a significant departure from the Gaussian null hypothesis. Figures 9.2(b) and 9.2(c) show similar graphs for five-minute and 30-minute returns. Again, the significance is apparent. (Interestingly, the graphs look similar.) Table 9.1 shows the results. As would be expected with so many observations, the results are highly significant. Figures 9.3(a)–(c), the V-statistic graphs, are summarized in Table 9.1. Again, all of the values are highly significant. No cycles are visible, which we will comment on below.

In fact, the values are too good. With trends this strong, it's hard to believe that anyone could *not* make money on them. When a natural system sampled at high frequency shows high significance, it seems reasonable to suspect that a short-memory process may be distorting our results. In the next section, we will see whether this is indeed the case.

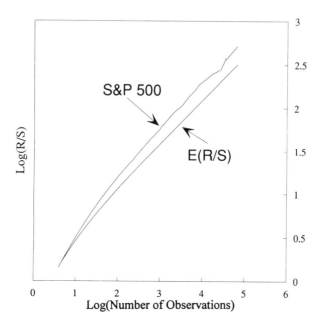

FIGURE 9.2a R/S analysis, S&P 500 unadjusted three-minute returns: 1989–1992.

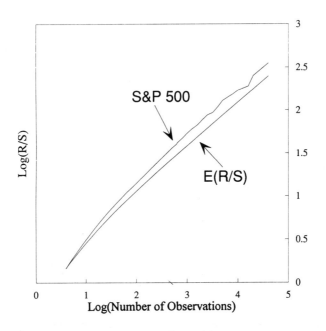

FIGURE 9.2b   R/S analysis, S&P 500 unadjusted five-minute returns: 1989–1992.

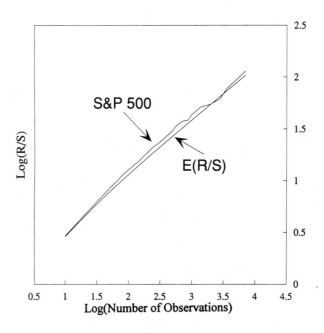

FIGURE 9.2c   R/S analysis, S&P 500 unadjusted 30-minute returns: 1989–1992.

Table 9.1   R/S Analysis, Raw S&P Tick Data

Interval (Minutes)	H	E(H)	Significance
3	0.603	0.538	23.436
5	0.590	0.540	12.505
30	0.653	0.563	10.260

THE AR(1) RESIDUALS

In this section, we will apply the methodology outlined in Chapter 7, and take AR(1) residuals. In this way, we should be able to minimize any short-memory effects. If short memory is not a major problem, then our results should not change much, as we saw in Chapter 8.

Sadly, this is not the case. Figures 9.4(a)–(c) show the V-statistic graphs for the same series, now using AR(1) residuals. The Hurst exponents have all dropped to levels that are not much different than a random walk. The results

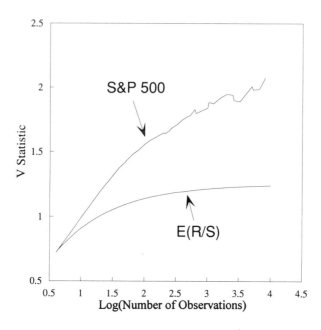

FIGURE 9.3a   V statistic, S&P 500 unadjusted three-minute returns: 1989–1992.

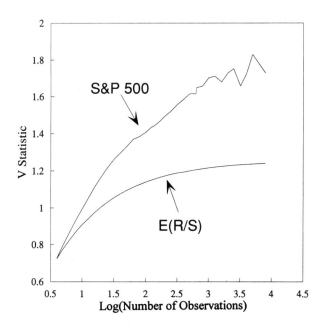

FIGURE 9.3b V statistic, S&P 500 unadjusted five-minute returns: 1989–1992.

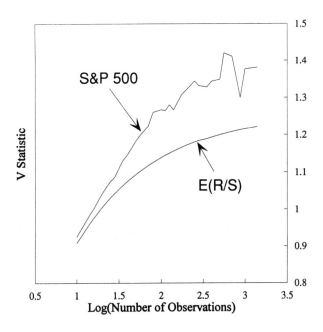

FIGURE 9.3c V statistic, S&P 500 unadjusted 30-minute returns: 1989–1992.

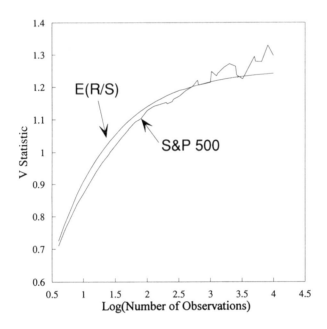

FIGURE 9.4a V statistic, S&P 500 AR(1) three-minute returns: January 1989–December 1992.

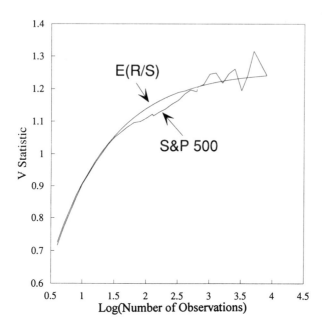

FIGURE 9.4b V statistic, S&P 500 AR(1) five-minute returns: January 1989–December 1992.

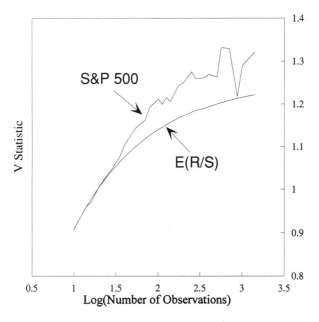

FIGURE 9.4c V statistic, S&P 500 AR(1) 30-minute returns: January 1989–December 1992.

are summarized in Table 9.2. For instance, the Hurst exponent for three-minute returns is 0.551, when the Gaussian null is 0.538. However, the number of observations is so large (over 130,000) that this slight difference is still significant at the 99.9 percent level. Therefore, we can conclude that the markets are not random walks, even at the three-minute return frequency.

The difference is statistically different, but not practically different. Remember, 2-H is the fractal dimension of the time series. The fractal dimension measures how jagged the time series is. Therefore, a random time series at the five-minute frequency would have an expected fractal dimension of 1.47, but the actual time series has a dimension of 1.46. The significant but low number

Table 9.2 R/S Analysis, AR(1) S&P Tick Data

Interval (Minutes)	H	E(H)	Significance
3	0.551	0.538	4.619
5	0.546	0.540	1.450
30	0.594	0.563	3.665

shows that there is so much noise at the five-minute frequency that we can only barely measure the determinism beneath the noise. The actual time series is dominated by a short-memory (probably an AR(1)) process, instead of a long-memory fractal system. As such, it is highly unlikely that a high-frequency trader can actually profit in the long term.

Interestingly, neither test shows evidence of intraday cycles; that is, there are no high-frequency cycles superimposed over the longer cycles found in Chapter 8. Based on the Weirstrass function analyzed in Chapter 6, we should be able to see any such cycles when sampling at high frequency. The fact that none is apparent leads us to conclude that there are no deterministic cycles at high frequency.

IMPLICATIONS

Analyzing high- and low-frequency data in this chapter and in Chapter 8 has given us some important insights into both market mechanisms and the usefulness of R/S analysis.

First, we have seen how influential a short-memory process can be on R/S analysis, and the importance of taking AR(1) residuals when analyzing systems. This is much more of a problem for high-frequency data than for low-frequency data. Comparing the results of Chapter 8 with those in this chapter, we can see that, by the time we get to a daily frequency, short-memory processes have less of an impact. With monthly returns, there is virtually no impact, and we have always known that oversampling the data can give statistically spurious results, even for R/S analysis.

Second, we have gained important insight into the U.S. stock market—insight that we may extend to other markets, although we leave the analysis to future research. As has always been suspected, the markets are some form of autoregressive process when analyzed at high frequency. The long-memory effect visible at high frequency is so small that it is barely apparent. Thus, we can infer that day traders have short memories and merely react to the last trade. In Chapter 8, we saw that this autoregressive process is much less significant once we analyze daily data. This gives us some evidence that conforms to the Fractal Market Hypothesis: Information has a different impact at different frequencies, and different investment horizons can have different structures. There is, indeed, local randomness and global structure. At high frequencies, we can see only pure stochastic processes that resemble white noise. As we step back and look at lower frequencies, a global structure becomes apparent.

We briefly discussed a similar process, called cell specialization, in Chapter 1. As a fetus develops, cells migrate to various locations to become heart cells, brain cells, and so on. Most cells make the journey safely, but some cells die along the way. Thus, at the local cell level, the chances of a cell's surviving are purely a matter of probability. However, the global structure that causes the organization of cells into an organism is purely deterministic. Only when we examine the organism's global structure does this determinism become apparent.

In the market, tick data are equivalent to the cell level. The data are so finely grained that we can barely see any structure at all. Only when we step back and look at longer time frames does the global structure, comparable to the whole organism, become apparent. In this way, we can see how local randomness and global determinism are incorporated into fractal time series.

10
Volatility: A Study in Antipersistence

Volatility is a much misunderstood concept. To the general public, it means turbulence. To academics and followers of the EMH, volatility is the standard deviation of stock price changes. It turns out that both concepts are equivalent, in ways that the founders of MPT probably did not envision.

Originally, standard deviation was used because it measured the dispersion of the percentage of change in prices (or returns) of the probability distribution. The probability distribution was estimated from unnormalized empirical data. The larger the standard deviation, the higher the probability of a large price change—and the riskier the stock. In addition, it was assumed (for reasons discussed earlier) that the returns were sampled from a normal distribution. The probabilities could be estimated based on a Gaussian norm. It was also assumed that the variance was finite; therefore, the standard deviation would tend to a value that was the population standard deviation. The standard deviation was, of course, higher if the time series of prices was more jagged, so standard deviation became known as a measure of the *volatility* of the stock. It made perfect sense that a stock prone to violent swings would be more volatile and riskier than a less volatile stock. Figure 10.1 shows the annualized standard deviation of 22-day returns for the S&P 500 from January 2, 1945, to August 1, 1990.

Volatility became an important measure in its own right because of the option pricing formula of Black and Scholes (1973):

$$C = P_S * N(d_1) - S * e^{r*(t-t*)} * N(d_2)$$

$$d_1 = \frac{\ln(P_S/S) + (r + 0.5*v^2)*(t* - t)}{v*\sqrt{t* - t}}$$

$$d_2 = \frac{\ln(P_S/S) + (r - 0.5*v^2)*(t* - t)}{v*\sqrt{t* - t}} \tag{10.1}$$

where c = fair value of the call option
$\quad\quad P_S$ = stock price
$\quad\quad S$ = exercise price of the option
$\quad\quad N(d)$ = cumulative normal density function
$\quad\quad r$ = risk-free interest rate
$\quad\quad t$ = current date
$\quad\quad t*$ = maturity date of the option
$\quad\quad v^2$ = variance of stock return

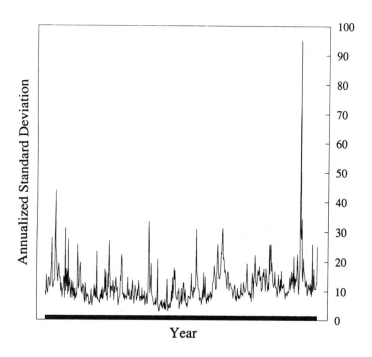

FIGURE 10.1   S&P 500, annualized standard deviation: January 2, 1945–August 1, 1990.

The option price estimated from this formula is sensitive to the variance number used within the calculation. In addition, variance is the only variable that is not known with certainty at the time of the trade. Option traders realized this and found it easier to calculate the variance that equated the current price of the option to the other values, instead of calculating the "fair price." This *implied volatility* became a measure of current uncertainty in the market. It was considered almost a forecast of actual volatility.

As option traders plumbed the depths of the Black–Scholes formula, they began buying and selling volatility as if it were an asset. In many ways, the option premium became a way to profit from periods of high (or low) uncertainty. Viewed increasingly as a commodity, volatility began to accumulate its own trading characteristics. In general, volatility was considered "mean reverting." Rises in volatility were likely to followed by declines, as volatility

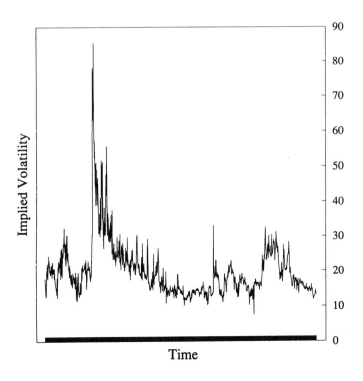

FIGURE 10.2 S&P 500, implied standard deviation: January 2, 1987–June 28, 1991.

reverted to the finite mean value implied from the normal distribution. Volatility had its own trends. Ironically, implied volatility was also highly volatile, a characteristic that caused many to question whether implied volatility was related to the realized population standard deviation. Figure 10.2 shows annualized implied volatility (calculated daily) from January 2, 1987, to June 28, 1991.

To test these assumptions, we will test both realized and implied volatility through R/S analysis. Are they trend reinforcing or mean reverting? We will examine their common characteristics. In keeping with the general approach of this book, we will study a broad index, the S&P 500, which has a long price history as well as a liquid option. The study of individual stocks and other asset types is left to the reader.

Volatility is an interesting subject for study using R/S analysis because we make so many assumptions about what it is, with so few facts to back us up. In fact, the study that follows should be disturbing to those who believe volatility has trends as well as stationarity, or stability. The study challenges, once again, our imposition of a Gaussian order on all processes.

REALIZED VOLATILITY

My earlier book gave a brief study of volatility. This section repeats those results, but with further explanation. The series is taken from a daily file of S&P composite prices from January 1, 1928, through December 31, 1989. The prices are converted into a series of log differences, or:

$$S_t = \ln(P_t/P_{(t-1)}) \tag{10.2}$$

where S_t = log return at time t
P_t = price at time t

The volatility is the standard deviation of contiguous 20-day increments of S_t. These increments are nonoverlapping and independent:

$$V_n = \frac{\sum_{t=1}^{n}(S_t - \overline{S})^2}{n - 1} \tag{10.3}$$

where V_n = variance over n days
$\overline{S}$ = average value of S

The log changes are calculated as in equation (10.2):

$$L_n = \ln(V_n / V_{(n-1)}) \tag{10.4}$$

where L_n = change in volatility at time n

R/S analysis is then performed as outlined in Chapter 7. Figure 10.3 shows the log/log plot. Table 10.1 summarizes the results.

Realized volatility has $H = 0.31$, which is *antipersistent*. Because $E(H) = 0.56$, volatility has an H value that is 5.7 standard deviations *below* its expected value. Up to this point, we had not seen an antipersistent time series in finance. Antipersistence says that the system reverses itself more often than a random one would. This fits well with the experience of traders who find volatility mean reverting. However, the term *mean reverting* implies that, in the system under study, both the mean and the variance are stable— that is, volatility has an average value that it is tending toward, and it reverses

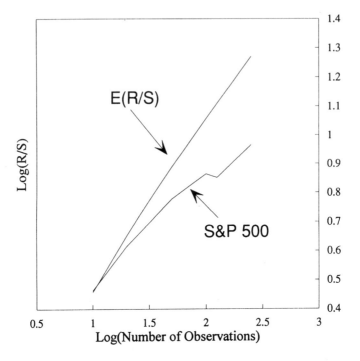

FIGURE 10.3 R/S analysis, S&P 500 realized volatility.

Table 10.1   Realized Volatility

	S&P 500		E(R/S)
Regression output:			
Constant	0.225889		−0.07674
Standard error			
of Y (estimated)	0.021117		0.005508
R squared	0.979899		0.99958
Number of observations	6		6
Degrees of freedom	4		4
Hurst exponent	0.309957		0.564712
Standard error			
of coefficient	0.022197		0.00579
Significance	−5.69649		

itself constantly, trying to reestablish an equilibrium value. We cannot make that assumption here.

In fact, in Chapter 13, we will find that an antipersistent Hurst exponent is related to the spectral density of turbulent flow, which is also antipersistent. Turbulent systems are also described by the stable Levy distributions, which have infinite mean and variance; that is, they have no average or dispersion levels that can be measured. By implication, volatility will be unstable, like turbulent flow.

This means that volatility will have no trends, but will frequently reverse itself. This may be a notion that implies some profit opportunity, but it must be remembered that the reversal is not even. A large increase in volatility has a high probability of being followed by a decrease of *unknown magnitude*. That is, the reversal is equally as likely to be smaller, as larger, than the increase. There is no guarantee that the eventual reversal will be big enough to offset previous losses in a volatility play.

IMPLIED VOLATILITY

Realized volatility is a statistical artifact, calculated as a characteristic of another process. Implied volatility falls out of a formula. Its tie to reality is a measure of how much the formula is tied to reality. A study of implied volatility is, in many ways, a test of the assumptions in the Black–Scholes formula. If volatility is really a finite process, then implied volatility, which is supposed to be a measure of instantaneous volatility, should also be finite and stable. It will be either a random walk or a persistent series that can be predicted as well as stock returns.

Figure 10.4 shows the log/log plot from R/S analysis. Table 10.2 summarizes the results.

Implied volatility is very similar to realized volatility. It has virtually the same Hurst exponent, H = 0.44, which is 3.95 standard deviations below E(H) = 0.56. There is, in fact, little to distinguish a time series of implied volatility from a time series of realized volatility. However, implied volatility does have a higher value of H, suggesting that it is closer to white noise than is realized volatility. From one aspect, this is encouraging to proponents of using the Black–Scholes formula for calculating implied volatility. The implied volatility calculation does, indeed, capture much of the relationship between volatility and option premium. However, it also brings into question the original practice of pricing options by assuming a stable, finite variance value when estimating a "fair" price based on this formula.

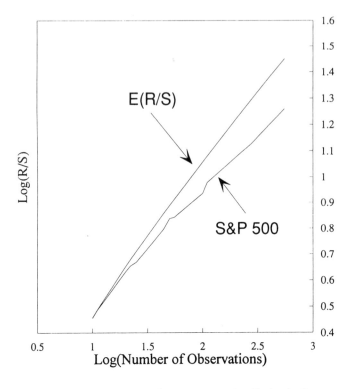

FIGURE 10.4 R/S analysis, S&P 500 implied volatility.

Table 10.2   Implied Volatility, 1,100 Observations

	S&P 500		E(R/S)
Regression output:			
Constant		0.05398	−0.07846
Standard error			
of Y (estimated)		0.017031	0.010699
R squared		0.994994	0.998767
Number of observations		12	12
Degrees of freedom		10	10
Hurst exponent	0.444502		0.563715
Standard error			
of coefficient	0.00997		0.006264
Significance	−3.95		

Antipersistence has interesting statistical characteristics; we will explore them further in Chapter 14. In addition, a relationship between persistent and antipersistent time series is well-exemplified by the persistent nature of stock price changes and the antipersistence of volatility. They appear to be mirror images of one another. One is not present without the other. This intriguing relationship will be covered when we discuss 1/f noises in Chapter 13.

SUMMARY

In this brief chapter, we have looked at two antipersistent series: realized and implied volatility. They were found to have similar characteristics. Antipersistence is characterized by more frequent reversals than in a random series. Therefore, antipersistence generates $0 < H < 0.50$. This results in $1.5 < D < 2.0$, which means an antipersistent time series is closer to the space-filling fractal dimension of a plane ($D = 2.0$) than it is to a random line ($D = 1.50$). However, this does not mean that the process is *mean* reverting, just that it is reverting. Antipersistence also implies the absence of a stable mean. There is nothing to revert to, and the size of the reversions is itself random.

27

11
Problems with Undersampling: Gold and U.K. Inflation

In Chapter 9, we saw the potential problem with oversampling—the distorting effects of testing data at too high a frequency. Among other statistical problems (serial correlation, for example), there lurks another danger: overconfidence of the analyst, because of the large sample size. This chapter deals with the reverse problem, undersampling. With undersampling, an analyst could accept a fractal time series as random, simply because there are not enough observations to make a clear determination.

There are two types of undersampling, and each has its own consequences. In what we will call Type I undersampling, we obtain a Hurst exponent that is different from a random walk, but we cannot be confident that the result is significant because there are too few observations. Type II undersampling is a "masking" of both persistence and cycle length because too few points are in a cycle. The process crosses over into a random walk for a small value of n, because n covers such a long length of time.

Each of these undersampling errors will be examined in turn, using the Dow Jones Industrials data from Chapter 8. The Dow data, in complete form, have already been shown to be significantly persistent, with a cycle length of approximately 1,000 trading days. Afterward, we will look at two studies that are intriguing, but inconclusive because of undersampling.

TYPE I UNDERSAMPLING: TOO LITTLE TIME

In Chapter 8, we saw that the Hurst exponent for a stable, persistent process does not change much when tested over time. We looked at three nonoverlapping 36-year periods, and found that their Hurst exponent changed little. If there truly is a Hurst process in place, the expected value of the Hurst exponent, using equation (5.6), also does not change significantly when the sample size is increased. What does change is the variance of E(H). The variance decreases as the total number of observations, T, increases. In Chapter 9, we saw how a low value of H could be statistically significant, if there are enough data points.

The analyst, however, does have a dilemma. If the same time period is kept but is sampled more frequently, then it is possible to oversample the data, as we saw in Chapter 9. If the frequency becomes too high, then noise and serial correlation can hide the signal. With market data, it is preferable to keep the sampling frequency to daily or longer, to avoid the oversampling problem. Unfortunately, the only alternative to high-frequency data is a longer time period. More time is not always possible to obtain, but it is preferable.

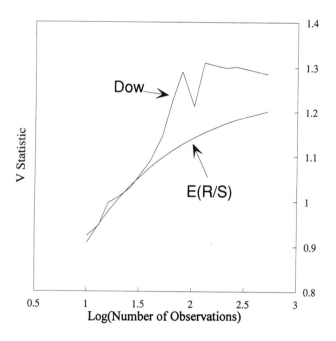

FIGURE 11.1   V statistic, Dow Jones Industrials, five-day returns: January 1970–December 1989.

Table 11.1   Dow Jones Industrials, Five-Day Returns,
January 1970–December 1989

	Dow Jones Industrials	E(R/S)
Regression output:		
Constant	−0.15899	−0.11082
Standard error of Y (estimated)	0.014157	0.008253
R squared	0.997421	0.998987
Number of observations	12	12
Degrees of freedom	10	10
X coefficient(s)	0.626866	0.583597
Standard error of coefficient	0.01008	0.005876
Significance	1.395384	

For instance, let us use 20 years of five-day Dow returns. This results in approximately 1,040 points. In investment finance, this seems like an adequate sample. The period under study covers January 1970 through December 1989. Figure 11.1 and Table 11.1 summarize the results of R/S analysis.

The Hurst exponent over the 20-year period is similar that in Chapter 8 for 108 years: H = 0.63. The E(H) still equals 0.58, and the cycle length still appears at approximately 200 weeks. However, the variance of E(H) is now $1/_{1,040}$ for a standard deviation of 0.031. Despite the fact that virtually all the values are the same as those in Chapter 8, the estimate of the Hurst exponent is now only 1.4 standard deviations from its expected value. Unfortunately, this is not high enough for us to reject the null hypothesis. The system could still be a random walk.

How many points do we need? If we increase the time period rather than the frequency, we can estimate the data requirements easily. If the Hurst exponent is stable, then the difference between E(H) and H will also be stable. In this case, the difference is 0.04. Therefore, we need to know the value of T (the total number of observations) that will make 0.04 a two standard deviation value, or:

$$(H - E(H))/(1/\sqrt{T}) = 2 \tag{11.1}$$

which simplifies to:

$$T = 4/(H - E(H))^2 \tag{11.2}$$

In this example, T = 2,500 weeks, or approximately 48 years of five-day data. To achieve a 99 percent confidence interval, the numerator on the right-hand side of equation (11.2) should be replaced with 9. We would need 5.625 weeks to achieve significance at the 1 percent confidence level, if H remained at 0.62 for the new interval. There is no guarantee that this will happen. H is remarkably stable in many but not all cases.

This numerator change works reasonably well if we keep the same sampling frequency but increase the time period. If we increase the sampling frequency within the same time frame, this approach is not reliable. For instance, in Chapter 8 we saw that increasing the frequency from 20-day to five-day to one-day returns changed the value of H from 0.72 to 0.62 to 0.59 respectively. Increase in sampling frequency is usually accompanied by an increase in noise and a decrease in the Hurst exponent. In this case, data sufficiency will increase at an ever-increasing rate as sampling frequency is increased.

TYPE II UNDERSAMPLING: TOO LOW A FREQUENCY

Suppose we now sample the Dow every 90 days. For the full Dow data set, this gives us 295 points covering 108 years. Figure 11.2 and Table 11.2 show the results. The Hurst exponent for four-year cycles cannot be seen, because it now occurs at n = 16. Because we typically begin at n = 10, we have no points for the regression. The standard deviation of E(H) is a large 0.058. There is no way to distinguish this system from a random one; the only alternative is to increase the sampling frequency. If increasing the frequency does not give a significant Hurst exponent, then we can conclude that the system is not persistent. Otherwise, we cannot be sure one way or the other.

TWO INCONCLUSIVE STUDIES

I have two data sets that suffer from undersampling problems. I have not pursued correcting these problems because the series studied are not important to my style of investment management. However, because many readers are interested in these time series, I present the inconclusive studies here to entice some reader into completing them.

Gold

I have 25 years of weekly gold prices from January 1968 to December 1992, or 1,300 observations. Figure 11.3 and Table 11.3 show the results of R/S

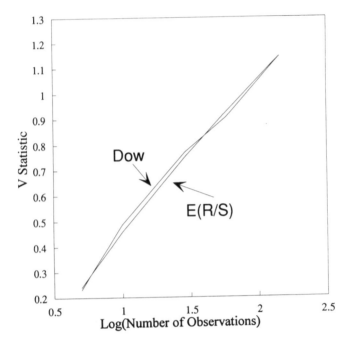

FIGURE 11.2   V statistic, Dow Jones Industrials, 90-day returns.

Table 11.2   Dow Jones Industrials, 90-Day Returns

	Dow Jones Industrials	E(R/S)
Regression output:		
Constant	−0.15456	−0.17121
Standard error		
of Y (estimated)	0.038359	0.021257
R squared	0.991328	0.997401
Number of observations	5	5
Degrees of freedom	3	3
X coefficient(s)	0.607872	0.61723
Standard error		
of coefficient	0.032825	0.018191
Significance	−0.16072	

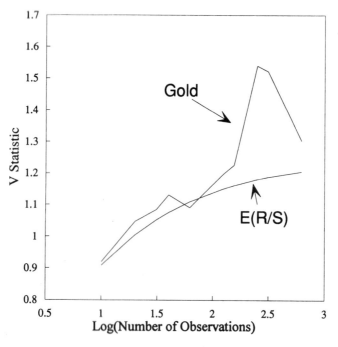

FIGURE 11.3   V statistic, weekly spot gold: January 1968–December 1992.

Table 11.3   Gold

		Gold		E(R/S)
Regression output:				
Constant		−0.15855		−0.10186
Standard error				
of Y (estimated)		0.028091		0.010688
R squared		0.992385		0.9987
Number of observations		8		8
Degrees of freedom		6		6
X coefficient(s)	0.624998	1.677234	0.577367	
Standard error				
of coefficient	0.022352		0.008504	

analysis. The V-statistic plot in Figure 11.3 indicates apparent 40-week and 248-week cycles. The long cycle is similar to the U.S. stock market cycle of four years. The shorter cycle is also intriguing. Unfortunately, the Hurst exponent is not significant. H = 0.62 and E(H) = 0.58. Thus, the Hurst exponent is 1.67 standard deviations above its expected value. According to equation (11.2), we need 4,444 weeks to achieve significance. Unfortunately, because dollar did not come off the gold standard until 1968, we cannot increase the time frame.

Our only alternative is to increase the frequency to daily pricing. This is clearly a Type I undersampling problem.

The gold results look intriguing, but need further study.

U.K. Inflation

A reader of my earlier book sent me an article from a 1976 issue of *The Economist* in which were listed annual estimates of U.K. inflation from 1662 to 1973—over 300 years. Although it is a very long time series, its annual

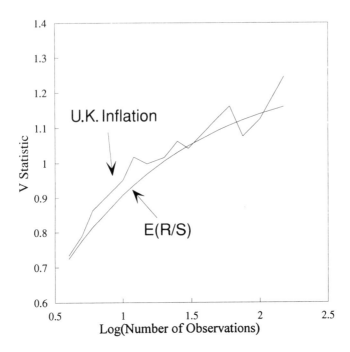

FIGURE 11.4   V statistic, U.K. annual inflation: 1662–1973.

Table 11.4   UK Inflation

	U.K. Inflation		E(R/S)
Regression output:			
Constant		−0.17106	−0.18656
Standard error			
of Y (estimated)		0.006444	0.001442
R squared		0.996196	0.999803
Number of observations		4	4
Degrees of freedom		2	2
X coefficient(s)	0.656017		0.645863
Standard error			
of coefficient	0.028665		0.006414
Significance	0.175883		

frequency makes it a classic Type II undersampling problem. In the United States, inflation appears to have a five-year cycle, as does the U.S. economy (Peters (1991a)). If the United Kingdom has a similar cycle, it would be overlooked because of infrequent sampling.

Figure 11.4 and Table 11.4 show the results of R/S analysis. This series is virtually indistinguishable from a random one. It stands to reason that, like U.S. inflation, U.K. inflation should have trends and cycles, but these data do not support that notion.

SUMMARY

In this chapter, we examined two types of undersampling problems. In Type I undersampling, there is too little time to support the frequency sampled. The preferred solution, if the first estimate of the Hurst exponent looks promising, is to increase the time span and keep the sampling frequency constant. In this way, an approximation to data sufficiency can be calculated.

In Type II undersampling, the frequency of sampling is too low, and cycles are missed. Given sufficient resources, such problems can usually be compensated for. Sometimes, however, the nature of the data set is not amenable to correction.

12
Currencies: A True Hurst Process

As we have stated in previous chapters, currencies are often confused with securities. When traders buy and sell currencies, they do not realize an investment income on the currencies themselves. Instead, currencies are bought and sold in order to invest in short-term interest-rate securities in the selected country. Currency "value" is not necessarily related to activity in the country's underlying economy. Currencies are tied to relative interest-rate movements in the two countries. In addition, the markets themselves are manipulated by their respective governments for reasons that may not be considered "rational" in an efficient market sense. For instance, if a country wants to stimulate exports, it will allow, or even encourage, the value of its currency to drop. On the other hand, if it wishes to encourage imports and reduce its trade surplus, it would like its currency to appreciate. Both objectives could be desirable, whether the country is in recession or expansion.

There are two ways in which the central bank of a country can manipulate its currency. First, it can raise or lower interest rates, making its government securities more or less attractive to foreign investors. Because this alternative can impact the overall economic growth of a country, it is generally considered a last resort, even though it has the most long-lasting effects.

The second method is more direct and usually occurs when the currency has reached a level considered acceptable by the central bank. Central banks typically buy or sell in massive quantities, to manipulate the value of the currency. At certain times, the largest trader in the currency market can be the central bank, which does not have a profit maximization objective in mind.

Because of these two factors, currency markets are different from other traded markets. For instance, they are not really a "capital market" because the objective of trading currency is not to raise capital, but to create the ability to trade in stocks and bonds, which are real markets for raising capital. Currencies are "pure" trading markets, because they are truly a zero sum game. In the stock market, asset values will rise and fall with the economy. Interest rates also rise and fall, in an inverse relationship with the economy. Both relationships are remarkably stable. However, currencies have no stable relationship with the economy. As a pure trading market, currencies are more inclined to follow fads and fashions. In short, currencies follow crowd behavior in a way that is assumed for stock and bond markets.

So far, we have examined markets that have some tie to economic activity. Stocks, bonds, and (probably) gold have nonperiodic cycles that have an average length. This latter characteristic is closely related to nonlinear dynamical systems and the Fractal Market Hypothesis. However, the pure Hurst process, as discussed in Part Two, does not have an average cycle length. The "joker" is a random event that can happen at any time. Because the drawing of random numbers from the probability pack of cards occurs with replacement, the probability of the joker's occurring does not increase with time. The change in "bias" truly does occur at random.

In the currency market, we see exactly these characteristics. In Chapter 2, we saw that the term structure of volatility for the yen/dollar exchange rate was different than for U.S. stocks and bonds. In Chapter 4, we saw evidence of a persistent Hurst exponent for the yen/dollar exchange rate. In this chapter, we will examine this and other exchange rates in more detail. The study will still be limited.

Besides currencies, it is possible that other "trading markets" are also pure Hurst processes, particularly in commodity markets such as pork bellies, which are known to be dominated by speculators. Other researchers will, I hope, investigate these markets.

THE DATA

Currency markets have the potential for Type I undersampling problems. Like gold, currency fluctuations in the United States did not occur in a free market environment until a political event—in this case, another Nixon Administration event: the floating of the U.S. dollar and other currencies, as a result of the Bretton Woods Agreement of 1972. In the period following World War II, the U.S. dollar became the world currency. Foreign exchange rates were fixed relative to the U.S. dollar by their respective governments. However, in the late 1960s, the global economy had reached a different state, and the current structure of floating rates manipulated by central banks developed. We therefore have less than 20 years' data. In the U.S. stock market, 20 years' daily data are insufficient to achieve a statistically significant Hurst exponent. Unless daily currency exchange rates have a higher Hurst exponent than the U.S. stock market, we may not achieve significance. Luckily, this does turn out to be the case.

YEN/DOLLAR

We have already examined some aspects of the yen/dollar exchange rate in Chapters 2 and 4. This exchange rate is, along with the mark/dollar exchange rate, an extremely interesting one. For one thing, it is very heavily traded, and has been since 1972. The postwar relationship between the United States and Japan, and the subsequent development of the United States as the largest consumer of Japanese exports, has caused the exchange rate between the two countries to be one long slide against the dollar. As the trade deficit between the two countries continues to widen, the value of the U.S. currency continues to decline. R/S analysis should give us insight into the structure of this actively traded and widely watched market.

Table 12.1 summarizes the results, and Figure 12.1 shows the V-statistic graph for this currency. The Hurst exponent is higher than the daily U.S. stock value, with H = 0.64. This period has 5,200 observations, so the estimate is over three standard deviations above its expected value. Therefore, it is highly persistent compared with the stock market. However, no long-range cycle is apparent. This is consistent with the term structure of volatility, which also has no apparent long-range reduction in risk. Therefore, we can conclude that the yen/dollar exchange rate is consistent with a fractional brownian motion, or Hurst process. However, unlike the stock and bond market, there is no crossover to longer-term "fundamental" valuation. Technical information continues to dominate all investment horizons. This would lead us to believe that this process is a true "infinite memory," or Hurst process, as opposed to the long, but finite memory process that characterizes the stock and bond markets.

Table 12.1 R/S Analysis

		Yen
Regression output:		
Constant		−0.187
Standard error of Y (estimated)		0.012
R squared		0.999
H	0.642	
E(H)	0.553	
Observations	4,400.000	
Significance	5.848	

		Pound		Yen/Pound
Regression output:				
Constant		−0.175		−0.139
Standard error				
of Y (estimated)		0.018		0.027
R squared		0.998		0.995
Number of observations		24.000		24.000
Degrees of freedom		22.000		22.000
Hurst exponent	0.626		0.606	
Standard error				
of coefficient	0.006		0.009	
Significance	4.797		3.440	

		Mark
Regression output:		
Constant		−0.170
Standard error of Y (estimated)		0.012
R squared		0.999
Number of observations		24.000
Degrees of freedom		22.000
X coefficient(s)	0.624	
Standard error of coefficient	0.004	
Significance	4.650	

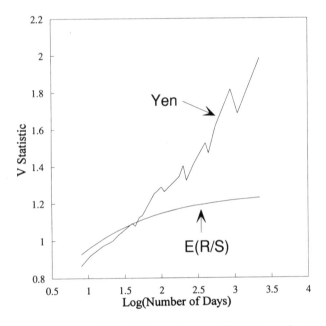

FIGURE 12.1   V statistic, daily yen, January 1972–December 1990.

MARK/DOLLAR

The mark/dollar exchange rate, like the yen/dollar, is tied to postwar expansion—in this case, Germany, as the United States helped its old adversary recover from the yoke of Nazism. Interestingly, R/S analysis of the mark/dollar exchange rate is virtually identical to the yen/dollar analysis. H = 0.62, slightly lower than the yen/dollar, but not significantly so. This gives us a significance of more than four standard deviations (see Figure 12.2). Again, there is no break in the log/log plot, implying that there is either no cycle or an extremely long cycle. The latter is always a possibility, but seems unlikely.

POUND/DOLLAR

The pound/dollar exchange rate is so similar to the other two (see Figure 12.3) that there is very little to comment on, except that, unlike the stocks studied in my earlier book, all three currency exchange rates have values of H that are virtually identical. This could prove to be very useful when we examine the Hurst exponent of portfolios.

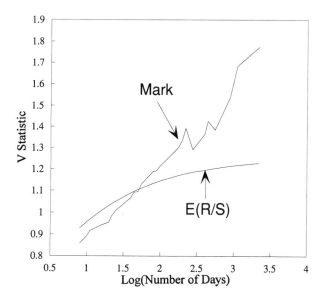

FIGURE 12.2   V statistic, daily mark, January 1972–December 1990.

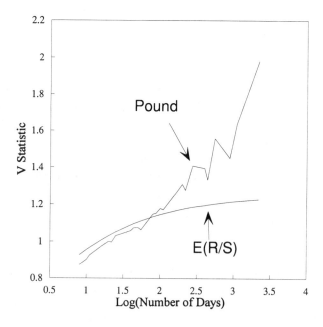

FIGURE 12.3   V statistic, daily pound, January 1972–December 1990.

YEN/POUND

The yen/pound is slightly different from the other exchange rates. Japan and the U.K. are not major trading partners; the currency trading that occurs between them is far less active. In addition, the forward market, where the majority of currency hedging occurs, is quoted in U.S. dollar exchange rates. Thus, the yen/pound exchange rate is derived from the ratio of the yen/dollar exchange rate and the pound/dollar exchange rate, rather than being quoted directly. As a result, the yen/pound exchange rate looks essentially random at periods shorter than 100 days. The other exchange rates have similar characteristics, but the yen/pound exchange rate is virtually identical to a random walk at the higher frequencies. Figure 12.4 shows how tightly the V statistic follows its expected value for less than 100 days.

Even though the yen/pound is not an exchange rate that garners much attention, it too has no apparent cycle length. The long memory is either extremely long or infinite.

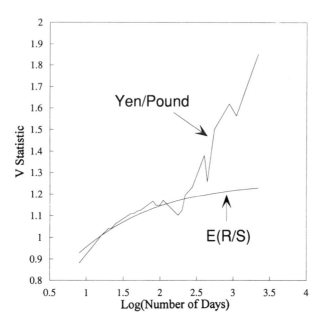

FIGURE 12.4   V statistic, daily yen/pound, January 1972–December 1990.

SUMMARY

Currencies have interesting statistical and fundamental characteristics that differentiate them from other processes. Fundamentally, currencies are not securities, although they are actively traded. The largest participants, the central banks, are not return maximizers; their objectives are not necessarily those of rational investors. At the same time, there is little evidence of cycles in the currency markets, although they do have strong trends.

These characteristics, taken together, lead us to believe that currencies are true Hurst processes. That is, they are characterized by infinite memory processes. Long-term investors should be wary of approaching currencies as they do other traded entities. In particular, they should not assume that a buy-and-hold strategy will be profitable in the long term. Risk increases through time, and does not decline with time. A long-term investor who must have currency exposure should consider actively trading those holdings. They offer no advantage in the long term.

PART FOUR
FRACTAL NOISE

13
Fractional Noise and R/S Analysis

In the previous chapters, we have seen evidence that markets are, at least in the short term, persistent Hurst processes, and volatility, a statistical by-product, is antipersistent. The Fractal Market Hypothesis offers an economic rationale for the self-similar probability distributions observed, but it does not offer a mathematical model to examine expected behavior. In this and the following chapters, we will examine such models. They must be consistent with the Fractal Market Hypothesis, as outlined in Chapter 3.

We have seen that short-term market returns generate self-similar frequency distributions characterized by a high peak at the mean and fatter tails than the normal distribution. This could be an ARCH or ARCH-related process. As noted in Chapter 4, ARCH is generated by correlated conditional variances. Returns are still independent, so some form of the EMH will still hold. However, we also saw in Part Two that the markets are characterized by Hurst exponents greater than 0.50, which implies long memory in the returns, unlike the GARCH and ARCH processes that were examined in Chapter 4. In addition, we found that variance is not a persistent process; instead, it is antipersistent. Based on R/S analysis, neither ARCH nor its derivations conforms with the persistence or long-memory effects that characterize markets. Therefore, we need an alternative statistical model that has fat-tailed distributions, exhibits persistence, and has unstable variances.

There is a class of noise processes that fits these criteria: 1/f or fractional noises. Unlike ARCH, which relies on a complicated statistical manipulation, fractional noises are a generalization of brownian motion processes. They seem to be everywhere. The ubiquitous nature of 1/f noise has both puzzled and intrigued scientists for some time. 1/f noise is particularly common to phase transitions, where intrinsic scales of length or time cease to exist; that is, correlations become infinite. Because the Hurst process, in its pure form, is also characterized by infinite memory, it would seem reasonable to equate the two processes. Mandelbrot and Wallis (1969a–1969c) did just that, but the scientific and mathematical community has generally been unaware of R/S analysis and its relationship to 1/f noise. A notable exception is Schroeder (1991). However, 1/f noise has been extensively researched, both theoretically and empirically. By reconciling the Hurst infinite memory process and 1/f noise, we make available a wide array of tools for market analysis. In this chapter, we will begin this process, but this is only a start. I expect that research into fractional noise processes and markets will be one of the most fruitful areas for creating useful technology. In addition, there is the family of ARFIMA models, a generalized version of the ARIMA models discussed in Chapter 5. When we allow the differencing interval to be fractional, many characteristics of the Hurst long-memory process can be generated and mixed with short-term AR or MA processes. The chapter ends with an examination of this interesting and useful area of study.

THE COLOR OF NOISE

When most people think of noise, they think of "white" or random noise. This type of noise is the hiss that is audible on blank audio tapes. Because it has no intrinsic scale, the hiss sounds the same no matter what the speed of the tape. Its integrand is called "brown" noise, or brownian motion. Brown noise is simply the running sum of white noise. It sounds like something is there, but no information really exists in brown noise.

These noises can be characterized by their power spectra, which follow simple inverse power laws. The power spectra are calculated through the Fourier transform, developed in the early 1800s by Jean-Baptiste Fourier, and are often called *spectral analysis*. The Fourier transform translates a time series into a function defined by its frequencies. It assumes that any time series can be represented by the sum of sine (or cosine) waves of different frequencies and infinite durations. The coefficients of the Fourier function define a "spectrum" in the same way that light has a spectrum, at many frequencies, or time increments. At frequencies that have sharp peaks, there is a periodic component in the original time series. Thus, spectral analysis assumes that (1) the time series under study is periodic in nature, and (2) cycles are periodic in nature.

However, when fractional noise is present, the power spectra are featureless and they scale according to inverse power laws. These inverse power laws are a function of a frequency, f, and follow the form f^{-b}. The power spectra follow the inverse power law because of the self-similar nature of the system under study. The frequencies scale, like all fractals, according to power laws. The scaling factor, or spectral exponent, b, can range from 0 to 4. For white noise, b = 0; that is, the power spectrum of white noise is not related to frequency. At all frequencies, white noise remains the same, which is why the hiss on the tape sounds the same at all speeds (or frequencies). Fractal dimension calculation of white noise in phase space is similar. The white noise fills the embedding dimension (which, in this case, is a frequency) that it is placed in. There is no scaling law. When white noise is integrated, then b = 2, the power spectra for brown noise. Thus, brown noise has the form $1/f^2$. As in most random processes, the scaling factor is a square.

There are other values for b as well. If $0 < b < 2$, we have *pink* noise. Pink noise is often referred to as 1/f noise, but that is a bit of a misnomer. Pink noise seems to be widespread in nature and has become useful in modeling turbulence, particularly when b assumes fractional values between 1 and 2. Beyond brown noise, there is *black* noise, where $b > 2$. Black noise has been used to model persistent systems, which are known to have abrupt collapses. Thus, we now have a relationship between fractional noises and the Hurst process:

$$b = 2*H + 1 \tag{13.1}$$

where b = the spectral exponent
       H = the Hurst exponent

Black noise is related to long-memory effects ($H > 0.50$, $2.00 < b \le 4.00$); pink noise is related to antipersistence ($H < 0.50$, $1 \ge b > 2$). This relationship between power spectra and the Hurst exponent was postulated by Mandelbrot and Van Ness (1968), who also suggested that the derivative of fractional brownian motion has a spectral exponent of $1 - 2*H$.

Although these relationships were postulated by Mandelbrot and Van Ness (1968) and were largely accepted, they were rigorously defined recently by Flandrin (1989).

PINK NOISE: 0 < H < 0.50

It has long been thought that $0 < H < 0.50$ is the "less interesting case," to quote Mandelbrot (1982). However, this is not so. Because of equation (13.1) and the results of Chapter 10, antipersistence can be very important. The relationship between volatility and turbulent flow will go far toward increasing our understanding of markets. It will also reduce a number of misconceptions about the relationship between physical systems and markets.

Schmitt, Lavallee, Schertzer, and Lovejoy (1992) and Kida (1991) have published the connection between fractal (i.e., Levy) distributions and turbulent flow. Equation (13.1) shows the connection between turbulent flow and the Hurst exponent. Antipersistent values of H correspond to pink noise. Thus, understanding pink noise increases our understanding of the structure of antipersistence and volatility.

Relaxation Processes

1/f noise is closely related to relaxation processes. In fact, 1/f noise has been postulated by Mandelbrot (1982) to be the sum of a large number of parallel relaxation processes occurring over many different frequencies. These frequencies are equally spaced logarithmically, which explains the inverse power law behavior. We saw a similar structure in the Weirstrass function, in Chapter 6. The Weirstrass function was the sum of an infinite number of sine curves occurring over an infinite number of frequencies.

A *relaxation process* is a form of dynamic equilibrium. Imagine two species in equilibrium, contained within a closed environment. An exogenous force appears that benefits one species over the other: one species will begin growing in numbers as the other declines, until a new equilibrium is reached. The time it takes for the new equilibrium to be reached is the system's correlation or *relaxation* time.

Gardner (1978) related a simple method proposed by Richard Voss for simulating 1/f noise. Like Hurst's probability pack of cards, it offers a method for understanding how parallel relaxation processes can occur in nature and in markets.

Voss's method uses three dice. The first die is thrown and the number is noted for each observation. The second die is thrown every second time, and its number is added to the first die. The third die is included in the throw every fourth time, and its value is added to the other two. This method simulates 1/f noise over a small range of frequencies. The first die has a frequency of one, the second a frequency of two, and the third a frequency of four. By adding together the three throws, at different equally spaced intervals, we are simulating multiple relaxation times at different intervals, which are evenly spaced in $\log_2$ space.

In markets, the two "species" could be two trends, one based on sentiment and one on value. Some information, such as the level of long-term interest rates, may not benefit a particular company if it has little or no long-term debt. But if the market as a whole benefits, the improved sentiment may push a stock's price to a new "fair-value" position. This new fair value is a combination of the prospects of the company (which are tied to fundamental, balance sheet information), and the relative position of interest rates to the stock market as a whole. The time it takes for the stock market to fully value the shift in interest rates would be the relaxation time for that factor. It is likely that different stocks would value the information at different rates. Therefore, the market as a whole would have many different "parallel" relaxation times in reaction to the same information.

Under the Fractal Market Hypothesis, it is more likely that different investors, with different investment horizons, react to the information with multiple relaxation times; that is, the information affects different investors differently, depending on their investment horizon. Therefore, volatility, which is the measure of uncertainty in the marketplace, would undergo many parallel shifts with different correlation or relaxation times.

Schroeder (1991) proposed a formula for simulating $1/f$ noise, and it is more reliable than the three-dice method of Voss. It involves a generator of relaxation processes. This formula is repeated for frequency levels evenly separated in log space, and added together. The formula is simple and can be easily implemented by computers, even in a spreadsheet. The formula is:

$$x_{n+1} = \rho * x_n + \sqrt{1 - \rho^2} * r_n \tag{13.2}$$

where $x_0 = 0$

      r = a uniform random number

      ρ = a desired correlation time

ρ is related to the relaxation time, t, by the following relationship:

$$\rho = \exp(-1/t) \tag{13.3}$$

where t is the relaxation time. Three values of t, evenly separated in log space, are chosen, and three series, x, are generated. For instance, if the desired sequence is in $\log_{10}$ space, then t = 1, 10, and 100 are used. Values of ρ = 0.37, 0.90, and 0.99, respectively, would result. Schroeder says that three observations, evenly separated in log space, are all that is needed for a good approximation. In this case, the frequencies are separated by powers of 10. With dice, it was powers of 2. However, it is important to note that this is an approximation. In theory, 1/f noise consists of an infinite number of such relaxation processes, occurring in parallel at all different frequencies. The more "frequencies" we add to the simulation, the better the results.

Equation (13.2) can be easily simulated in a spreadsheet, using the following steps:

1. Place a column of 1,000 or so random numbers in column A.
2. In cell B1, place a 0.
3. In cell B2, place the following equation:

    0.37*B1 + @sqrt(1 − .37∧2)*A2

4. Copy cell B2 down for 1,000 cells.
5. Repeat steps 1 through 4 in columns C and D, but replace 0.37 in step 3 with 0.90.
6. Repeat steps 1 through 4 in columns E and F, but replace 0.37 in step 3 with 0.99.
7. Add columns A, C, and F together in column G.

Column G contains the pink noise series. Graph the series and compare it to a random one. Notice that there are many more large changes, both positive and negative, as well as more frequent reversals.

Equation (13.2) looks very simple, but there is a complex interaction between its parts. The first term on the right-hand side is a simple AR(1) process, like those we examined in Chapter 4. Therefore, this equation contains an infinite memory, as AR(1) processes do. However, we also saw in Chapter 4 that AR(1) systems are persistent for short time intervals. As we shall see, this series is antipersistent. Something in the second term must be causing the antipersistence.

The second term is a random shock. Its coefficient is inversely related to the correlation coefficient in the first term. For instance, when ρ = 0.37, the coefficient to the second term is 0.93; when ρ = 0.90, the coefficient to the second term is 0.43. That is, the stronger the AR(1) process, the less strong the random shock. However, the random shock enters the AR process in the next iteration, and becomes part of the infinite memory process.

The random shock keeps the system from ever reaching equilibrium. If the random element were not included, each x series would reach equilibrium by its relaxation time, t. However, the random element keeps perturbing the system; it is continually reversing itself and never settling down. This type of system can be expected to have an unstable variance and mean. We will examine this more fully in Chapter 14.

Figure 13.1 shows a log/log plot of power spectrum versus frequency for a series of 1,000 observations created according to equation (13.2). The slope of the line is −1.63, giving b = 1.63, or H = 0.31, according to equation (13.1). Figure 13.2 shows R/S analysis of the same series. R/S analysis gives H = 0.30, supporting equation (13.1). The values vary, again, because equation (13.1) gives the asymptotic value of H. For small numbers of observations, R/S values will be biased and will follow the expected values from equation (5.6). However, both results are in close agreement. More importantly, both give antipersistent values of H. They look very similar to the volatility studies of Chapter 9.

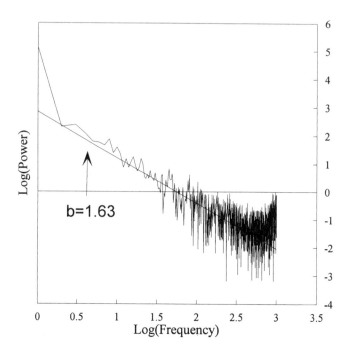

FIGURE 13.1   Power spectra, 1/f noise: multiple relaxation algorithm.

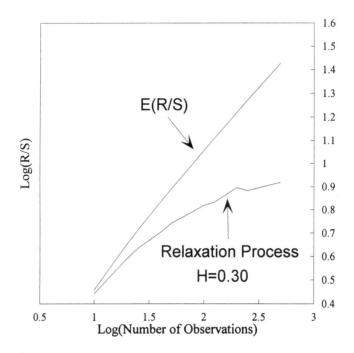

FIGURE 13.2   R/S analysis, antipersistence: relaxation process.

It is likely that the multiple parallel relaxation processes exist because of the market structure postulated in the Fractal Market Hypothesis. Each investment horizon (or frequency) has its own probability structure. This self-similar probability structure means that, in the short term, each investment horizon faces the same level of risk, after adjustment for scale. Therefore, each investment horizon has the same unstable volatility structure. The sum of these unstable volatilities is a 1/f noise with characteristic exponent b = 1.56, or H = 0.44. The reason volatility is unstable must wait for Chapter 14 and fractal statistics.

Intermittency

Interestingly, a characteristic value of b = 1.67, or H = 0.33, often shows up in nature. Kolmogorov (1941) predicted that the change in velocity of a turbulent fluid would have b = $5/3$. Recent studies of turbulence in the atmosphere by Kida (1991) and Schmitt et al. (1992) have shown that the actual exponent of turbulence is very close to the predicted value. Persistent values of H tend to be approximately 0.70; antipersistent values tend to be approximately 0.33. This suggests that there might be a relationship between turbulence and market volatility. Ironically, when most people equate turbulence with the stock market, they are thinking of the change in prices. Instead, turbulent flow might better model volatility, which can also be bought and sold through the options markets.

Turbulence is considered a *cascade* phenomenon. It is characterized by energy being transferred from large-scale to small-scale structures. In turbulence, a main force is injected into a fluid. This force causes numerous eddies, and smaller eddies split off from the larger eddies. This self-similar cascading structure was one of the first images of a dynamical fractal. However, it seems unlikely that this is the phenomenon that characterizes volatility, because it is an inverse power law effect. The markets are more likely power law phenomena, where large scales are the sum of the small scales (an amplification process). This amplification process underlies the long-memory process. In volatility, this may be the case:

1. We have seen the term structure of volatility in Chapter 2. In the stock, bond, and currency markets, volatility increased at a faster rate than the square root of time. This relationship of one investment horizon to another, amplifying the effects of the smaller horizons, may be the dynamical reason that volatility has a power law scaling characteristic. At any one time, the fractal structure of the markets (that is, many investors, who have different investment horizons, trading simultaneously) is a snapshot of the amplification process. This would be much like the snapshots taken of turbulent flow.

2. The stock and bond markets do have a maximum scale, showing that the memory effect dissipates as the energy in turbulent flow does. However, currencies do not have this property, and the energy amplification, or memory, continues forever. Volatility, which has a similar value of b to turbulent flow, should be modeled as such.

The well-known Logistic Equation is the simplest method for simulating the cascade model of turbulence. The Logistic Equation is characterized by a period-doubling route from orderly to chaotic behavior. This equation is often used as an example of how random-looking results (statistically speaking) can be generated from a simple deterministic equation. What is not well-known is that the Logistic Equation generates *antipersistent* results. This makes it an inappropriate model for the capital markets, although it may be a good model for volatility.

The Logistic Equation was originally designed to model population dynamics (as do relaxation processes) and ballistics. Assume we have a population that has a growth (or "birth") rate, r. If we simply apply the growth rate to the population, we will not have a very interesting or realistic model. The population will simply grow without bound, linearly, through time. As we know, when a population grows without bound, it will eventually reach a size at which it outstrips its resources. As resources become scarcer, the population will decline. Therefore, it is important to add a "death" rate. With this factor, as the population gets bigger, the death rate increases. The Logistic Equation contains this birth and death rate, and takes the following basic form:

$$X_{t+1} = r*X_t*(1 - X_t), \qquad 0 < X < 1 \tag{13.4}$$

where t = a time index

The Logistic Equation is an *iterated* equation: its output becomes the input the next time around. Therefore, each output is related to all of the previous outputs, creating a type of infinite memory process. The equation has a wealth of complex behavior, which is tied to the growth rate, r.

The Logistic Equation has been extensively discussed in the literature. I devoted a chapter to it in my previous book, but my primary concern was making the intuitive link between fractals and chaotic behavior. Here, I would like to discuss the Logistic Equation as an example of an antipersistent process that exhibits, under certain parameter values, the important characteristic of intermittency, as market volatility and turbulent flow do. The Logistic Equation is probably not *the* model of volatility, but it has certain characteristics that we will wish to see in such a model.

The process can swing from stable behavior to intermittent and then to chaotic behavior by small changes in the value of r. To return to the population dynamics analogy, at small values of r, the population eventually settles down to an equilibrium level; that is, the population reaches a size where supply and demand balance out. However, when r = 3.00, two solutions (often called "period 2" or a "2-cycle") appear. This event is called a *pitchfork bifurcation,* or period doubling. As r is increased, four solutions appear, then 16, and then 32. Finally, at approximately r = 3.60, the output appears random. It has become "chaotic." (A more complete description, including instructions for simulating the Logistic Equation in a common spreadsheet, is available in Peters (1991a).)

Figure 13.3(a) is the bifurcation diagram that appeared in my earlier book. The x-axis shows increasing values of r, while the y-axis shows the output of the equation x(t). Low values of r reach a single solution, but increasing the values results in successive bifurcations. This *period-doubling* route to chaos has been found to occur in turbulent flow. The period-doublings are related to the "cascade" concept discussed above. However, in the chaotic region (r > 3.60), there are also windows of stability. In particular, one large white band appears at approximately r = 3.82. Figure 13.3(b) is a magnification of this region.

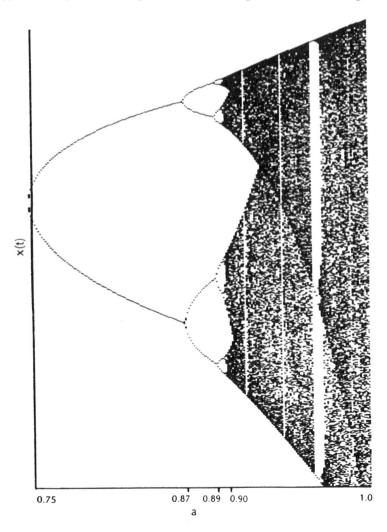

FIGURE 13.3a   The bifurcation diagram.

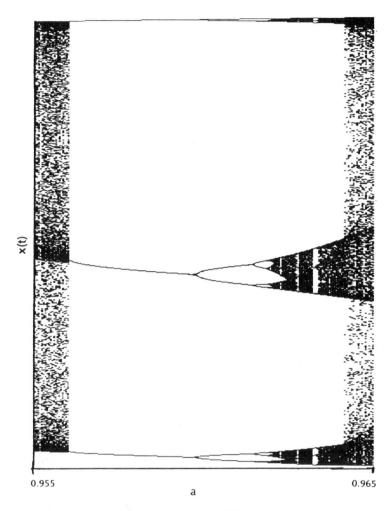

FIGURE 13.3b   Magnification of the chaotic region.

The critical value of r is actually $1 + \sqrt{8}$. At this point, a stable area of period 3 (three alternating solutions) develops. However, a little below this area the results alternate between a stable 3-cycle and a chaotic region. Figure 13.4 shows the results of iterating equation (13.4) in a spreadsheet with $r = 1 + \sqrt{8} - .0001$, after Schroeder (1991). The alternating areas illustrate *intermittent* behavior, or alternating periods of stability and instability. Intermittency, or bursts of chaos,

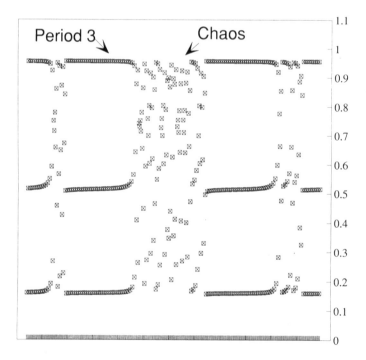

FIGURE 13.4 Intermittency, Logistic Equation: r = 3.8283 . . . .

are highly symptomatic of the time behavior of realized and implied market volatility.

Schroeder (1991) went into more detail about the geometrics of this event, which is called a *tangent bifurcation*. Conceptually, the system becomes trapped for a long period, alternating within a closely related set of three values. Then it breaks out, becoming wild and chaotic before being trapped once more. The "stable values" decay hyperbolically (examine the pitchforks in Figure 13.3(b)) before they become unstable. Many studies have noticed a similar behavior of volatility "spikes" followed by a hyperbolic decay. The hyperbolic decay would appear to be equivalent to the relaxation times discussed earlier.

Given this behavior, it was of interest to apply R/S analysis to the Logistic Equation. Figure 13.5 shows the results. We applied R/S analysis to 3,000 values from the Logistic Equation, with r = 4.0 in the chaotic region. H is calculated to be 0.37, or 10.2 standard deviations below E(H). These values are very similar to those found in Chapter 10 for market volatility.

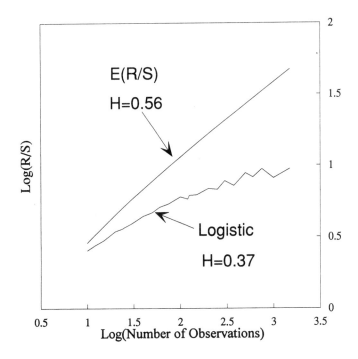

FIGURE 13.5   R/S analysis, Logistic Equation: r = 4.0.

We have seen two models of pink noise. The relationship between relaxation processes and the Logistic Equation should be obvious. Both model population dynamics as an iterated process. However, as similar as equations (13.2) and (13.4) are, they are also quite different. In the relaxation model, the decay is due to a correlation time and a random event. In the Logistic Equation, the decay is due to a nonlinear transformation of the population size itself. The Logistic Equation is a much richer model from a dynamics point of view. However, the relaxation model, with its multiple relaxation times, has great appeal as well, particularly in light of the Fractal Market Hypothesis and its view that markets are made up of the superimposition of an infinite number of investment horizons.

There is a significant problem with both models as "real" models of volatility. Neither process generates the high-peaked, fat-tailed frequency distribution that is characteristic of systems with $0 < H < 0.50$, as we will see in Chapter 14. In addition, we remain unable to explain why intermittency and relaxation processes should be related to volatility, which is, after all, a by-product of market price dynamics. There is a plausible link, but before we can discuss that, we must take a look at black noise processes.

BLACK NOISE: 0.50 < H < 1.0

The Hurst process, essentially a black noise process, has already been discussed extensively. Like pink noise, black noise processes seem to abound in nature. Pink noises occur in relaxation processes, like turbulence. Black noise appears in long-run cyclical records, like river levels, sunspot numbers, tree-ring thicknesses, and stock market price changes. The Hurst process is one possible explanation for the appearance of black noise, but there are additional reasons for persistence to exist in a time series. In Part Five, we will discuss the possibility of "noisy chaos." In this section, we will examine fractional brownian motion.

The Joseph Effect

Fractional brownian motion (FBM) is a generalization of brownian motion, which has long been used as a "default" defusion process, as we have discussed many times before. Essentially, if the process under study is unknown and a large number of degrees of freedom are involved, then brownian motion is as good an explanation as any. Because it has been so widely studied and its properties are well understood, it also makes available a large number of mathematical tools for analysis. However, as we have seen, it is a myth that random processes and brownian motion are widespread. Hurst found that most processes are persistent, with long-memory effects. This violates the assumption that makes a process random, thus reducing the reliability of most of those tools. Part of the problem is the restrictive assumption required for brownian motion—and the Gaussian statistics that underlie it. It becomes a special case, not the general case. Perhaps the most widespread error in time series analysis is the assumption that most series should be accepted as brownian motion until proven otherwise. The reverse should be the case.

Brownian motion was originally studied as the erratic movement of a small particle suspended in a fluid. Robert Brown (1828) realized that this erratic movement was a property of the fluid itself. We now know that the erratic movement is due to water molecules colliding with the particle. Bachelier (1900) recognized the relationship between a random walk and Gaussian statistics.

Einstein (1908) saw the relationship between brownian motion and a random walk. In 1923, Weiner (1976) modeled brownian motion as a random walk, with underlying Gaussian statistical structure. Feder (1988) explained the process in the following manner.

Take X(t) to be the position of a random particle at time, t. Let {e} be a Gaussian random process with zero mean and unit variance, consisting of a random number labeled e. The change in the position of the random particle from time t_0 to time t is given by:

$$X(t) - X(t_0) \approx e*|t - t_0|^H, \qquad \text{for } t \geq t_0 \tag{13.5}$$

where H = 0.50 for brownian motion

As Feder (1988) said, "[O]ne finds the position X(t) given the position $X(t_0)$ by choosing a random number e from a Gaussian distribution, multiplying it by the time increment $|t - t_0|^H$ and adding the result to the given position $X(t_0)$."

For fractional brownian motion, we generalize H so that it can range from 0 to 1. If we now set $B_H(t)$ as the position of a particle in FBM, the variance of the changes in position scale in time as follows:

$$V(t - t_0) \approx |t - t_0|^{2*H} \tag{13.6}$$

For H = 0.50, this reduces to the classical Gaussian case. The variance increases linearly with time, or the standard deviation increases at the square root of time. However, FBM has variances that scale at a faster rate than brownian motion, when 0.5 < H < 1. According to (13.3), standard deviation should increase at a rate equal to H. Thus, a persistent, black noise process will have variances that behave much like the scaling of capital markets that we examined in Chapter 2. However, those processes did increase at a slower value than H. The Dow Jones Industrials scaled at the .53 root of time, while H = 0.58. Likewise, the standard deviation of the yen/dollar exchange rate scaled at the 0.59 root of time, while H = 0.62. The concept behind equation (13.6) is correct, but is in need of further refinement. We leave that to future research. Meanwhile, we can say that there is a relationship between the scaling of variance and H. The *exact* nature of that relationship remains unclear.

In addition, the correlation between increments, C(t), is defined as follows:

$$C(t) = 2^{(2*H-1)} - 1 \tag{13.7}$$

This equation expresses the correlation of changes in position of a process over time t with all increments of time t that precede and follow it. Thus, in market terms, it would be the correlation of all one-day returns with all future and past one-day returns. It would also apply to the correlation of all five-day returns with all past and future five-day returns. In fact, theoretically, it would apply to all time increments. It is a measure of the strength of the long-memory effect, and it covers all time scales.

When a process is in brownian motion, with H = 0.50, then C(t) is zero. There is no long-memory effect. When $0 < H < 0.50$, C(t) is negative. There is a reversal effect, which takes place over multiple time scales. We saw a similar effect for an antipersistent, pink noise process. However, when the process is black noise, with $0.5 < H < 1.0$, we have infinite long-run correlations; that is, we have a long-memory effect that occurs over multiple time scales, or in capital markets' investment horizons. We know that equation (13.5) is not completely true, so we can expect that equation (13.6) is also in need of correction. Again, that is left to future research.

Thus, the equation defining FBM uses this infinite memory effect:

$$B_H(t) = [1 / \Gamma(H + 0.50)] * [\int_{-\infty}^{0} (|t - t'|^{H-0.50} - |t'|^{H-0.50}) dB(t')$$
$$+ \int_{0}^{t} |t - t'|^{H-0.50} dB(t')] \qquad (13.8)$$

As before, when H = 0.50, equation (13.8) reduces to ordinary brownian motion. If we examine (13.8) more closely, we see that a number of other interesting properties appear for FBM. The first is that FBM is not a stationary process, as has been often observed of the capital markets. However, the changes in FBM are not only stationary, but self-similar. Equation (13.8) can be simplified, for simulation purposes, into a form that is easier to understand:

$$B_H(t) - B_H(t-1) = [n^{-H} / \Gamma(H + 0.50)] * \left[\sum_{i=1}^{n*t} i^{H-0.50} * r_{(1+n*(M+t)-i)} \right.$$
$$\left. + \sum_{i=1}^{n*(M-1)} ((n+1)^{H-0.50} - i^{H-0.50} * r_{(1+n*(M-1+t)-i)} \right] \qquad (13.9)$$

where r = a series of M Gaussian random variables

Equation (13.9) is a discrete form of equation (13.8). Essentially, it says the same thing, replacing the integrals with summations. The equation is a moving average over a finite range of random Gaussian values, M, weighted by a power law dependent on H. The numerical values in Figure 6.6 were generated using this algorithm. (A BASIC program for using this algorithm was provided in my earlier book.)

In its basic form, the time series (or "time trace") of the black noise series becomes smoother, the higher H or b is. In the simulation, the smoothness is a product of the averaging process. In theory, it is caused by increased correlations among the observations. The long-memory effect causes the appearance of trends and cycles. Mandelbrot (1972) called this *the Joseph effect* after the biblical story of seven fat years followed by seven lean years. The Joseph effect is represented by the power law summation in equation (13.9).

The Noah Effect

As shown in Figure 6.6, equation (13.9) produces time traces with the appropriate value of H or the right amount of jaggedness; that is, it duplicates the fractal dimension of the time trace, and the Joseph or long-memory effect. Black noise has an additional characteristic: catastrophes. Equations (13.8) and (13.9) do not induce catastrophes because they are fractional *Gaussian* noises. They explain only one aspect of black noise: long memory.

Black noise is also characterized by discontinuities in the time trace: there are abrupt discontinuous moves up and down. These discontinuous catastrophes cause the frequency distribution of black noise processes to have high peaks at the mean, and fat tails. Mandelbrot (1972) called this characteristic *the Noah effect,* after the biblical story of the deluge. Figure 13.6 shows the frequency distribution of changes for the FBM used to produce Figures 6.6(a) and (b). This series has H = 0.72, according to R/S analysis, and its frequency distribution is similar to normal Gaussian noise. We can see (1) that FBM simulation algorithms do not necessarily capture all the characteristics we are looking for, and (2) the one great shortcoming of R/S analysis: *R/S analysis cannot distinguish between fractional Gaussian noises and fractional non-Gaussian noises.* Therefore, R/S analysis alone is not enough to conclude that a system is black noise. We also need a high-peaked, fat-tailed frequency distribution. Even then, there is the third possibility of noisy chaos, which we will examine more fully in Part Five.

The Noah effect, an important aspect of black noise, is often overlooked because it adds another layer of complexity to the analysis. It occurs because the large events are *amplified* in the system; that is, something happens that causes an iterated feedback loop, much like the Logistic Equation. However, in

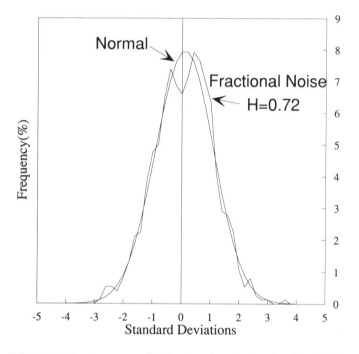

FIGURE 13.6   Frequency distribution, fractional noise: H = 0.72.

the Logistic Equation, the catastrophes occurred frequently, as they do for pink noise processes. In black noise, they happen more infrequently; the system remains persistent rather than becoming antipersistent.

Statistically, we seem to be unable to reproduce the Noah effect in simulation. However, we can reproduce it in nonlinear dynamics, as we shall see.

THE MIRROR EFFECT

Pink noises and black noises are commonly found in nature, but is there a relationship between the two? Will finding one necessarily lead to the other? In the spectrum of 1/f noises, this could well be the case.

Mandelbrot and van Ness (1968), as well as Schroeder (1991), have shown that brown noise is the integrand of white noise; that is, brown noise is simply the running sum of white noise. It also follows that the derivative or velocity of brown noise is white noise. Therefore, in the 1/f spectrum, a white noise series can easily be translated into brown noise through a type of "mirror" effect.

In equation (13.1), the spectral exponent, b, was equivalent to $2*H + 1$. We also mentioned, for the derivative of FBM, the spectral exponent is $2*H - 1$. Thus, a persistent series with $0.50 < H < 1.00$ will have a spectral exponent greater than 2.0, signaling a black noise process. However, the derivative of the black noise process will have $b < 1.0$, making it a pink noise process.

It is not surprising, therefore, that the volatility of stock market prices is antipersistent. Market returns are a black noise process, so their acceleration or volatility should be a pink noise process, as we found. We have also confirmed that it is a misconception to say that market returns are like "turbulence," which is a well-known pink noise process. The incorrect term is similar to saying that moving water is turbulent. The turbulence we measure is not the fluid itself, but the velocity of the fluid. Likewise, the turbulence of the market is in the velocity of the price changes, not the changes themselves.

As a further test of the relationship of pink and black noise, we can examine the second difference—the changes in the changes—through R/S analysis. According to this relationship, if the first difference is a black noise, then the second difference should be a pink noise. Figure 13.7 shows the log/log R/S plot for five-day Dow Jones Industrials returns used in Chapter 8. Note that $H = 0.28$, which is consistent with an antipersistent, pink noise process. I have found this to be true for any process with $H > 0.50$.

FRACTIONAL DIFFERENCING: ARFIMA MODELS

In addition to the more exotic models of long memory that we have been discussing, there is also a generalized version of the ARIMA (autoregressive integrated moving average) models we discussed in Chapter 5. ARIMA models are homogeneous nonstationary systems that can be made stationary by successively differencing the observations. The more general ARIMA(p,d,q) model could also include autoregressive and moving average components, either mixed or separate. The differencing parameter, d, was always an integer value. Hosking (1981) further generalized the original ARIMA(p,d,q) value for fractional differencing, to yield an autoregressive fractionally integrated moving average (ARFIMA) process; that is, d could be any real value, including fractional values. ARFIMA models can generate persistent and antipersistent behavior in the manner of fractional noise. In fact, an ARFIMA(0,d,0) process is the fractional brownian motion of Mandelbrot and Wallis (1969a–1969d). Because the more general ARFIMA(p,d,q) process can include short-memory AR or MA processes over a long-memory process, it has potential in describing

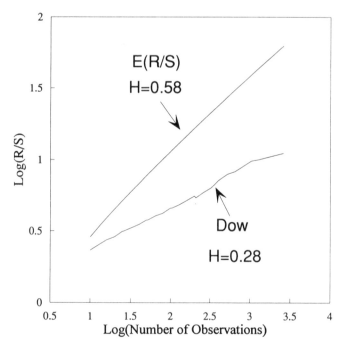

FIGURE 13.7 R/S analysis, Dow Jones Industrials, five-day returns: second difference.

markets. In light of the Fractal Market Hypothesis, it has particular appeal, because the very high-frequency terms can be autoregressive (as we found in Chapter 9), when superimposed over a long-memory Hurst process. Thus, ARFIMA models offer us an adaptation of a more conventional modeling technique that can be fully integrated into the Fractal Market Hypothesis. Most of the following discussion is a paraphrase of Hosking (1981). Readers interested in more detail are referred to that work.

Fractional differencing sounds strange. Conceptually, it is an attempt to convert a continuous-process, fractional brownian motion into a discrete one by breaking the differencing process into smaller components. Integer differencing, which is only a gross approximation, often leads to incorrect conclusions when such a simplistic model is imposed on a real process.

In addition, there is a direct relationship between the Hurst exponent and the fractional differencing operator, d:

$$d = H - 0.50 \tag{13.10}$$

Thus, $0 < d < 0.50$ corresponds to a persistent black noise process, and $-0.50 < d < 0$ is equivalent to an antipersistent pink noise system. White noise corresponds to $d = 0$, and brown noise corresponds to $d = 1$ or an ARIMA(0,1,0) process, as well known in the literature. Brown noise is the trail of a random walk, not the increments of a random walk, which are white noise.

It is common to express autoregressive processes in terms of a backward shift operator, B. For discrete time white noise, $B(x_t) = x_{t-1}$, so that

$$\Delta x_t = (1 - B)*x_t = a_t$$

where the a_t are IID random variables. Fractionally differenced white noise, with parameter, d, is defined by the following binomial series:

$$\Delta^d = (1 - B)^d = \sum_{k=0}^{\infty} \binom{d}{k} (-B)^k$$

$$= 1 - d*B - \frac{1}{2}*d*(1 - d)*B^2 - \frac{1}{6}*d(1 - d)*(2 - d)*B^3 - \ldots \quad (13.11)$$

Characteristics of ARFIMA(0,d,0)

Hosking developed the characteristics of the ARFIMA equivalent of fractional noise processes, ARFIMA(0,d,0)—an ARFIMA process with no short-memory effects from p and q. I will state the relevant characteristics here.

Let $\{x_t\}$ be an ARFIMA(0,d,0) process, where k is the time lag and a_t is a white noise process with mean zero and variance σ_a^2. These are the characteristics:

1. When $d < 0.50$, $\{x_t\}$ is a stationary process and has the infinite moving-average representation:

    $$x_t = \psi(B)a_t = \sum_{k=0}^{\infty} \psi_k * a_{t-k} \quad (13.12)$$

    where:

    $$\psi_k = \frac{d(1 + d) \ldots (k - 1 + d)}{k!} = \frac{(k + d - 1)!}{k!(d - 1)!} \quad (13.13)$$

    As $k \to \infty$, $\psi_k \sim \frac{k^{d-1}}{(d - 1)!}$

2. When $d > -0.50$, $\{x_t\}$ is invertible and has the infinite autoregressive representation:

$$\pi(B)x_t = \sum_{k=0}^{\infty} \pi_k * x_{t-1} \tag{13.14}$$

where:

$$\pi_t = \frac{-d*(1-d) \ldots (d-1-d)}{k!} = \frac{(k-d-1)!}{k!*(d-1)!} \tag{13.15}$$

As $k \to \infty, \pi_k \sim \dfrac{k^{-d-1}}{(-d-1)!}$

3. The spectral density of $\{x_t\}$ is:

$$s(\omega) = (2*\sin\frac{\omega}{2})^{-2*d} \tag{13.16}$$

for $0 < \omega \le \pi$.

4. The covariance function of $\{x_t\}$ is:

$$\gamma_k = E(x_t x_{t-k}) = \frac{(-1)^k(-2d)!}{(k-d)!*(-k-d)!} \tag{13.17}$$

5. The correlation function of $\{x_t\}$ is:

$$\rho_k \sim \frac{(-d)!}{(d-1)!} * k^{2*d-1} \tag{13.18}$$

as k approaches infinity.

6. The inverse correlations of $\{x_t\}$ are:

$$\rho_{inv,k} \sim \frac{d!}{(-d-1)!} * k^{-1-2*d} \tag{13.19}$$

7. The partial correlations of $\{x_t\}$ are:

$$\varphi_{kk} = \frac{d}{k-d}, (k = 1,2, \ldots) \tag{13.20}$$

Commentary on the Characteristics

The most relevant characteristics to the Fractal Market Hypothesis deal with the decay of the autoregressive process. For $-0.5 < d < 0.5$, both φ_k and π_k decay hyperbolically (that is, according to a power law) rather than exponentially, as they would through a standard AR process. For $d > 0$, the correlation function, equation (13.18) is also characterized by power law decay. Equation (13.18) also implies that $\{x_t\}$ is asymptotically self-similar, or it has a statistical fractal structure. For $d > 0$, the partial and inverse correlations also decay hyperbolically, unlike a standard ARIMA(p,0,q) process. Finally, for long (or low) frequencies, the spectrum implies a long-memory process. All of the hyperbolic decay behavior in the correlations is also consistent with a long-memory, stationary process for $d > 0$.

For $-0.5 < d < 0$, the ARFIMA(0,d,0) process is antipersistent, as described in Chapter 4. The correlations and partial correlations are all negative, except $\rho_0 = 1$. They also decay, according to a power law, to zero. All of this is consistent with the antipersistent process previously discussed.

ARFIMA(p,d,q)

This discussion has dealt with the ARFIMA(0,d,0) process, which, as we mentioned, is equivalent to fractional noise processes. It is also possible to generalize this approach to an ARFIMA(p,d,q) process that includes short-memory AR and MA processes. The result is short-frequency effects superimposed over the low-frequency or long-memory process.

Hosking discussed the effect of these additional processes by way of example. In particular, he said: "In practice ARIMA(p,d,q) processes are likely to be of most interest for small values of p and q . . . ." Examining the simplest examples, AFRIMA(1,d,0) and ARFIMA(0,d,1) processes are good illustrations of the mixed systems. These are the equivalent of short-memory AR(1) and MA(0,1) superimposed over a long-memory process.

An ARFIMA(1,d,0) process is defined by:

$$(1 - \varphi^*B)\Delta^d y_t = a_t \tag{13.21}$$

where a_t is a white noise process. We must include the fractional differencing process in equation (13.12), where $\Delta^a x_t = a_t$, so we have $x_t = (1 - \varphi^*B)^*y_t$. The ARIMA(1,d,0) variable, y_t, is a first-order autoregression with ARIMA (0,d,0) disturbances; that is, it is an ARFIMA(1,d,0) process. y_t will have short-term behavior that depends on the coefficient of autoregression, φ, just like a normal AR(1) process. However, the long-term behavior of y_t will be similar to x_t. It will exhibit persistence or antipersistence, depending on the value of d. For stationarity and invertibility, we assume $|d| < 0.50$, and $|\varphi| < 1$.

Of most value is the correlation function of the process, ρ_k^y. Using $F(a,b;c;z)$ as the hypergeometric function, as $k \to \infty$:

$$\rho_k^y \sim \frac{(-d)!}{(d-1)!} * \frac{(1+\varphi)}{(1-\varphi)^2} * \frac{k^{2*d-1}}{F(1,1+d;1-d;\varphi)} \tag{13.22}$$

Hosking (1981) provided the following example. Let $d = 0.2$ and $\varphi = 0.5$. Thus, $\rho_1 = 0.711$ for both processes. (See Table 13.1.) By comparing the correlation functions for the ARFIMA(1,d,0) and AR(1) processes (as discussed in Chapter 5) for longer lags, we can see the differences after even a few periods. Remember that an AR(1) process is also an infinite memory process.

Figure 13.8 graphs the results. The decay in correlation is, indeed, quite different over the long term but identical over the short term.

Hosking described an ARFIMA(0,d,1) process as "a first-order moving average of fractionally different white noise." The MA parameter, θ, is used such that $|\theta| < 1$; again, $|d| < 0.50$, for stationarity and invertibility. The ARFIMA(0,d,1) process is defined as:

$$y_t = (1 - \theta * B) * x_t \tag{13.23}$$

The correlation function is as follows, as $k \to \infty$:

$$\rho_k^y \sim \frac{(-d)!}{(d-1)!} * a * k^{2*d-1} \tag{13.24}$$

where:

$$a = \frac{(1-\theta)^2}{(1+\theta^2 - (2*\theta*d / (1-d)))} \tag{13.25}$$

To compare the correlation structure of the ARFIMA(0,d,1) with the ARFIMA(1,d,0), Hosking chose two series with $d = 0.5$, and lag parameters that gave the same value of ρ_1. (See Figure 13.9.) Specifically, the ARFIMA(1,d,0) parameter, $\varphi = 0.366$, and the ARFIMA(0,d,1) parameter, $\theta = -.508$, both give $\rho_1 = 0.60$. (See Table 13.2.)

Table 13.1   ARFIMA (1,d,0) Correlations, p_k; d = 0.2,
ϕ = 0.5, and an AR(1) with ϕ = 0.711

k	ARFIMA	AR	k	ARFIMA	AR
1	0.711	0.711	7	0.183	0.092
2	0.507	0.505	8	0.166	0.065
3	0.378	0.359	9	0.152	0.046
4	0.296	0.255	10	0.141	0.033
5	0.243	0.181	15	0.109	0.001
6	0.208	0.129	20	0.091	0.000

The short-term correlation structure is different, with the MA process dropping more sharply than the AR process. However, as the lag increases, the correlations become more and more alike and the long-memory process dominates. The studies of the U.S. stock market in Chapters 8 and 9 were very similar. Chapter 8 used the Dow Jones Industrials and Chapter 9 used the S&P 500, but there is enough similar behavior in these broad market indices to come

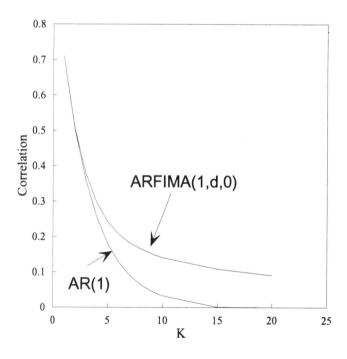

FIGURE 13.8   ARFIMA(1,d,0) versus AR(1), correlations over lag, K.

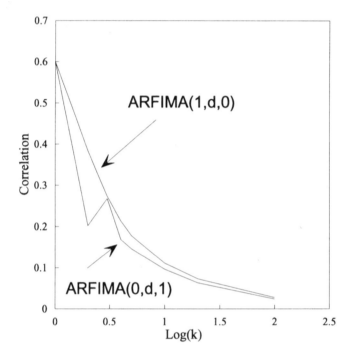

FIGURE 13.9 ARFIMA(1,d,0) versus ARFIMA(0,d,1), correlations over log(k).

Table 13.2 Correlation Comparison o
ARFIMA (1,d,0) and ARFIMA (0,d,1)

k	ARFIMA(1,d,0)	ARFIMA(0,d,1)
1	0.600	0.600
2	0.384	0.267
3	0.273	0.202
4	0.213	0.168
5	0.178	0.146
10	0.111	0.096
20	0.073	0.063
100	0.028	0.024

to a conclusion. In Chapter 9, we found the high-frequency "tick" data to be an AR process, with scant evidence of a long-memory process. However, in Chapter 8, we had found the reverse. There was little evidence of an AR process (except at the daily frequency), but much evidence of long memory. This would imply that the U.S. stock market is likely an ARFIMA(p,d,0) process, although more extensive study is needed.

Hosking gave the following procedure for identifying and estimating an ARFIMA(p,d,q) model:

1. Estimate d in the ARIMA(0,d,0) model $\Delta^d y_t = a_t$.
2. Define $u_t = \Delta^d y_t$.
3. Using Box–Jenkings modeling procedure, identify and estimate the φ and θ parameters in the ARFIMA(p,0,q) model $\varphi * B * u_t = \theta * B * a_t$.
4. Define $x_t = (\theta * B)^{-1} * (\varphi * B * y_t)$.
5. Estimate d in the ARFIMA(0,d,0) model $\Delta^d x_t = a_t$.
6. Check for the convergence of the d, φ, and θ parameters; if not convergent, go to step 2.

Hosking specifically suggested using R/S analysis to estimate d in steps 1 and 5, using equation (13.10).

The ARFIMA model has many desirable characteristics for modeling purposes. It also falls within a more traditional statistical framework, which may make it acceptable to a wide group of researchers. I expect that much future work will be devoted to this area.

SUMMARY

In this chapter, we examined some complex but important relationships. We found that noise can be categorized according to color and that the color of noise can be directly related to the Hurst exponent, H, and the Hurst process. Antipersistent time series, like market volatility, are pink noise and akin to turbulence. Persistent series are black noise, characterized by infinite memory and discontinuous abrupt changes. We also looked at the ARFIMA family of models as a potential modeling tool. We examined the characteristics of these noises, but we have not yet looked at their statistics. Because statistics is the primary tool of financial economics, it would appear to be useful to study fractal statistics. We turn to that next.

14
Fractal Statistics

We have stated, a number of times, that the normal distribution is not adequate to describe market returns. Up to this point, we have not specifically stated what should replace it. We will make a suggestion, which many readers are not going to like. First, we must reexamine the reasons for the widespread acceptance of the Gaussian Hypothesis (markets are random walks and are well described by the normal distribution).

The normal distribution has a number of desirable characteristics. Its properties have been extensively studied. Its measures of dispersion are well understood. A large number of practical applications have been formulated under the assumption that processes are random, and so are described in the limit by the normal distribution. Many sampled groups are, indeed, random. For a while, it seemed that the normal distribution could describe any situation where complexity reigned.

West (1990) quoted Sir Francis Galton, the 19th-century English mathematician and eccentric:

> I know of scarcely anything so apt to impress the imagination as the wonderful form of cosmic order expressed by the "law of frequency of error." The law would have been personified by the Greeks and deified if they had known of it. It reigns with serenity and in complete self-effacement amidst the wildest confusion. The larger the mob, and the greater the apparent anarchy, the more perfect is its sway. It is the supreme law of Unreason. Whenever a large sample of chaotic elements are taken in hand and marshaled in the order of their magnitude, an unsuspected and most beautiful form of regularity proves to have been latent all along.

Galton was, evidently, a disciple of Plato and a true believer in the creations of the Good. To Galton, and to most mathematicians, the normal distribution is the ultimate imposition of order on disorder. Galton studied many groups and showed them to be normally distributed, from the useful (life spans) to the ridiculous (the frequency of yawns). Unfortunately, there are many processes that are not normal. The "supreme law of Unreason" often does not hold sway, even for systems that appear overwhelmingly complex.

The reasons for its failure rest on its assumptions. Gauss showed that the limiting distribution of a set of independent, identically distributed (IID) random variables was the normal distribution. This is the famous *Law of Large Numbers*, or, more formally, the *Central Limit Theorem*. It is because of Gauss's formulation that we often refer to such processes as Gaussian. However, there are situations in which the law of large numbers does not hold. In particular, there are instances where amplification occurs at extreme values. This occurrence will often cause a long-tailed distribution.

For instance, Pareto (1897), an economist, found that the distribution of incomes for individuals was approximately log-normally distributed for 97 percent of the population. However, for the last 3 percent, it was found to increase sharply. It is unlikely that anyone will live five times longer than average, but it is not unusual for someone to be five times wealthier than average. Why is there a difference between these two distributions? In the case of life spans, each individual is truly an independent sample, family members aside. It is not much different from the classic problem in probability—pulling red or black balls out of an urn. However, the more wealth one has, the more one can risk. The wealthy can leverage their wealth in ways that the average, middle-income individual cannot. Therefore, the wealthier one is, the greater his or her ability to become wealthier.

This ability to leverage is not limited to wealth. Lotka (1926) found that senior scientists were able to leverage their position, through graduate students and increased name recognition, in order to publish more papers. Thus, the more papers published, the more papers could be published, once the extreme tail of the distribution was reached.

These long-tailed distributions, particularly in the findings of Pareto, led Levy (1937), a French mathematician, to formulate a generalized density function, of which the normal as well as the Cauchy distributions were special cases. Levy used a generalized version of the Central Limit Theorem. These distributions fit a large class of natural phenomena, but they did not attract much attention because of their unusual and seemingly intractable problems. Their unusual properties continue to make them unpopular; however, their other properties are so close to our findings on capital markets that we must examine them. In addition, it has now been found that stable Levy distributions are useful in describing the statistical properties of turbulent flow and 1/f noise—and, they are fractal.

FRACTAL (STABLE) DISTRIBUTIONS

Levy distributions are *stable* distributions. Levy said that a distribution function, F(x), was stable if, for all b_1, $b_2 > 0$, there also exists $b > 0$ such that:

$$F(x/b_1)*F(x/b_2) = F(x/b) \tag{14.1}$$

This relationship exists for all distribution functions. F(x) is a general characteristic of the class of stable distributions, rather than a property of any one distribution.

The characteristic functions of F can be expressed in a similar manner:

$$f(b_1*t)*f(b_2*t) = f(b*t) \tag{14.2}$$

Therefore, $f(b_1*t)$, $f(b_2*t)$, and $f(b*t)$ all have the same *shaped* distribution, despite their being products of one another. This accounts for their "stability."

Characteristic Functions

The actual representation of the stable distributions is typically done in the manner of Mandelbrot (1964), using the log of their characteristic functions:

$$\emptyset(t) = \ln[f(t)] = \ln[E(e^{i*x*t})]$$
$$= i*\delta*t - |c*t|^{\alpha}*(1 - i*\beta*(t/|t|))*\tan(\pi*\alpha/2), \alpha \neq 1,$$
$$= i*\delta*t - |c*t|*(1 + i*\beta*(2/\pi)*\ln|t|), \alpha = 1 \tag{14.3}$$

The stable distributions have four parameters: α, β, c, and δ. Each has its own function, although only two are crucial.

First, consider the relatively unimportant parameters, c and δ. δ is the *location parameter*. Essentially, the distribution can have different means than 0 (the standard normal mean), depending on δ. In most cases, the distribution under study is normalized, and $\delta = 0$; that is, the mean of the distribution is set to 0.

Parameter c is the *scale parameter*. It is most important when comparing real distributions. Again, within the normalizing concept, c is like the sample deviation; it is a measure of dispersion. When normalizing, it is common to subtract the sample mean (to give a mean of 0) and divide by the standard deviation, so that units are in terms of the sample standard deviation. The normalizing operation is done to compare an empirical distribution to the standard normal distribution with mean = 0 and standard deviation of 1. c is used to set the units by which the distribution is expanded and compressed about δ. The default value of c is 1. These two parameters' only purpose is setting the scale of the distribution, regarding mean and dispersion. They are not really characteristic to any one distribution, and so are less important. When c = 1 and δ = 0, the distribution is said to take a *reduced* form.

Parameters α and β determine the shape of the distribution and are extremely important. These two parameters are dependent on the generating process; c and δ are not. β is the *skewness parameter*. It takes values such that $-1 \leq \beta \leq +1$. When $\beta = 0$, the distribution is symmetrical around δ. When the skewness parameter is less than 0, the distribution is negatively skewed; when it is greater than 0, the distribution is positively skewed.

Parameter α, the *characteristic exponent,* determines the peakedness at δ and the fatness of the tails. The characteristic exponent can take the values $0 < \alpha \leq 2$. When $\alpha = 2.0$, the distribution is normal, with variance equal to $2*c^2$. However, when $\alpha < 2.0$, the second moment, or population variance, becomes infinite or undefined. When $1 < \alpha < 2.0$, the first moment or population mean exists; when $\alpha \leq 1$, the population mean also becomes infinite.

Infinite Variance and Mean

To most individuals who are trained in standard Gaussian statistics, the idea of an infinite mean or variance sounds absurd or even perverse. We can always calculate the variance or mean of a sample. How can it be infinite? Once again, we are applying a special case, Gaussian statistics, to all cases. In the family of stable distributions, the normal distribution is a special case that exists when $\alpha = 2.0$. In that case, the population mean and variance do exist. Infinite variance means that there is no "population variance" that the distribution tends to at the limit. When we take a sample variance, we do so, under the Gaussian assumption, as an estimate of the unknown population variance. Sharpe (1963) said that betas (in the Modern Portfolio Theory (MPT) sense) should be calculated from five years' monthly data. Sharpe chose five years because it gives a statistically significant sample variance needed to estimate the population variance. Five years is statistically significant only if the underlying distribution is Gaussian. If it is not Gaussian and $\alpha < 2.0$, the sample variance tells nothing about the population variance, because there is no population variance. Sample variances would be expected to be unstable and not tend to any value, even as the sample size increases. If $\alpha \leq 1.0$, the same goes for the mean, which also does not exist in the limit.

Figures 14.1 and 14.2 show how infinite mean and variance affect stable distributions using the sequential mean and standard deviation, after Fama (1965b).

Figure 14.1 uses the 8,000 samples from the well-known Cauchy distribution, which has infinite mean and variance. The Cauchy distribution is described in more detail below. The series used here has been "normalized" by subtracting the mean and dividing by the sample standard deviation. Thus, all units are expressed in standard deviations. For comparison, we use 8,000 Gaussian random variables that have been similarly normalized. It is important to understand that the two steps that follow will always end at mean 0 and standard deviation of 1, because they have been normalized to those values. Converging means that the time series rapidly goes to a stable value.

Figure 14.1(a) shows the *sequential mean,* which calculates the mean as observations are added one at a time. For a system with a finite mean, the sequential mean will eventually converge to the population mean, when enough data are used. In this case, it will be 0. In Figure 14.1(a), the time series of Gaussian random numbers converges to within .02 standard deviation of the mean by about 500 observations. Although it wanders around the mean of 0, it does so in a random, *uniform* fashion. By contrast, although the Cauchy series does not wander far from 0, it does so in a systematic, discontinuous fashion; that is, there are discrete jumps in the sequential mean, after which it begins to rise systematically.

Figure 14.2(a) shows the *sequential standard deviation* for the same two series. The sequential standard deviation, like the sequential mean, is the calculation of the standard deviation as observations are added one at a time. In this case, the difference is even more striking. The random series rapidly converges to a standard deviation of 1. The Cauchy distribution, by contrast, never converges. Instead, it is characterized by a number of large discontinuous jumps, and by large deviations from the normalized value of 1.

Figure 14.1(b) graphs the sequential mean of the five-day Dow Jones Industrials data used in Chapter 8 and elsewhere in this book, but it has also been normalized to a mean of 0 and a standard deviation of 1. After about 1,000 days, the graph converges to a value within 0.01 standard deviation of 0. A Gaussian

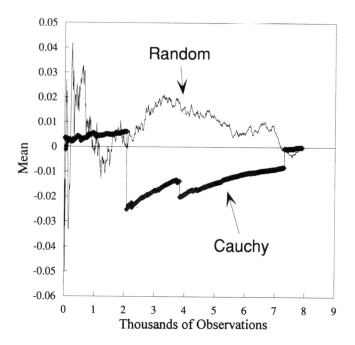

FIGURE 14.1a   Convergence of sequential mean, Cauchy function.

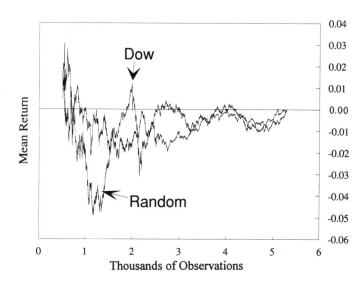

FIGURE 14.1b   Convergence of sequential mean, Dow Jones Industrials, five-day returns: 1888–1990.

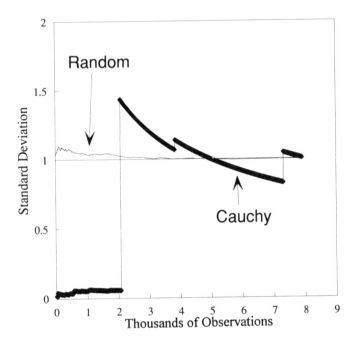

FIGURE 14.2a Convergence of sequential standard deviation, Cauchy function.

random time series shows similar behavior. The mean of the Dow returns appears to be stable, as one would expect from a stable fractal distribution. The behavior is uniform and continuous. It does not show the discrete jumps found in the Cauchy function, with its infinite mean.

Figure 14.2(b) shows a very different story. The sequential standard deviation for the Dow data does not converge. It ends at 1 because the time series was normalized to a standard deviation of 1, but it does not converge. On the other hand, the Gaussian random time series appears to converge at about 100 observations, and the large changes in Dow standard deviation are jumps—the changes are discontinuous. Even at the end of the graph, where we have over 5,200 observations, the discontinuities appear. The fluctuations seem to have become less violent, but this is because a daily change in price contributes less to the mean. Figure 14.3 is a "blow-up" of the end of Figure 14.2(b). We can see that the discontinuities are continuing. This is the impact of "infinite variance." The population variance does not exist, and using sampling variances as estimates can be misleading. There is a striking similarity between the behavior of the Cauchy sequential standard deviation and the Dow.

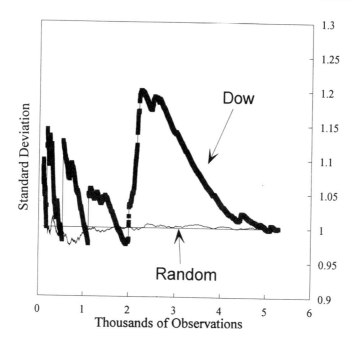

FIGURE 14.2b   Sequential standard deviation, Dow Jones Industrials, five-day returns: 1888–1990.

These graphs support the notion that, in the long term, the Dow is characterized by a stable mean and infinite memory, in the manner of stable Levy or fractal distributions.

I must add some qualifications at this point. When I state that the market is characterized by infinite variance, I do not mean that the variance is truly infinite. As with all fractal structures, there is eventually a time frame where fractal scaling ceases to apply. In earlier chapters, I said that trees are fractal structures. We know that tree branches do not become infinitely small. Likewise, for market returns, there could be a sample size where variance does, indeed, become finite. However, we can see here that after over 100 years of daily data, the standard deviation has still not converged. Therefore, for all practical purposes, market returns will behave as if they are infinite variance distributions. At least we can assume that, within our lifetime, they will behave as if they have infinite variance.

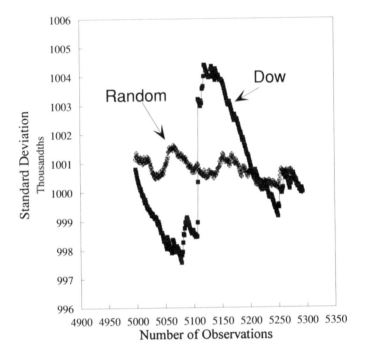

FIGURE 14.3 Convergence of sequential standard deviation, Dow Jones Industrials, five-day returns.

The Special Cases: Normal and Cauchy

Embedded within the characteristic function of the stable distributions are two well-known distributions as special cases. Using the notation $S(x; \alpha, \beta, c, \delta)$ to represent the parameters of a stable distribution, x, we will briefly examine these distributions:

1. For $S(x; 2, 0, c, \delta)$, equation (14.3) reduces to:

    $$\emptyset(t) = i*\delta*t - (\sigma^2/2)*t^2 \tag{14.4}$$

    where σ^2 = the variance of a normal distribution

    This is the standard Gaussian case, with $c = 2*\sigma^2$. If we also have $\delta = 0$, then it becomes the standard normal distribution with mean 0 and standard deviation of 1.

2. For S(x; 1, 0, c, δ), equation (14.4) reduces to:

$$\phi(t) = i*\delta*t - c*|t| \tag{14.5}$$

This is the log of the characteristic function for the Cauchy distribution, which is known to have infinite variance and mean. In this case, δ becomes the median of the distribution, and c, the semi-interquartile range.

These two well-known distributions, the Cauchy and normal, have many applications. They are also the only two members of the family of stable distributions for which the probability density functions can be explicitly derived. In all other fractional cases, they must be estimated, typically through numerical means. We will discuss one of these methods in a later section of this chapter.

Fat Tails and the Law of Pareto

When $\alpha < 2$ and $\beta = 0$, both tails follow the Law of Pareto. As we stated earlier, Pareto (1897) found that the log normal distribution did not describe the frequency of income levels in the top 3 percent of the population. Instead, the tails became increasingly long, such that:

$$P(U > u) = (u/U)^\alpha \tag{14.6}$$

Again, we have a scaling factor according to a power law. In this case, the power law is due to the characteristic exponent, α, and the probability of finding a value of U that is greater than an estimate u is dependent on alpha. To return to Pareto's study, the probability of finding someone with five times the average income is directly connected to the value of α.

The behavior of the distribution for different values of β, when $\alpha < 2$, is important to option pricing, which will be covered in Chapter 15. Briefly, when β takes the extreme values of $+1$ or -1, the left (or right) tail vanishes for the respective values of beta, and the remaining tail keeps its Pareto characteristics.

STABILITY UNDER ADDITION

For portfolio theory, the normal distribution had a very desirable characteristic. The sum of series of IID variables was still IID and was governed by the normal distribution. Stable distributions with the same value of alpha have the same characteristic. The following explanation is adapted from Fan, Neogi, and Yashima (1991).

Applying equation (14.2) to equation (14.3), we have:

$$E(e^{i*t*b_1*x_1})*E(e^{i*t*b_2*x_2}) = E(e^{i*t*b*x}) \qquad (14.7)$$

where x1, x2, and x are *reduced* stable independent random variables as described above.

Then:

$$E(e^{i*t*(b_1*x_1+b_2*x_2)}) = E(e^{i*t*b*x}) \qquad (14.8)$$

or, if " $\sim d \sim$ " means "same distribution,"

$$b_1*x_1 + b_2*x_2 \sim d \sim b*x \qquad (14.9)$$

Applying this relation to the characteristic functions using equation (14.3), we find the following relationship:

$$\exp[-(b_1^\alpha + b_2^\alpha)*|t|^\alpha*(1 + i*\beta*(t/|t|)*\tan(\alpha*\pi/2))$$
$$= \exp[-b^\alpha*|t|^\alpha*[1 + i*\beta*(t/|t|)*\tan(\alpha*\pi/2)] \qquad (14.10)$$

We can now see that:

$$b_1^\alpha + b_2^\alpha = b^\alpha \qquad\qquad \alpha \qquad (14.11)$$

Equation (14.11) reduces to the more well-known Gaussian, or normal case when alpha equals 2.

Based on equation (14.11), we can see that if two distributions are stable, with characteristic exponent α, their sum is also stable with characteristic exponent α. This has an application to portfolio theory. If the securities in the portfolio are stable, with the same value of alpha, then the portfolio itself is also stable, with that same value of alpha. Fama (1965b) and Samuelson (1967) used this relationship to adapt the portfolio theory of Markowitz (1952) for infinite variance distributions. Before we examine the practicality of those adaptations, we must first review the characteristics of the stable, fractal distributions.

CHARACTERISTICS OF FRACTAL DISTRIBUTIONS

Stable Levy distributions have a number of desirable characteristics that make them particularly consistent with observed market behavior. However, these same characteristics make the usefulness of stable distributions questionable, as we shall see.

Self-Similarity

Why do we now call these distributions fractal, in addition to stable, which was Levy's term? The scale parameter, c, is the answer. If the characteristic exponent, α, and the skewness parameter, β, remain the same, changing c simply rescales the distribution. Once we adjust for scale, the probabilities stay the same at all scales with equal values of α and β. Thus, α and β are not dependent on scale, although c and δ are. This property makes stable distributions self-similar under changes in scale. Once we adjust for the scale parameter, c, the probabilities remain the same. The series—and, therefore, the distributions—are *infinitely divisible*. This self-similar statistical structure is the reason we now refer to stable Levy distributions as fractal distributions. The characteristic exponent α, which can take fractional values between 1 and 2, is the fractal dimension of the probability space. Like all fractal dimensions, it is the scaling property of the process.

Additive Properties

We have already seen that fractal distributions are invariant under addition. This means that stable distributions are additive. Two stocks with the same value of α and β can be added together, and the resulting probability distribution will still have the same values of α and β, although c and δ may change. The normal distribution also shares this characteristic, so this aspect of MPT remains intact, as long as all the stocks have the same values of α and β. Unfortunately, my earlier book shows that different stocks can have different Hurst exponents and different values of α. Currently, there is no theory on combining distributions with different alphas. The EMH, assuming normality for all distributions, assumed $\alpha = 2.0$ for all stocks, which we now know to be incorrect.

Discontinuities: Price Jumps

The fat tails in fractal distributions are caused by amplification, and this amplification in a time series causes jumps in the process. They are similar to the jumps in sequential variance for the Cauchy and the Dow. Thus, a large change in a fractal process comes from a small number of large changes, rather than a large number of small changes, as implied in the Gaussian case. These changes tend to be abrupt and discontinuous—another manifestation of the Noah effect. Mandelbrot (1972, 1982) referred to it as the *infinite variance syndrome.*

These large discontinuous events are the reason we have infinite variance. It is easy to see why they occur in markets. When the market stampedes, or panics, fear breeds more fear, whether the fear is of capital loss or loss of opportunity. This amplifies the bearish/bullish sentiment and causes discontinuities in the executed price, as well as in the bid/asked prices. According to the Fractal Market Hypothesis, these periods of instability occur when the market loses its fractal structure: when long-term investors are no longer participating, and risk is concentrated in one, usually short, investment horizon. In measured time, these large changes affect all investment horizons. Despite the fact that long-term investors are not participating during the unstable period (because they either have left the market or have become short-term investors), the return in that horizon is still impacted. The infinite variance syndrome affects all investment horizons in measured time.

MEASURING α

Fama (1965a) describes a number of different ways to measure α. It now appears that R/S analysis and spectral analysis offer the most reliable method for calculating α, but these alternative methods can be used as confirmation.

The original method recommended by Mandelbrot (1964) and Fama (1965b) came from the relationship between the tails and the Law of Pareto, described in equation (14.6). By dividing both sides of equation (14.6) by the right-hand term and then taking logarithms, we obtain:

$$\log(P(U_1 > u)) = -\alpha * (\log(u) - \log(U_1)) \tag{14.7a}$$

$$\log(P(U_2 < u)) = -\alpha * (\log|u| - \log(U_2)) \tag{14.7b}$$

Equations (14.7a) and (14.7b) are for the positive and negative tails respectively. These equations imply that the slope of a log/log plot should asymptotically have a slope equal to $-\alpha$. The accepted method for implementing this analysis is to perform a log/log plot of the frequency in the positive and negative tail versus the absolute value of the frequency. When the tail is reached, the slope should be approximately equal to α, depending on the size of the sample. Figure 14.4 is taken from Mandelbrot (1964) and shows the theoretical log/log plot for various values of α.

Figure 14.5 shows the log/log chart for the daily Dow file used throughout this book. The tail area for both the positive and negative tails has ample observations for a good reading of α. The approximate value of 1.66 conforms to earlier studies by Fama (1965b).

The double-log graphical method works well in the presence of large data sets, such as the daily Dow time series. However, for smaller data sets, it is less reliable. This method was criticized by Cootner (1964), who stated that fat tails alone are not conclusive evidence that the stable distribution is the one of choice. That criticism is even more compelling today, with the advent of ARCH models and other fat-tailed distributions. Therefore, the graphical method should be used in conjunction with other tests.

R/S Analysis

Mandelbrot was not aware of rescaled range (R/S) analysis until the late 1960s. Even at that time, his work using R/S analysis was primarily confined to its field of origin, hydrology. When Fama wrote his dissertation (1965a), he was not aware of R/S analysis either. However, he was familiar with range analysis, as most economists were, and developed a relationship between the scaling of the range of a stable variable and α. In Chapter 5, we saw that Feller's work (1951) primarily dealt with the scaling of the range, and its relationship to the Hurst exponent. Here, we will modify Fama's work, and make an extension to the rescaled range and the Hurst exponent.

The sum of stable variables with characteristic exponent alpha results in a new variable with characteristic exponent alpha, although the scale will have changed. In fact, the scale of the distribution of the sums is $n^{1/\alpha}$ times the scale of the individual sums, where n is the number of observations. If the scale increases from daily to weekly, the scale increases by $5^{1/\alpha}$, where 5 is the number of days per week.

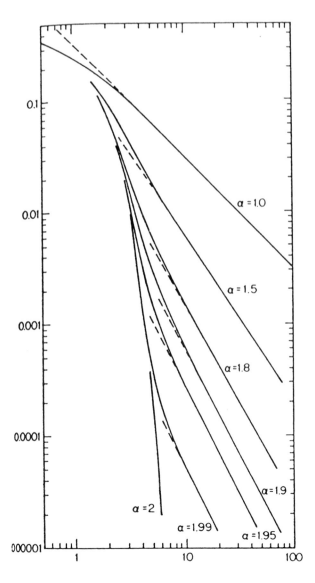

FIGURE 14.4 Log/log plot for various values of α. (From Mandelbrot (1964). Reproduced with permission of M.I.T. Press.)

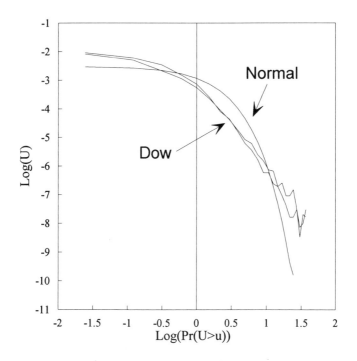

FIGURE 14.5 Estimating alpha, graphical method: daily Dow Jones Industrials.

If we define the sum, R_n, as the sum of a stable variable in a particular interval n, and R_1 as the initial value, then the following relationship holds:

$$R_n = R_1 * n^{1/\alpha} \tag{14.8}$$

This equation is close to equation (4.7) for the rescaled range. It states that the sum of n values scales as $n^{1/\alpha}$ times the initial value. That is, the sum of five-day returns with characteristic alpha is equivalent to the one-day return times $5^{1/\alpha}$. By taking logs of both sides of equation (14.8) and solving for alpha, we get:

$$\alpha = \frac{\log(n)}{\log(R_n) - \log(R_1)} \tag{14.9}$$

You will remember from equation (4.x) that

$$H = \frac{\log(R/S)}{\log(n)}$$

If the log of the range, $R_n - R_1$, is approximately equal to the rescaled range R/S, then we can postulate the following relationship:

$$\alpha = \frac{1}{H} \tag{14.10}$$

The fractal dimension of the probability space is in this way related to the fractal dimension of the time series. As is often the case, the two fractal dimensions will have similar values, although they measure different aspects of the process. H measures the fractal dimension of the time trace by the fractal dimension $2 - H$, but it is also related to the statistical self-similarity of the process through the form of equation (14.10). However, $1/H$ measures the fractal dimension of the probability space.

Fama (1965a) mentioned most of the shortcomings of R/S analysis that we have already discussed, particularly the fact that the range can be biased if a short-memory process is involved. We have already dealt with biases. In general, Fama found that range analysis gave stable values of alpha that conformed with the results of the double-log graphical method. R/S analysis gives even more stable values, because it makes the range dimensionless by expressing it in terms of local standard deviation.

Spectral Analysis

We have already seen, in Chapter 13, the relationship between the Hurst exponent, H, and the spectral exponent, β_s. (We will now refer to the spectral exponent as β_s, to distinguish it from the exponent of skewness, β.) Equation (14.10) allows us to express a relationship with β_s:

$$\alpha = \frac{\beta_s - 1}{2} \tag{14.11}$$

In Chapter 13, we found $\beta_s = 2.45$ for the daily Dow data. This implies that $\alpha = 1.73$, which is also close to the value of 1.7 estimated by Fama (1965a).

MEASURING PROBABILITIES

As we have stated before, the major problem with the family of stable distributions is that they do not lend themselves to closed-form solutions, except in the special cases of the normal and Cauchy distributions. Therefore, the probability density functions cannot be solved for explicitly. The probabilities can be solved for only numerically, which is a bit tedious. Luckily, a number of researchers have already accomplished solutions for some common values.

Holt and Crow (1973) solved for the probability density functions for $\alpha = 0.25$ to 2.00 and $\beta = -1.00$ to $+1.00$, both in increments of 0.25. The methodology they used interpolated between the known distributions, such as the Cauchy and normal, and an integral representation from Zolotarev (1964/1966). Produced for the former National Bureau of Standards, the tables remain the most complete representation of the probability density functions of stable distributions.

Some readers may find the probability density function useful; most are more interested in the cumulative distributions, which can be compared directly to frequency distributions, as in Chapter 2. Fama and Roll (1968, 1971) produced cumulative distribution tables for a wide range of alphas. However, they concentrated on symmetric stable distributions, thus constraining β to 0. Markets have been shown numerous times to be skewed, but the impact of this skewness on market risk is not obvious. We can assume that these symmetric values will suffice for most applications.

Appendix 3 reproduces the cumulative distributions of the Fama and Roll studies. The appendix also briefly describes the estimation methodology.

INFINITE DIVISIBILITY AND IGARCH

The ARCH family of distributions has been mentioned numerous times in this book. The reason is obvious: ARCH is the only plausible alternative to the family of fractal distributions. Among the many reasons for its popularity, ARCH appears to fit the empirical results. ARCH processes are characterized by probability distributions that have high peaks and fat tails, as we have seen empirically for numerous markets. Logically, it is appealing to believe that conditional variance is important. As investors, we are aware of recent market volatility, so it is fitting that future volatility be a reaction to our recent experience.

However, there are shortcomings as well. ARCH processes are not long-memory processes, as measured by R/S analysis. However, it is possible that the two processes can coexist—in fact, it is highly likely that they measure different aspects of the same thing.

ARCH is a *local* process. It states that future volatility is measured by our experience of past volatility. However, it only works for specific investment horizons. One cannot, for instance, take the volatility of weekly returns and predict future daily volatility. It is investment-horizon-specific, and analysis only works within that local time frame.

Fractal processes, on the other hand, are *global* structures; they deal with all investment horizons simultaneously. They measure unconditional variance (not conditional, as ARCH does). In Chapter 1, we examined processes that have local randomness and global structure. It is possible that GARCH, with its finite conditional variance, is the local effect of fractal distributions, which have infinite, unconditional variance. With the example of the pine tree, in Chapter 1, the overall structure of the tree was apparent only when we looked at the entire structure, examining all of its branches simultaneously. When examining each individual branch, we entered a realm of local randomness. There may be a similarity in the relationship between the ARCH and its variants, and the fractal family of distributions.

As it turns out, some members of the ARCH family do fit this criterion. In particular, the integrated variance, or IGARCH, models of Engle and Bollerslev (1986) are characterized by infinite unconditional variance. The linear GARCH(p,q) model of equation (5.12) contains an approximate unit root in the autoregressive polynomial such that $f_1 + \ldots + f_q + g_1 + \ldots + g_p = 1$. As stated by Bollerslev, Chou, and Kroner (1990): "As in the martingale model for conditional means, current information remains important for forecasts of the conditional variance *for all horizons*. To illustrate, in the simple IGARCH(1,1) model with $f_1 + g_1 = 1$, the minimum mean square error forecast for the conditional variance s steps ahead is equal to $\omega^*(s - 1) + \sigma_{t+1}^2$" (italics added). As a result of this infinite memory process, the unconditional memory for the IGARCH(p,q) model does not exist. In addition, there is a strong relationship to the ARIMA class of models, discussed in Chapter 5, which already have a fractional form.

This relationship is merely postulated here without proof, but it is intriguing and it fits the fractal market hypothesis. In addition, it fits with the fractal structure of other systems; with local randomness, characterized by ARCH; and with the global structure of unconditional infinite variance consistent with fractal distributions. We leave the formal proof to future research.

SUMMARY

In this chapter, we have examined fractal statistics. Like other fractals, its statistical equivalent does not lend itself to clean, closed-form solutions. However, fractal distributions have a number of desirable characteristics:

1. Stability under addition: the sum of two or more distributions that are fractal with characteristic exponent α keeps the same shape and characteristic exponent α.
2. Self-similarity: fractal distributions are infinitely divisible. When the time scale changes, α remains the same.
3. They are characterized by high peaks at the mean and by fat tails, which match the empirical characteristics of market distributions.

Along with these desirable characteristics, there are inherent problems with the distributions:

1. Infinite variance: second moments do not exist. Variance is unreliable as a measure of dispersion or risk.
2. Jumps: large price changes can be large and discontinuous.

These characteristics are undesirable only from a mathematical point of view. As any investment practitioner will agree, these mathematical "problems" are typical of the way markets actually behave. It appears that it would be wiser to adjust our models to account for this bit of reality, rather than the other way around. Plato may have said that this is not the real world, but he was not investing his money when he said so.

The next chapter will deal with two areas in which we must at least make an adjustment to standard theory: portfolio selection and option pricing.

15
Applying Fractal Statistics

In the previous chapter, we saw a possible replacement for the normal distribution as the probability function to describe market returns. This replacement has been called, alternatively, *stable Levy distributions, stable Paretian distributions,* or *Pareto–Levy distributions.* Now, we can add *fractal distributions,* a name that better describes them. Because the traditional names honor the mathematicians who created them, we will use all these names interchangeably.

We have seen that these distributions have a singular characteristic that makes them difficult to assimilate into standard Capital Market Theory (CMT). These distributions have infinite or undefined variance. Because CMT depends on variance as a measure of risk, it would appear to deal a major blow to the usefulness of Modern Portfolio Theory (MPT) and its derivatives. However, in the early days of MPT, there was not as high a consensus that market returns were normally distributed. As a result, many of the brightest minds of the time developed methods to adapt CMT for stable Levy distributions. Fama (1965b) and Samuelson (1967) independently developed a technique for generalizing the mean/variance optimization method of Markowitz (1952). The technique was further described in Fama and Miller (1972) and Sharpe (1970), but, at that time, it was decided by academia that there was not enough evidence to reject the Gaussian (random walk) Hypothesis and substitute the stable Paretian Hypothesis. At least, there was not enough evidence for the trouble that stable Paretian distributions caused mathematically.

We have now seen substantial support for fractal distributions, so it would seem appropriate to revive the earlier work of Fama and Samuelson, in the hope that other researchers will develop the concepts further. In this chapter, we will do just that. In addition, we will examine work by McCulloch (1985), who developed an alternative to the Black–Scholes option pricing formula, using stable Levy distributions. Given the widespread use of the Black–Scholes formula, it would seem appropriate to examine a more general form of it.

The work that follows has its shortcomings. For instance, the Fama and Samuelson adaptations assume that all securities have the same characteristic exponent, α. The Gaussian Hypothesis assumed that all stocks had $\alpha = 2.0$, so assuming a universal value of 1.7 did not seem to be much of a change. Despite this limitation, the work is well worth reexamining, and, with apologies to the original authors, I will do so in this chapter.

PORTFOLIO SELECTION

Markowitz (1952) made the great breakthrough in CMT. He showed how the portfolio selection problem could be analyzed through mean–variance optimization. For this, he was awarded the Nobel prize in economics. Markowitz reformulated the problem into a preference for risk versus return. Return was the *expected* return for stocks, but was the less controversial part of the theory. For a portfolio, the expected return is merely the weighted average of the expected returns of the individual stocks in the portfolio. Individual stock risk was the standard deviation of the stock return, or σ. However, the risk of a portfolio was more than just the risk of the individual stocks added together. The covariance of the portfolio had to be taken into account:

$$\sigma^2_{a,b} = \sigma^2_a + \sigma^2_b + 2*\rho_{a,b}*\sigma_a*\sigma_b \qquad (15.1)$$

where $\rho_{a,b}$ = the correlation between stock a and b

In order to calculate the risk of a portfolio, it became important to know that the two stocks could be correlated. If there was positive correlation, then the risk of two stocks added together would be greater than the risk of the two separately. However, if there was negative correlation, then the risk of the two stocks added together would be less than either one separately. They would diversify one another. Equation (15.1) calculates the risk of two stocks, a and b, but it can be generalized to any number of stocks. In the original formulation, which is widely used, the expected return and risk are calculated for each combination of all the stocks in the portfolio. The portfolio with the highest expected return for a given level of risk was called an *efficient* portfolio. The collection of all the efficient portfolios was called the *efficient frontier.* Optimizing mean return versus variance gave rise to the term mean/variance efficiency, or optimization. In this way, Markowitz quantified how portfolios could be rationally constructed and how diversification reduced risk. It was a marvelous achievement.

However, using fractal distributions, we have two problems: (1) variance and (2) correlation coefficient. The obvious problem deals with variance. In the mean/variance environment, variance is the measure of a stock's and portfolio's risk. Fractal distributions do not have a variance to optimize. However, there is the dispersion term, c, which can also be used to measure risk. A more difficult problem deals with the correlation coefficient, ρ. In the stable family, there is no comparable concept, except in the special case of the normal distribution. At first glance, the lack of a correlation coefficient would be a strike against the applicability of fractal distributions for markets. Correlation coefficients are often used, particularly in formulating hedging strategies. However, correlations are notoriously unstable, as many a hedger has found.

The lack of correlation between securities under the fractal hypothesis makes traditional mean/variance optimization impractical. Instead, the single-index model of Sharpe (1964) can be adapted. The single-index model gave us the first version of the famous relative risk measure, beta. However, we have already used the Greek letter β twice in this book. Therefore, we shall refer to this beta as b. It is important to note that the beta of the single-index model is different from the one developed by Sharpe at a later date for the CAPM. The single-index model beta is merely a measure of the sensitivity of the stocks returns to the index return. It is not an economic construct, like the CAPM beta.

The single-index model is expressed in the following manner:

$$R_i = a_i + b_i*I + d_i \tag{15.2}$$

where b_i = the sensitivity of stock i to index I
a_i = the nonindex stock return
d_i = error term, with mean 0

The parameters are generally found by regressing the stock return on the index return. The slope is b, and the intercept is a. In the stable Paretian case, the distribution of the index returns, I, and the stock returns, R, can be assumed to be stable Paretian with the same characteristic exponent, α. The ds are also members of the stable Paretian family, and are independent of the stock and index returns.

The risk of the portfolio, c_p, can be stated as follows:

$$c_p = \sum_{i=1}^{N} X_i^{\alpha} {}^* c_{d_i} + b_p^{\alpha} {}^* c_I \tag{15.3}$$

where X_i = weight of stock i

      c_p = dispersion parameter of the portfolio

      c_{d_i} = dispersion parameter of d_i

      c_I = dispersion parameter of the index, I

      $b_p = \sum_{i=1}^{N} X_i {}^* b_i$ = sensitivity of the portfolio returns to I

Again, for the normal distribution, $\alpha = 2.0$, and $c_j = \sigma_j^2 / 2$, for $j = p, d_i$, and I. However, for the other members of the stable family, the calculations can be quite complex. For instance, we have not yet discussed how to estimate the measure of dispersion, c. We can use an alternative to the stable Paretian parameter, c; that is, we can use the mean absolute deviation, or the first moment. Although second moments do not exist in the stable family, first moments are finite. Fama and Roll (1971) formulated a method for estimating c. The mean absolute deviation is easier to calculate, but Fama and Roll found, through Monte Carlo simulations, that the mean absolute deviation is a less efficient estimate of c than their estimate. Table 3 in Appendix 3 is reproduced from their 1971 paper. It is important to note that all of Fama and Roll's calculations (1969, 1971) were done for the reduced case, $c = 1$ and $\delta = 0$.

They estimated c from the sample fractiles shown as Table 3 in Appendix 3. They found that the .72 fractile is appropriate because it varies little for different levels of alpha. Therefore, using the .72 fractile will cause the estimate of c to be little affected by the level of alpha. They found a "sensible estimator of c" to be:

$$\hat{c} = (1/(2^*0.827))^*(\hat{x}_{.72} - \hat{x}_{.28}) \tag{15.4}$$

where $\hat{x}_f$ is the $(f)(N + 1)$st order statistic from Table 3 in Appendix 3, used to estimate the 0.28 and 0.72 fractiles. Fama and Roll (1971) found the estimate of c in equation (15.4) to be the best unbiased estimate.

However, one consequence of equation (15.3) is that the diversification effect of the original market model is retained. The number of assets does not reduce the market risk directly, but it does reduce the nonmarket risk, d, of the i individual stocks. If we take the simple case where all $X_i = 1/N$, then the error term in equation (15.3) becomes:

$$c_p^\alpha = \left(\frac{1}{N}\right)^\alpha * \sum_{i=1}^{N} c_i^\alpha \qquad (15.5)$$

As long as $\alpha > 1$, the residual risk, c_p, decreases as the number of assets, N, increases. Interestingly, if alpha equals 1, there is no diversification effect; if alpha is less than 1, increasing the portfolio size increases the nonmarket risk.

Fama and Miller (1972) used the following example. Suppose that $c_i^\alpha = 1$ and $X_i = 1/N$ for all stocks, i, in the portfolio. In other words, all stocks are equally weighted with risk of 1.0. Equation (15.5) then reduces to:

$$c_i^\alpha = N^{1-\alpha} \qquad (15.6)$$

Table 15.1 and Figure 15.1 show the diversification effect for various α and N, using equation (15.6). The reader can also generate these numbers simply in a spreadsheet. As predicted, for $\alpha < 1.0$, diversification does reduce the non-market risk of the portfolio. The rate of diversification decreases with decreasing α until, with $\alpha = 1.0$, diversification does nothing for a portfolio. The Central Limit Theorem does not apply when $\alpha = 1$, and works in reverse for $\alpha > 1$.

In the context of fractal statistics, this makes perfect sense. Antipersistent series have more jagged time series than do persistent or random ones. Adding together antipersistent systems would only result in a noisier system.

On the other hand, market exposure is not a matter of diversification; it is the weighted average of the b's of the individual securities in the portfolio. Therefore, as in the traditional market model, diversification reduces nonmarket risk, not market risk.

The adaptation of traditional CMT to stable distributions was ingenious, but fell mostly on deaf ears. It was simply too complicated compared to the standard Gaussian case. At the time, there was not enough conclusive evidence to show that the markets were not Gaussian.

Now, we have more convincing evidence. However, the adaptation has its own problems. Foremost among them is the retention of the sensitivity factor, b, from the traditional market model. This was usually established as a linear relationship between individual securities and the market portfolio, I. This relationship was retained because, at the time, Fama, Roll, and Samuelson were

Table 15.1   The Effects of Diversification: Nonmarket Risk

N	Alpha (α)					
	2.00	1.75	1.50	1.25	1.00	0.50
10	0.1000	0.1778	0.3162	0.5623	1.0000	3.1623
20	0.0500	0.1057	0.2236	0.4729	1.0000	4.4721
30	0.0333	0.0780	0.1826	0.4273	1.0000	5.4772
40	0.0250	0.0629	0.1581	0.3976	1.0000	6.3246
50	0.0200	0.0532	0.1414	0.3761	1.0000	7.0711
60	0.0167	0.0464	0.1291	0.3593	1.0000	7.7460
70	0.0143	0.0413	0.1195	0.3457	1.0000	8.3666
80	0.0125	0.0374	0.1118	0.3344	1.0000	8.9443
90	0.0111	0.0342	0.1054	0.3247	1.0000	9.4868
100	0.0100	0.0316	0.1000	0.3162	1.0000	10.0000
110	0.0091	0.0294	0.0953	0.3088	1.0000	10.4881
120	0.0083	0.0276	0.0913	0.3021	1.0000	10.9545
130	0.0077	0.0260	0.0877	0.2962	1.0000	11.4018
140	0.0071	0.0246	0.0845	0.2907	1.0000	11.8322
150	0.0067	0.0233	0.0816	0.2857	1.0000	12.2474
160	0.0063	0.0222	0.0791	0.2812	1.0000	12.6491
170	0.0059	0.0212	0.0767	0.2769	1.0000	13.0384
180	0.0056	0.0203	0.0745	0.2730	1.0000	13.4164
190	0.0053	0.0195	0.0725	0.2693	1.0000	13.7840
200	0.0050	0.0188	0.0707	0.2659	1.0000	14.1421
250	0.0040	0.0159	0.0632	0.2515	1.0000	15.8114
300	0.0033	0.0139	0.0577	0.2403	1.0000	17.3205
350	0.0029	0.0124	0.0535	0.2312	1.0000	18.7083
400	0.0025	0.0112	0.0500	0.2236	1.0000	20.0000
450	0.0022	0.0102	0.0471	0.2171	1.0000	21.2132
500	0.0020	0.0095	0.0447	0.2115	1.0000	22.3607
550	0.0018	0.0088	0.0426	0.2065	1.0000	23.4521
600	0.0017	0.0082	0.0408	0.2021	1.0000	24.4949
650	0.0015	0.0078	0.0392	0.1980	1.0000	25.4951
700	0.0014	0.0073	0.0378	0.1944	1.0000	26.4575
750	0.0013	0.0070	0.0365	0.1911	1.0000	27.3861
800	0.0013	0.0066	0.0354	0.1880	1.0000	28.2843
850	0.0012	0.0064	0.0343	0.1852	1.0000	29.1548
900	0.0011	0.0061	0.0333	0.1826	1.0000	30.0000
950	0.0011	0.0058	0.0324	0.1801	1.0000	30.8221
1,000	0.0010	0.0056	0.0316	0.1778	1.0000	31.6228

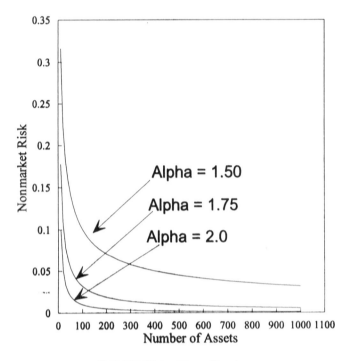

FIGURE 15.1 Diversification.

not aware of Hurst's work and the importance of persistence and antipersistence. However, given a large enough portfolio, it can be expected that the diversification effect described above, relative to a market portfolio, will be fairly stable. Thus, optimizing a portfolio relative to a market index would be more stable than a straight mean/variance optimization.

A second problem lies in the value of α itself. The adaptation assumes that all of the securities in the portfolio have the same value of α. This is necessary because the sum of stable Paretian variables with the same characteristic exponent, α, will result in a new distribution that still has the same characteristic exponent, α. This is the additive property discussed in Chapter 14. However, I have shown that different stocks can have different Hurst exponents and, therefore, different values of α. (See Peters (1991a, 1992).) Unfortunately, there is no theory for the effect of adding together distributions with different values of α.

It seems reasonable that this process should now be revisited and that further work should be done to generalize the approach and minimize the effects of these still troublesome problems.

OPTION VALUATION

In Chapter 10, we discussed the Black–Scholes (1973) formula. It is important to remember that the basic formula is for "European" options—options that can be exercised only at expiration. We discussed the use of equation (10.1) to study volatility, but its original purpose was to calculate the fair price of an option. The formula seems to work reasonably well when the option is at-the-money, or close, but most options traders find the formula to be unreliable when options are deep out-of-the-money. Options will always have a value, even when the Black–Scholes formula says they should be worth virtually zero. There are many explanations for this systematic departure from the formula. The most reasonable one is the fatness of the negative tail in the observed frequency distribution of stock returns. The market knows that the likelihood of a large event is larger than the normal distribution tells us, and prices the option accordingly.

An additional problem lies in the discontinuity of pricing itself. The normal distribution is a continuous one. If stock returns are governed by the normal distribution, then, when a stock price moves from 50 to 45, it is supposed to pass through all of the prices in between to get there. However, experience shows that all security prices are subject to discontinuities. A stock will often jump over the intervening prices during extreme moves, as will currencies or bonds. Merton (1976) proposed the class of Poisson-driven jump processes for large movements against a background of Gaussian changes for small movements. This process is infinitely divisible, as are stable distributions. However, McCulloch (1985) has pointed out that the stable process "is preferable by the criterion of Occam's razor, however, since it provides both large jumps and continual movement. At the same time, it is more parsimonious with parameters than Merton's specification. A stable process actually entails an infinite number of Poisson-driven jump processes, whose relative frequencies are governed by the characteristic exponent α."

There is an additional qualification. The calculation of option values for stable distributions is quite complex and requires extensive tables that were inappropriate in length for this book. (They are available from McCulloch.) Therefore, the discussion of McCulloch's work here is a paraphrase, to give some basic information to readers interested in the calculation of "fair values" using stable distributions. Given that the statistical distribution under conditional volatility may be defined by GARCH distributions, there are probably simpler methods. Readers are forewarned that the discussion here will not be complete, and they may wish to pursue study and research upon completion.

Those uninterested in the particulars given here are encouraged to skip ahead to Chapter 16.

McCulloch's Approach

McCulloch (1985) developed an option-pricing formula to account for stable distributions. He did so by using a particular property of stable distributions. Remember, the skewness variable, β, can range from -1 to $+1$. When it is equal to 0, then the distribution is symmetric. All of Fama and Roll's work was done assuming the symmetric case. However, when $\beta = +1(-1)$, the lower (upper) tail loses its Paretian characteristic and declines faster than the normal distribution. The opposite tail becomes even longer and fatter, so that the distribution resembles a "log normal" distribution—unimodel (single-humped), with a long positive (negative) tail and a short, finite negative (positive) tail. Zolotarev (1983) showed that, when a stable random variable, x, has parameters $(\alpha, -1, c, \delta)$, the characteristic function for $\alpha \neq 1$ is:

$$\log(E(e^x)) = \delta*(-c)^{\alpha}*\sec\left(\frac{\pi*\alpha}{2}\right) \tag{15.7}$$

McCulloch used this equation to develop a formula for valuing European options with "log stable uncertainty." This section is a summary of McCulloch's work. It fits in well with the Fractal Market Hypothesis, and shows a practical application of fractal statistics. McCulloch deserves much credit for formulating this work before there was accepted evidence that markets were described by fractal distributions.

Spot and Forward Prices

We begin by defining spot and forward prices in terms of stable distributions. The derivative security, A_2, will be worth X at a future time, T, in terms of a spot security A_1. U_1 and U_2 represent the marginal utility, or value, of A_1 and A_2, respectively, for the investor. If $\log(U_1)$ and $\log(U_2)$ are both stable with a common characteristic exponent, then:

$$\log(X) = \log(U_2/U_1) \tag{15.8}$$

is also stable, with the same characteristic exponent, as discussed in Chapter 14.

We must now examine the forward price, F, that makes an investor indifferent to investing in either the derivative security, A_2, or the underlying security, A_1:

$$F = \frac{E(U_2)}{E(U_1)} \tag{15.9}$$

McCulloch pointed out that, if $\log(U_1)$ and $\log(U_2)$ are stable with alpha less than 2.0, then both logarithms must also have the skewness parameter, β, equal to -1; that is, they must be *maximally negatively skewed*. This applies to the utility functions, but X itself does not need to be so constrained. Beta can equal anything between -1 and $+1$.

We now take two factors, u_1 and u_2, which are independent and asset-specific. u_1 has a negative impact on $\log(U_1)$; u_2 has a negative impact on $\log(U_2)$. There is a third factor, u_3, which has a negative impact on *both* $\log(U_1)$ and $\log(U_2)$. u_1 is stable, with parameters $(\alpha, + 1, c_1, \delta_1)$. u_2 is stable as well, with parameters $(\alpha, + 1, c_2, \delta_2)$. u_3 is independent of u_1 and u_2. However, it is also stable, with parameters $(\alpha, + 1, c_3, \delta_3)$. All three factors are maximally and positively skewed, as shown by their skewness parameters of $+1$. The three factors contribute to $\log(U_1)$ and $\log(U_2)$ in the following manner:

$$\log(U_1) = -u_1 - u_3 \tag{15.10}$$

$$\log(U_2) = -u_2 - u_3 \tag{15.11}$$

$$\log(X) = u_1 - u_2 \tag{15.12}$$

Log(X) is defined by parameters $(\alpha, \beta, c, \delta)$. In this formulation, α, β, c, and F are assumed to be known—a large assumption. The other parameters are unknown. However, using the additive property in equation (14.11), we can infer the following relationships:

$$\delta = \delta_1 - \delta_2, \alpha \neq 1 \tag{15.13}$$

$$c = c_1^\alpha + c_2^\alpha \tag{15.14}$$

$$\beta * c^\alpha = c_1^\alpha - c_2^\alpha \tag{15.15}$$

Adding equation (15.14) and equation (15.15) and solving for c_1, we have:

$$c_1 = \left(\frac{1 + \beta}{2}\right)^{1/\alpha} * c \tag{15.16}$$

Likewise, subtracting equation (15.15) from equation (15.14) and solving for c_2, we have:

$$c_2 = \left(\frac{1 - \beta}{2}\right)^{1/\alpha} *c \tag{15.17}$$

Now we can use equation (15.7), which simplified the characteristic function for stable variables that are maximally and negatively skewed, such as U_1 and U_2:

$$E(\log(U_2)) = e^{-\delta_2 - \delta_3 - (c_2^\alpha + c_3^\alpha)*\sec(\pi*\alpha/2)} \tag{15.18}$$

$$E(\log(U_1)) = e^{-\delta_1 - \delta_3 - (c_1^\alpha + c_3^\alpha)*\sec(\pi*\alpha/2)} \tag{15.19}$$

Using these relationships in equation (15.9), we can now state the value of the forward price, F, in terms of the stable parameters of X:

$$F = e^{-\delta_1 - \delta_2 - (c_1^\alpha + c_2^\alpha)*\sec(\pi*\alpha/2)}$$

$$= e^{\delta + \beta*c^\alpha*\sec(\pi*\alpha/2)} \tag{15.20}$$

The final transformation comes from the relationships in equations (15.13) through (15.15).

The forward price, F, is expressed in terms of the characteristic distribution of X. This forward rate equation is now used as the expected forward security price in pricing options.

Pricing Options

In keeping with tradition, we shall call the price of a European call option C, at time 0. The option can be unconditionally exercised at time T, for one unit (or share) of an asset we shall call A_2. A_1 is the currency we use to pay for the option. The risk-free rate of interest on A_1 is r_1, which also matures at time T. Therefore, C units of A_1 is equivalent to $C*e^{r_1*T}$ units at time T. The exercise price is X_0. If $X > X_0$ at time T, then the owner will pay X_0 units of A_1 to receive one share of A_2, less the $C*e^{r_1*T}$ paid for the option. This includes the price of the option, C, plus the time value of that money at expiration.

McCulloch set up a formula that equates the expected advantage of buying or selling the option to 0. This is an indifference equation:

$$0 = \int_{X>X_0} (U_2 - X_0*U_1)dP(U_1,U_2) - C*e^{r_1*T} * \int_{all-X} U_1dP(U_1,U_2) \tag{15.21}$$

McCulloch then used equation (15.9) and solved for C:

$$C = e^{-r_1*T} * \left[\frac{F}{E(U_2)} * \int_{x>x_0} U_2 dP(U_1,U_2) - \frac{X_0}{E(U_1)} * \int_{x>x_0} U_1 dP(U_1,U_2) \right] \quad (15.22)$$

$P(U_1,U_2)$ represents the joint probability distribution of U_1 and U_2.

The final step is to describe C in terms of the family of stable distributions. McCulloch did so by defining two functions, s(z) and S(z), as being *standard* maximally and *positively* skewed; that is, β equals $+1$, so that the density and distribution functions are defined as $(\alpha,1,1,0)$. Then McCulloch showed that equation (15.22) can be converted into equation (15.23). The proof is beyond the scope of this book. The final form of C is as follows:

$$C = F*e^{-r_1*T+c_2^q*\sec(\pi*\alpha/2)}*I_1 - X_0*e^{-r_1*T+c_1^q*\sec(\pi*\alpha/2)}*I_2 \quad (15.23)$$

where:

$$I_1 = \int_{-\infty}^{\infty} e^{-c_2*Z}*s(z)* \left[1 - S\left(\frac{c_2*z - \log\left(\frac{F}{X_0}\right) + \beta*c^\alpha*\sec(\pi*\alpha/2)}{c_1} \right) \right] dz \quad (15.24)$$

$$I_2 = \int_{-\infty}^{\infty} e^{-c_1*Z}*s(z)*S\left(\frac{c_1*z + \log\left(\frac{F}{X_0}\right) - \beta*c^\alpha*\sec(\pi*\alpha/2)}{c_2} \right) dz \quad (15.25)$$

Equations (15.16) and (15.17) show how to determine c_1 and c_2. The remainder of the formula shows that the price of the option is a function of three values and the three stable parameters; that is, the price depends on (1) the forward price (F), (2) the strike price (X_0), and (3) the current risk-free rate (r_1). In addition, it depends on the α, β, and c values of the distribution of X. δ is contained in F, and the "common component of uncertainty," u_3, drops out.

The Black–Scholes formula was complicated, but it could be understood in terms of a simple arbitrage argument. The McCulloch formula has a similar arbitrage argument, but the formula itself appears even more complicated than its predecessor. It also seems less precise. The Black–Scholes formula stated the call price based on the relationship between the stock price and the exercise price; the McCulloch formula does so between the forward price and the exercise price. McCulloch was aware of this problem, and stated: "If the forward rate, F, is unobserved for any reason, we may use the spot price, S, to construct a proxy for it if we know the default-free interest rate r_2 on A_2 denominated loans, since arbitrage requires:

$$F = S*e^{(r_1-r_2)*T}"$$

(15.26)

The normal distribution is no longer used. Stable distributions s and S are used instead. Variance, likewise, is replaced by c.

The formula for the price of a put option is similar to the Black–Scholes derivation:

$$P = C + (X_0 - F)*e^{-r_1*T}$$

(15.27)

This, again, is a European put option, which gives the holder the right, not the obligation, to sell 1 unit of A_2 at the striking price, X_0.

Pseudo-Hedge Ratio

McCulloch stated a hedge ratio, but gave it important qualifications. Primarily, fractal systems, as we have extensively discussed, are subject to discontinuities in the time trace. This makes the arbitrage logic of Black and Scholes (1973) useless under the most severe situations (the large events that cause the fat tails), when the hedger needs it the most. This failure in the Black–Scholes approach caused the strategy called "Portfolio Insurance" to offer only partial protection during the crash of 1987.

McCulloch did offer a pseudo-hedge ratio. Essentially, the risk exposure of writing a call option can be *partially* hedged by taking a long forward position on the underlying asset. The units needed are derived in the following equation:

$$\frac{\partial(C*e^{r_1*T})}{\partial F} = e^{c_2^{\alpha}*\sec(\alpha*\pi/2)}*I_1$$

(15.28)

However, because there is no cure for the discontinuities in the time trace of market returns, a "perfect" hedge is not possible in a fractal environment. This will always be an imperfect hedge.

Numerical Option Values

McCulloch calculated a number of option values as examples. He used the following argument to calculate option values from the standard tables, such as those found in Appendix 3.

Suppose we are interested in a call on 1 unit of A_2 at the exercise price of X_0, as we have stated this problem throughout the chapter. We define $C(X_0,F,\alpha,\beta,c,r_1,T)$ as the call price. This can be written in the following manner:

$$C(X_0,F,\alpha,\beta,c,r_1,T) = e^{-r_1*T}*F*C'\left(\frac{X_0}{F},\alpha,\beta,c\right) \quad (15.29)$$

where:

$$C'\left(\frac{X_0}{F},\alpha,\beta,c\right) = C\left(\frac{X_0}{F},1,\alpha,\beta,c,0,1\right) \quad (15.30)$$

A similar transformation can be done for the put price P, and P'. In addition, using equation (15.27), we can compute P' from C':

$$P'\left(\frac{X_0}{F},\alpha,\beta,c\right) = C'\left(\frac{X_0}{F},\alpha,\beta,c\right) + \frac{X_0}{F} - 1 \quad (15.31)$$

A call on 1 share of A_2 at a price of X_0 is equivalent to a put on X_0 shares of A_1, at a strike price of $1/X_0$. The value of the latter option in units of A_2 is:

$$X_0*P\left(\frac{1}{X_0},\frac{1}{F},\alpha, - \beta,c,r_2,T\right)$$

because the forward price is $1/F$ units of A_2.

The $\log(1/x) = -\log(x)$, and also has parameters $\alpha, -\beta,c$. This can be reformulated as:

$$C(X_0,F,\alpha,\beta,c,r_1,T) = S\left[X_0*P\left(\frac{1}{X_0},\frac{1}{F},\alpha,-\beta,c,r_2,T\right)\right] \quad (15.32)$$

Using equation (15.26), this can be restated as:

$$C'\left(\frac{X_0}{F},\alpha,\beta,c:\right)\frac{X_0}{F}*C'\left(\frac{F}{X_0},\alpha,-\beta,c\right)+1-\frac{X_0}{F} \qquad (15.33)$$

Therefore, options prices for a combination of the different factors can be calculated from tables of

$$C'\left(\frac{X_0}{F},\alpha,\beta,c\right) \text{ for } \frac{X_0}{F} \geq 1.$$

In Tables 15.2 and 15.3, we reproduce two of McCulloch's tables. Values are shown for 100 options priced at $C'(X_0/F,\alpha,\beta,c)$. The tables show the value in amounts of A_1 for 100 shares or units of A_2. If the option is on IBM (A_2), payable in dollars (A_1), the table shows the value, in dollars, for an option of $100 worth of IBM.

In Table 15.2, $c = 0.1$, and $X_0/F = 1.0$. Because X_0 is the strike price and F is the forward price, the option is at-the-money. α and β are allowed to vary. Decreasing α causes a rise in the option price because stable distributions have a higher peak at the mean, and so are more likely to be at-the-money than a normal distribution. When $\alpha = 2.0$, beta has no impact. However, for other values of beta, the price goes up with skewness.

In Table 15.3, also reproduced from McCulloch (1985), alpha and beta are held constant at 1.5 and 0.0 respectively; c and X_0/f are varied instead. As would be expected, increasing c (which is equivalent to increasing volatility in the Black–Scholes formula) results in increasing option values. The same is true of being increasingly in-the-money.

Table 15.2 Fractal Option Prices: $c = 0.1$, X0/F = 1.0

Alpha	Beta (β)				
	−1.0	−0.5	0.0	0.5	1.0
2.0	5.637	5.637	5.637	5.637	5.637
1.8	6.029	5.993	5.981	5.993	6.029
1.6	6.670	6.523	6.469	6.523	6.670
1.4	7.648	7.300	7.157	7.300	7.648
1.2	9.115	8.455	8.137	8.455	9.115
1.0	11.319	10.200	9.558	10.200	11.319
0.8	14.685	12.893	11.666	12.893	14.685

Table 15.3   Fractal Option Prices: $\alpha = 1.5$, $\beta = 0.0$

c	XO/F			
	0.5	1.0	1.1	2.0
0.01	50.007	0.787	0.079	0.014
0.03	50.038	2.240	0.458	0.074
0.10	50.240	6.784	3.466	0.481
0.30	51.704	17.694	14.064	3.408
1.00	64.131	45.642	43.065	28.262

A Final Word

I said, at the beginning of this section, that fractal option pricing is quite involved and requires much study. It is not clear that the complicated methodology used here is necessary, but it is certainly worth examining again. With the enormous amounts of money channeling into the option markets, there is bound to be profit in knowing the shape of the underlying distribution. If nothing else, it should give pause to those who use a traditional hedging ratio and expect it to give them a "perfect hedge." We have seen, in this chapter, that such an animal may not exist.

SUMMARY

This chapter examined earlier work that used stable distributions in two traditional areas of quantitative financial economics. The first area was portfolio selection. Fama and Samuelson independently developed a variant on Sharpe's market model, which allowed for efficient portfolio selection in a fractal environment. There are limitations to that work: the characteristic exponent, α, had to be the same for all securities in the portfolio. Stocks seem to have different values of the Hurst exponent, and so, different values of α. Further work in this area would be very useful.

The second area we examined was McCulloch's derivation of an option pricing model for stable distributions. This model appears to be correct, but it is exceptionally complicated, as most things are in the real world. It is left to the reader to decide whether this level of complexity will be profitable for further study.

PART FIVE
NOISY CHAOS

16
Noisy Chaos and
R/S Analysis

In Part Four, we examined fractional brownian motion (FBM) as a possible model for market returns. FBM has a number of important characteristics that conform to the Fractal Market Hypothesis. Among these are a statistical self-similarity over time, and persistence, which creates trends and cycles. The statistical self-similarity conforms to the observed frequency distribution of returns examined in Chapter 2. We saw them to be similar in shape at different time scales. Persistence is consistent with the notion that information is absorbed unevenly, at different investment horizons. Finally, the fact that market returns appear to be a black noise, while volatility is a pink noise, is consistent with the theoretical relationship between those two colored noises.

FBM is not consistent with one aspect of markets like stocks and bonds. There is no reward for long-term investing. We saw, in Chapter 2, that stocks and bonds are characterized by increasing return/risk ratios after four years. FBMs, on the other hand, do not have bounded risk characteristics; that is, the term structure of volatility, in theory, does not stop growing.

In addition, there is no link to the economy or other deterministic mechanisms. Statistical theory is more concerned with describing the risks than analyzing the mechanisms. Figure 16.1 shows the S&P 500 versus various economic indicators, for the period from January 1957 through April 1993. Visually, we can see a link, and it is reasonable to think that there should be one, in the long term.

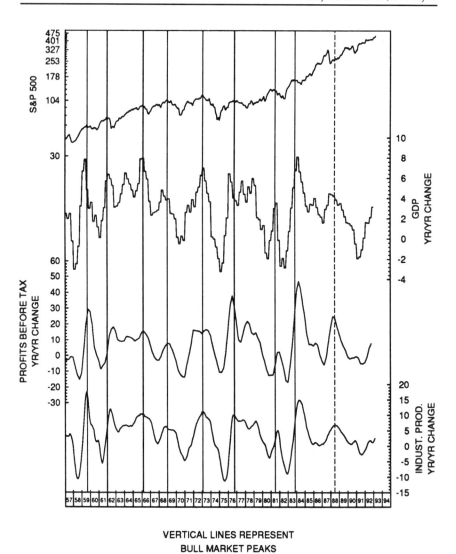

VERTICAL LINES REPRESENT
BULL MARKET PEAKS

FIGURE 16.1   Stock market and peak rates of economic growth. (Used with permission of Boston Capital Markets Group.)

The link to the economy is still tied to investor expectations, but these expectations are more related to fundamental factors than to crowd behavior. Thus, we should expect that, as investment horizons lengthen, fundamental and economic information should have a greater influence than technical factors. The investor interpretation of economic information will, of necessity, be nonlinear.

INFORMATION AND INVESTORS

There have been many different models of information absorption by investors. The simplest versions assume instantaneous, homogeneous interpretation of information at all investment horizons. This results in a "fair" price at all times, and is the bedrock of the Efficient Market Hypothesis (EMH). To explain discontinuities in the pricing structure, and the fat tails, Miller (1991) and Shiller (1989) have proposed that information arrives in a "lumpy," discontinuous manner. Investors still react to information homogeneously, but the arrival of information is discontinuous. This theory preserves the assumption of independence, so important to the EMH, but recognizes that the shape of the frequency distribution of returns and the discontinuities in the pricing structure are too severe to be dismissed as outliers. Yet, both theories ignore one fact: People do not make decisions this way.

As we discussed in Chapter 4, a particular piece of information is not necessarily important to investors at each investment horizon. When an important piece of information has obvious implications, then the market can, and often does, make a quick judgment. A recent example was the announcement by Philip Morris to cut the price of its Marlboro cigarettes. Most analysts knew immediately what the effect on earnings would be. The stock opened at a price commiserate with that level ($50 a share), and stayed within that level afterward.

Other information is not as easily valued, particularly if the data are noisy. The noise can be due either to volatility in the particular indicator for structural reasons, or to measurement problems. Both contribute to the inability of the marketplace to uniformly value the information.

There is another possibility: The new information may contribute to increased levels of uncertainty, rather than increased levels of knowledge. In general, economists consider new information a positive development. New information increases knowledge of current conditions and facilitates judgment about the future. Our increased knowledge results in fairer security prices. However, there is also information that raises uncertainty, negating what we thought we already knew. The Arbitrage Pricing Theory refers to this as unexpected changes in a variable, but the impact of these unexpected changes is not taken into account. For instance, suppose there is an unexpected rise in inflation. If the rise is large enough, then uncertainty about the status of inflation increases. Is it rising again, or not? Suppose money supply growth has been dropping at this point. The unexpected rise in inflation may actually have the effect of negating the value of the previous information, which was considered valuable. This rise in uncertainty with the arrival of new information may actually result in increased uncertainty about the level of the "fair" price, rather than the automatic incorporation of price. We may get increased volatility, or merely a noisy jitter. This kind of noise probably occurs most often at high frequencies, where the market is trying to figure out the value of information concurrently with its arrival.

The problem of noise is not simple. Measurement error is not the only source of noise. It can be a part of the system itself. Both types of noise are possible.

Measurement noise (also referred to as observational noise) is by far the most common problem with economic data. Measuring economic activity is an imprecise science made more so by data collection problems. As a result, we often do not know when a recession has ended or begun for months, or sometimes years, after the fact. In December 1992, the U.S. Department of Commerce announced that the last recession had ended in April 1991, some 18 months before. Most numbers are frequently revised, adding to the uncertainty of the value of the data. This measurement noise is comparable to the observational noise discussed in Chapter 4.

The second type of noise occurs when the indicator itself is volatile. One of the most widely followed economic indicators is commodity prices, which are followed to discern price inflation trends. Commodity prices themselves are subject to their own market swings. The Consumer Price Index (CPI) is often analyzed with the "volatile food and energy" component removed. The resulting less volatile inflation figure is called the "core rate." Even so, a change in the CPI can be interpreted many different ways. Markets seem to react to recent trends in the CPI, and similar volatile indicators, rather than the published monthly change, unless it is perceived that the trend has changed. The trend is not perceived to have changed unless it had already done so some time ago. For instance, if we have been in a long period of low inflation, an unexpected rise in the rate of inflation will usually be rationalized away as a special event, and not a change in trend. However, if inflation continues rising, and a change in trend is perceived, then the markets will react to all the inflation changes they had ignored up to that point. This is a nonlinear reaction. The volatility in the CPI is symptomatic of another type of noise, usually referred to as *system* noise, or dynamical noise.

At longer frequencies, the market reacts to economic and fundamental information in a nonlinear fashion. In addition, it is not unreasonable to assume that the markets and the economy should be linked. This implies that a nonlinear dynamical system would be an appropriate way to model the interaction, satisfying the aspect of the Fractal Market Hypothesis left unresolved by fractional brownian motion. Nonlinear dynamical systems lend themselves to non-periodic cycles and to bounded sets, called attractors. The systems themselves fall under the classification of chaotic systems. However, in order to be called chaotic, very specific requirements must be met.

CHAOS

Chaotic systems are typically nonlinear feedback systems. They are subject to erratic behavior, amplification of events, and discontinuities. There are two basic requirements for a system to be considered chaotic: (1) the existence of a fractal dimension, and (2) a characteristic called *sensitive dependence on initial conditions.* A more complete discussion of these characteristics appeared in my earlier book, but a basic review is in order because fractional noise and noisy chaos are difficult to distinguish from one another, especially when examining empirical data. However, as we shall see, R/S analysis is a very robust way of distinguishing between them. In addition, finding chaos in experimental data has been very frustrating. Most methods are not robust with respect to noise. By contrast, R/S analysis is not only robust with respect to noise, it thrives on it. R/S analysis would be a useful addition to the toolbox of not only the market analyst, but the scientist studying chaotic phenomena.

Phase Space

A chaotic system is analyzed in a place called phase space, which consists of one dimension for each factor that defines the system. A pendulum is a simple example of a dynamical system with two factors that define its motion: (1) velocity and (2) position. Plotting either velocity or position versus time would result in a simple sine wave, or harmonic oscillator, because the position and velocity rise and fall as the pendulum goes back and forth, rising and falling. However, when we plot velocity versus position, we remove time as a dimension. If there is no friction, the pendulum will swing back and forth forever, and its phase plot will be a closed circle. However, if there is friction, or damping, then each time the pendulum swings back and forth, it goes a little slower, and its amplitude decreases until it eventually stops. The corresponding phase plot will spiral into the origin, where velocity and position become zero.

The phase space of the pendulum tells us all we need to know about the dynamics of the system, but the pendulum is not a very interesting system. If we take a more complicated process and study its phase space, we will discover a number of interesting characteristics.

We have already examined one such phase space, the Lorenz attractor (Chapter 6). Here, the phase plot never repeats itself, although it is bounded by the "owl eyes" shape. It is "attracted" to that shape, which is often called its "attractor." If we examine the lines within the attractor, we find a self-similar structure of lines, caused by repeated folding of the attractor. The nonintersecting structure of lines means that the process will never completely fill its space. Its dimension is, thus, fractional. The fractal dimension of the Lorenz attractor is approximately 2.08. This means that its structure is slightly more than a two-dimensional plane, but less than a three-dimensional solid. It is, therefore, also a creation of the Demiurge.

In addition, the attractor itself is bounded to a particular region of space, because chaotic systems are characterized by growth and a decay factor. Each trip around the attractor is called an orbit. Two orbits that are close together initially will rapidly diverge, even if they are extremely close at the outset. But they will not fly away from one another indefinitely. Eventually, as each orbit reaches the outer bound of the attractor, it returns toward the center: The divergent points will come close together again, although many orbits may be needed to do so. This is the property of sensitive dependence on initial conditions. Because we can never measure current conditions to an infinite amount of precision, we cannot predict where the process will go in the long term. The rate of divergence, or the loss in predictive power, can be characterized by measuring the divergence of nearby orbits in phase space. A rate of divergence (called a "Lyapunov exponent") is measured for each dimension in phase space. One positive rate means that there are divergent orbits. Combined with a fractal dimension, it means that the system is chaotic. In addition, there must be a negative exponent to measure the folding process, or the return to the attractor. The formula for Lyapunov exponents is as follows:

$$L_i = \lim_{t \to \infty}[(1/t)*\log_2(p_i(t)/p_i(0))] \tag{16.1}$$

where L_i = the Lyapunov exponent for dimension i

$p_i(t)$ = position in the ith dimension, at time t

Equation (16.1) measures how the volume of a sphere grows over time, t, by measuring the divergence of two points, p(t) and p(0), in dimension i. The distance is similar to a multidimensional range. By examining equation (16.1), we can see certain similarities to R/S analysis and to the fractal dimension calculation. All are concerned with scaling. However, chaotic attractors have orbits that decay exponentially rather than through power laws.

APPLYING R/S ANALYSIS

When we studied the attractor of Mackey and Glass (1988) briefly in Chapter 6, we were concerned with finding cycles. In this chapter, we will extend that study and will see how R/S analysis can distinguish between noisy chaos and fractional noise.

The Noise Index

In Chapter 6, we did not disclose the value of the Hurst exponent. For Figure 6.8, H = 0.92. As would be expected, the continuous, smooth nature of the chaotic flow makes for a very high Hurst exponent. It is not equal to 1 because of the folding mechanism or the reversals that often occur in the time trace of this equation. In Figure 6.11, we added one standard deviation of white, uniform noise to the system. This brought the Hurst exponent down to 0.72 and illustrated the first application of R/S analysis to noisy chaos: Use the Hurst exponent as an index of noise.

Suppose you are a technical analyst who wishes to test a particular type of monthly momentum indicator, and you plan to use the Mackey–Glass equation to test the indicator. You know that the Hurst exponent for monthly data has a value of 0.72. To make the simulation realistic, one standard deviation of noise should be added to the data. In this manner, you can see whether your technical indicator is robust with respect to noise.

Now suppose you are a scientist examining chaotic behavior. You have a particular test that can distinguish chaos from random behavior. To make the test practical, you must show that it is robust with respect to noise. Because most observed time series have values of H close to 0.70 (as Hurst found; see Table 5.1), you will need enough noise to make your test series have H = 0.70. Or, you could gradually add noise and observe the level of H at which your test becomes uncertain.

Figure 16.2 shows values of H as increasing noise is added to the Mackey–Glass equation. The Hurst exponent rapidly drops to 0.70 and then gradually

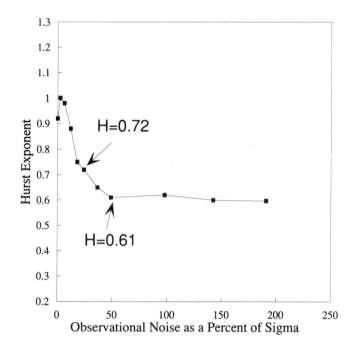

FIGURE 16.2   Mackey–Glass equation, Hurst exponent sensitivity to noise.

falls toward 0.60. However, after adding two standard deviations of noise, H is still approximately 0.60. This means that the frequent values of H = 0.70, which so intrigued Hurst (1951), may have been due to the fact that adding noise to a nonlinear dynamical system quickly makes the value of H drop to 0.70. On the other hand, readings of H below 0.65, which are found in markets, are probably not caused by merely adding measurement or additive noise to a chaotic attractor, but may instead be caused by fractional noise. This possibility further supports the idea that markets are fractional noise in the short term, but noisy chaos in the long term.

System Noise

Besides the additive noise we have been examining, there is another type of noise called "system noise." System noise occurs when the output of an iterative system becomes corrupted with noise, but the system cannot distinguish the noisy signal from the pure one, and uses the noisy signal as input for the next iteration.

This is quite different from observational noise, which occurs because the observer is having difficulty measuring the process. The process continues, oblivious to our problem. However, with system noise, the noise invades the system itself. Because of the problem of sensitive dependence on initial conditions, system noise increases the problem of prediction.

In markets, system noise, not observational noise, is more likely to be a problem. Face it: We have no problem knowing the value of the last trade, but we do not know whether it was a fair price or not. Perhaps the seller was desperate and needed to sell at any price to make margin requirements. We react to this "noisy" output, not knowing its true value. If system noise is involved, then prediction becomes more difficult and tests should be adjusted accordingly.

The impact of system noise on the Hurst exponent is similar to additive noise, and is shown as Figure 16.3.

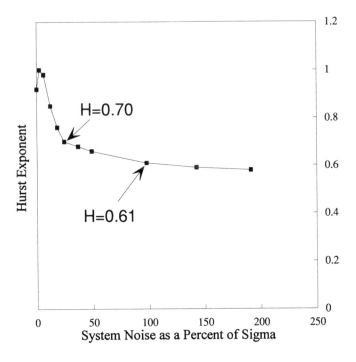

FIGURE 16.3 Mackey–Glass equation, Hurst exponent sensitivity to noise.

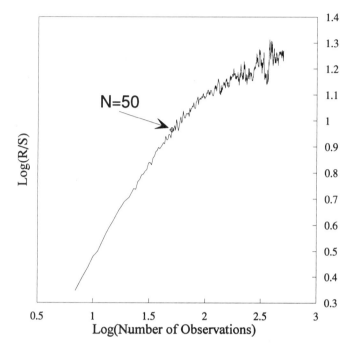

FIGURE 16.4 R/S analysis, Mackey–Glass equation with system noise.

Cycles

We have already discussed in Chapter 6 how R/S analysis can distinguish a cycle even in the presence of one standard deviation of observational noise. Figure 16.4 shows R/S analysis of the Mackey–Glass equation with one standard deviation of system noise incorporated. The Hurst exponent is virtually identical (H = 0.72), and the 50 observations cycle is still discernible.

The V statistic is shown in Figure 16.5, where, again, the cycle is easily discernible.

What does it mean when the slope of the log/log plot crosses over to a random walk? There are two possible explanations:

1. The process can be fractional brownian motion with a long but finite memory. There is no causal explanation for the finite memory, but it may be a function of the number of observations. Scaling often stops because enough observations do not exist for large values of n.

2. The system is a noisy chaotic system, and the finite memory length measures the folding of the attractor. The diverging of nearby orbits in phase space means that they become uncorrelated after an orbital period (Wolf, Swift, Sweeney, & Vastano, 1985). Therefore, the memory process ceases after an orbital cycle. In essence, the finite memory length becomes the length of time it takes the system to forget its initial conditions.

From a graphical standpoint, once the system passes through an orbit, it travels over the length of the attractor. Once it covers the length of the attractor, the range cannot grow larger because the attractor is a bounded set. A fractional noise process is not a bounded set, and so the range will not stop growing. This physical characteristic of attractors also fits in with the characteristics of the rescaled range.

Both explanations are plausible, particularly when we are using short data sets. How do we decide which is which?

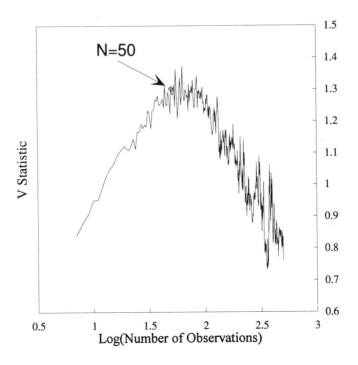

FIGURE 16.5 V statistic, Mackey–Glass equation with system noise.

DISTINGUISHING NOISY CHAOS FROM
FRACTIONAL NOISE

The most direct approach is to imitate the analysis of the Dow Jones Industrials in Chapter 8. If the break in the log/log plot is truly a cycle, and not a statistical artifact, it should be independent of the time increment used in the R/S analysis. For the Dow data, the cycle was always 1,040 trading days. When we went from five-day to 20-day increments, the cycle went from 208 five-day periods to 52 20-day periods. If the cycle is not dependent on sample size, then we can be fairly certain that we are examining noisy chaos and not fractional noise. In the case of the Dow data, reducing the size of the data set by 75 percent (as far as number of observations are concerned) did not affect the memory length. This is strong evidence that we are measuring a fold in phase space, not a statistical artifact.

If we are faced with a small data set to begin with, then we have a problem. We can use the cycle length estimate as another piece of confirming evidence, but, by itself, it is not decisive. For instance, suppose we use R/S analysis on a data set of 500 observations. We find a significant Hurst exponent ($0.50 < H < 1.0$) and a cycle length of 50 observations. This implies that we have ten cycles of observations, with 50 observations per cycle. According to Wolf et al. (1985), this is an adequate amount of data to estimate the largest Lyapunov exponent. Using the method outlined by Wolf et al. and Peters (1991a), we calculate an estimate of the largest Lyapunov exponent. If that exponent is positive, we have a good basis for concluding that the process is chaotic. If the inverse of the largest Lyapunov exponent is approximately equal to the cycle length (as suggested by Chen (1987)), then we can be more certain.

Those of you familiar with my earlier studies of the S&P 500 (Peters (1991a, 1991b)), will recognize that this was my criterion for concluding that the S&P 500 is, in the long term, chaotic, as suggested in the Fractal Market Hypothesis. The results are controversial, but I believe that the conclusions, which are drawn from independent tests, are valid.

The BDS Test

Three economists, Brock, Dechert, and Scheinkman (1987), developed an additional test—the "BDS test"—which is widely used by scientists. The BDS statistic, a variant on the correlation dimension, basically measures the statistical significance of the correlation dimension calculations. It is a powerful test for distinguishing random systems from deterministic chaos or from non-linear stochastic systems. However, it cannot distinguish between a nonlinear deterministic system and a nonlinear stochastic system. Essentially, it finds nonlinear dependence. Used in conjunction with other tests for chaos and with R/S analysis, it can be very useful.

According to the BDS test, the correlation integrals should be normally distributed if the system under study is independent, much like the distribution of H we discussed in Chapter 5.

The correlation integral is the probability that any two points are within a certain length, e, apart in phase space. As we increase e, the probability scales according to the fractal dimension of the phase space. The correlation integrals are calculated according to the following equation:

$$C_m(e) = (1/N^2) * \sum_{i,j=1}^{T} Z(e - |X_i - X_j|), \qquad i \neq j \qquad (16.2)$$

where $Z(x) = 1$ if $e - |Xi - Xj > 0$; 0 otherwise

$\qquad$ T = the number of observations

$\qquad$ e = distance

$\qquad$ C_m = correlation integral for dimension m

The function, Z, counts the number of points within a distance, e, of one another. According to theory, the C_m should increase at the rate e^D, with D the correlation dimension of the phase space, which is closely related to the fractal dimension. Calculating the correlation requires us to know what the phase space looks like. In real life, not only do we not know the factors involved in the system, we do not even know how many there are! Usually, we have only one observable, like stock price changes. Luckily, a theorem by Takens (1981) says that we can reconstruct the phase space by lagging the one time series we have for each dimension we think exists. If the number of "embedding dimensions" is larger than the fractal dimension, then the correlation dimension stabilizes to one value. My earlier book outlines the procedures for doing this calculation with experimental data taken from Wolf et al. (1985).

The BDS statistic is based on the statistical properties of the correlation integral. Much of the following discussion is taken from Hsieh (1989), where a more mathematical treatment of the BDS statistic can be found.

The correlation integral, from equation (16.2), calculates the probability that two points that are part of two different trajectories in phase space are e units apart. Assume that the X_i in the time series X (with T observations) are independent. We lag this series into "N histories"; that is, we use the Takens time delay method to create a phase space of dimension N from the time series, X. We then calculate the correlation integral, $C_N(e,T)$, using equation (16.2). Brock et al. showed that, as T approaches infinity:

$$C_N(e,T) \Rightarrow C_1(e)^N \qquad \text{with 100\% probability} \qquad (16.3)$$

This is the typical scaling feature of random processes. The correlation integral simply fills the space of whatever dimension it is placed in. Brock et al. showed that $|C_N(e,T) - C_1(e,T)^N| * \sqrt{T}$ is normally distributed with a mean of 0. The BDS statistic, w, that follows is also normally distributed:

$$w_N(e,T) = |C_N(e,T) - C_1(e,T)^N| * \sqrt{T}/s_N(e,T) \qquad (16.4)$$

where $s_N(e,T)$ = the standard deviation of the correlation integrals

Thus, the BDS statistic, w, has a standard normal probability distribution. When it is greater than 2.0, we can reject, with 95 percent confidence, the null hypothesis that the system under study is random. When it is greater than 3.0, we can reject with 99 percent confidence. However, the BDS test will find linear as well as nonlinear dependence in the data. Therefore, it is necessary to take AR(1) residuals for this test, as we did for R/S analysis. In addition, like R/S analysis, the dependence can be stochastic (such as the Hurst process, or GARCH), or it can be deterministic (such as chaos).

I obtained a program of the BDS statistic from Dechert and used it for the following tests. To do the tests, one must choose a value of e, the radius, and, m, the embedding dimension. As in the correlation dimension calculations described in my earlier book, there is a range of e values where probabilities can be calculated. This range depends on the number of observations, T. If e is too small, there will not be enough points to capture the statistical structure; if e is too large, there will be too many points. Following the example of LeBaron (1990) and Hsieh (1989), we will use e = 0.50 standard deviation of the data sets. By setting the value of e to the size of the data, we can, perhaps, overcome these problems.

We must choose an embedding dimension that will make the resulting phase space reconstruction neither too sparse nor too crowded. If m is too small, the points will be tightly packed together. If m is too large, the points will be too distant. For the purposes of this example, we will use m = 6. Hsieh (1989) tested many embedding dimensions on currencies, and m = 6 gave results comparable to the other higher (and lower) embedding dimensions.

The examples given here are not new. LeBaron (1990) did a study of stock prices, as did Brock (1988). Hsieh (1989) did extensive tests of currencies and performed a comprehensive set of Monte Carlo experiments, which we will describe below.

I have examined the Mackey–Glass equation without noise, with one standard deviation of observational noise, and with one standard deviation of system noise. I have also tested the fractional noise with H = 0.72, which we have used earlier, as well as the simulated GARCH series used in Chapter 5. In keeping with earlier statements about linear dependence, I have used AR(1) residuals again for all tests in this chapter. Table 16.1 shows the results.

The noise-free Mackey–Glass equation shows a highly significant BDS statistic of 112, as would be expected. In addition, the noise-contaminated Mackey–Glass systems have significant BDS statistics, although at lower levels. The simulated GARCH series also shows a significant BDS statistic of 6.23, as does the fractional noise series at 13.85. In these simulated series, the BDS statistic is shown to be sensitive to nonlinear dependence in both deterministic and stochastic form. It is robust with respect to noise, when used in analyzing a deterministic system.

Table 16.2 shows the results of the Dow 20-day and five-day series used in Chapter 8, as well as the daily yen. Again, all are significant—and surprisingly large. However, the Japanese daily yen statistic of 116.05 is consistent with Hsieh's (1989) value of 110.04 for the same values of R and m. LeBaron (1990), using weekly S&P 500 data from 1928 to 1939, found w = 23.89 for m = 6.

Table 16.1   BDS Statistic: Simulated Processes

Process	BDS Statistic	Epsilon	Embedding Dimension	Number of Observations
Mackey–Glass				
No noise	56.88	0.12	6	1,000
Observational noise	13.07	0.06	6	1,000
System noise	−3.12	0.08	6	1,000
Fractional noise (H = 0.72)	13.85	0.07	6	1,400
GARCH	6.23	0.01	6	7,500
Gaussian noise	0.03	0.06	6	5,000

Table 16.2 BDS Statistic: Market Time Series

Market	BDS Statistic	Epsilon	Embedding Dimension	Number of Observations
Dow—five-day	28.72	0.01	6	5,293
Dow—20-day	14.34	0.03	6	1,301
Yen/Dollar—daily	116.05	0.03	6	4,459

This is very close to our finding of w = 28.72 for five-day Dow returns (1888 to 1990), even though our data cover a much longer time frame. LeBaron found that the value of w varied greatly over ten-year periods. Given the four-year stock market cycle found through R/S analysis, this variability over short time frames is not unusual. After all, ten years is only 2.50 orbits.

Hsieh (1989) and LeBaron (1990) performed Monte Carlo simulations of the BDS statistic and found it to be robust with respect to the Gaussian null hypothesis. Thus, like R/S analysis, it can easily find dependence. Once linear dependence is filtered out, the BDS statistic is a significant test for nonlinearity. Unfortunately, it cannot distinguish between fractional noise and deterministic chaos, but, used in conjunction with other tests, it is a powerful tool.

Combining Tests

In the absence of a long data set (both in time and number of observations), it is best to turn to multiple independent tests that should confirm one another. R/S analysis offers yet another tool for doing so. It is extremely robust with respect to noise, and should be considered as an additional test (along with the BDS statistic) on all data sets that are suspected of being chaotic.

Implications for the FMH

For the Fractal Market Hypothesis, the break in the R/S graph for the Dow data confirms that the market is chaotic in the long term and follows the economic cycle. Currencies, however, do not register average nonperiodic cycles, despite the fact that the daily Hurst exponent for most currencies is more significant than the daily Dow or T-Bond yields. This would further confirm that currencies are fractional noise processes, even in the long term.

SUMMARY

We have seen that R/S analysis is an additional tool for examining noisy chaotic time series. We have also seen that it is extremely robust with respect to noise, and that the Hurst exponent can be used as a noise index when preparing simulated data. These qualities make R/S analysis a useful process for studying chaotic systems.

We are finally brought to the relationship between fractal statistics and noisy chaos. Can noisy chaos be the cause of the fat-tailed, high-peaked distributions that are so common in the financial markets, as well as in other natural time series? In Chapter 17, we will find out.

17
Fractal Statistics, Noisy Chaos, and the FMH

In Chapter 16, we saw that capital market and economic time series share certain similarities with noisy "chaotic" systems. In particular, their Hurst exponents are consistent with values of H calculated from the spectral exponent, β. We also found that R/S analysis could estimate the average length of a nonperiodic cycle by a "break" in the log/log plot. This cycle length was similar to cycles found by R/S analysis for the capital markets and for economic time series. Popular stochastic processes, such as GARCH, which are also used as possible models, do not have these characteristics.

Based on the results in previous chapters, noisy chaos seems like a reasonable explanation for capital market movements. Except for currencies, noisy chaos is consistent with the long-run, fundamental behavior of markets, and fractional brownian motion is more consistent with the short-run, trading characteristics. Both behaviors are consistent with the Fractal Market Hypothesis as outlined in Chapter 3.

A final question concerns the relationship between noisy chaos and stable, or fractal, distributions. Can the high-peaked, fat-tailed distributions observed empirically, as well as intermittent dynamical behavior, also be tied to noisy chaos? In this chapter, we will examine this question. Noisy chaos can be offered as a possible explanation, but we will find that there is much that is unexplained, as well.

In the closing section of this chapter, I attempt to reconcile the different elements of time series analysis that appear to give significant results: ARCH, fractional noise, and noisy chaos will be united into one framework. The applicability of each process depends on individual investment horizons. We must first examine the relationship between fractal statistics and noisy chaos.

FREQUENCY DISTRIBUTIONS

The frequency distribution of changes is an obvious place to start. It is well known that the changes in a system characterized by deterministic chaos have a frequency distribution with a long positive tail. Figure 17.1 shows the frequency distribution Mackey–Glass equation, using the changes in the graph shown as Figure 6.7. The changes have been "normalized" to a mean of 0 and a standard deviation of 1. The result is a "log normal" looking distribution; that is, it is single-humped, with a long positive tail and a finite negative tail.

Adding noise to these systems changes their frequency distributions dramatically. Figures 17.2(a) and 17.2(b) show the Mackey–Glass equation with observational and system noise respectively. Enough noise has been added to generate a Hurst exponent of 0.70, as shown in Chapter 16. The frequency distribution is

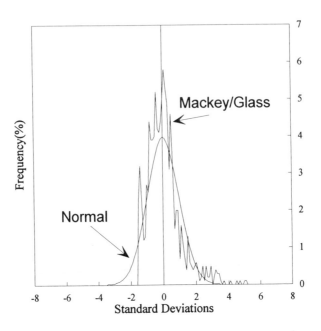

FIGURE 17.1   Mackey–Glass equation: no noise.

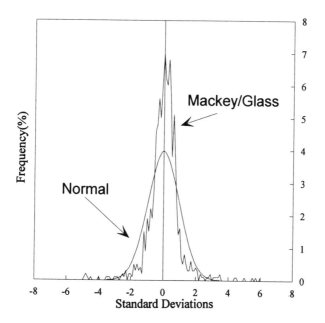

FIGURE 17.2a   Mackey–Glass equation: observational noise.

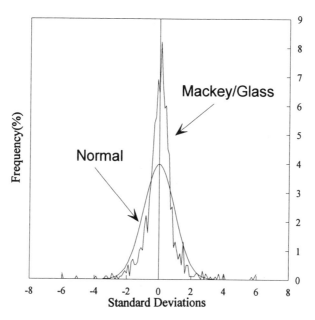

FIGURE 17.2b   Mackey–Glass equation: system noise.

now the familiar high-peaked, fat-tailed distribution. Figures 17.3(a)–17.3(c) show the differences between the distributions and the normal distribution. The systems with noise resemble the Dow graphs of Figures 2.4(a)–2.4(e), but the no-noise graph looks quite different. Why?

Adding normally distributed Gaussian noise has the impact of lowering the Hurst exponent, as we have examined previously. In addition, it shifts the mean toward the center (bringing the mean and median closer together), extends the negative tail, and adds more (negative) values. The positive tail is reduced by the mean shift and by the addition of smaller values. However, the original distribution had a high peak and a long positive tail. Where did the long negative tail come from?

In the Mackey–Glass equation shown in Figure 6.7, I took equation (6.4) and added 10 to the resulting values. This transformation was necessary because equation (6.4) produces negative values, and one cannot take the log of a negative number. Adding 10 had the result of moving all of the values up into positive territory. The noise added was white Gaussian noise. As a result, the noise had a bigger impact on the changes at the troughs in the system, than on those at the peaks. Hence, the longer negative tail.

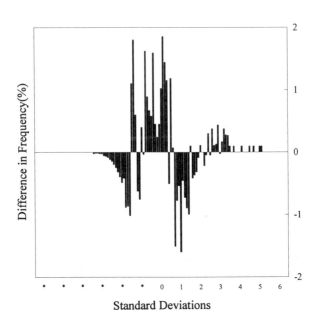

FIGURE 17.3a   Mackey–Glass equation: no noise—normal.

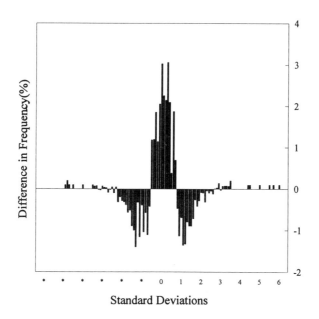

FIGURE 17.3b   Mackey–Glass equation: observational noise—normal.

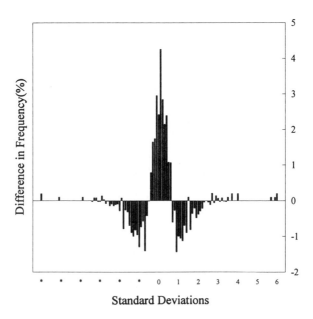

FIGURE 17.3c   Mackey–Glass equation: system noise—normal.

With system noise, the change is different. The negative tail is quite long—
almost as long as the positive tail. The similarity of the system noise frequency
distributions to the capital market distributions we saw in Chapter 2 is striking. In fact, this is the first simulated series, other than ARCH and its derivatives, that has this characteristic.

VOLATILITY TERM STRUCTURE

In Chapter 2, we looked at the volatility term structure of the stock, bond,
and currency markets. The term structure of volatility is the standard deviation of returns over different time horizons. If market returns are determined
by the normal distribution, then volatility should increase with the square
root of time. That is, five-day returns should have a standard deviation equivalent to the standard deviation of daily returns times the square root of five.
However, we found that stocks, bonds, and currencies all have volatility term
structures that increase at a faster rate than the square root of time, which is
consistent with the properties of infinite variance distributions and fractional brownian motion (FBM). For a pure FBM process, such scaling should
increase forever. We found that currencies appeared to have no limit to their
scaling, but U.S. stocks and bonds were bounded at about four years; that is,
10-year returns had virtually the same standard deviation as four-year returns. No explanation was given for this bounded behavior, but the four-year
limit is remarkably similar to the four-year cycle found by R/S analysis.
Could there be a connection?

Conceptually, yes, there is a connection. In a chaotic system, the attractor is
a bounded set. After the system travels over one cycle, changes will stop growing. Therefore, it would not be surprising to find that chaotic systems also have
bounded volatility term structures. In fact, bounded volatility term structures
may be another way to test for the presence of nonperiodic cycles.

Figure 17.4(a) shows the volatility term structure of the Mackey–Glass
equation with a 50-iteration lag. The scaling stops just prior to 50 iterations.
Figure 17.4(b) shows the volatility term structure for the Mackey–Glass equation with observational and system noise added. These are the same noise-
added time series used throughout the book. They both have $H \approx 0.70$, versus
$H = 0.92$ for the no-noise version. The series with noise added are even more
convincing than the Mackey–Glass attractor without noise. The peak in both
plots occurs, without question, at $n = 50$ iterations, the average nonperiodic
cycle of the system.

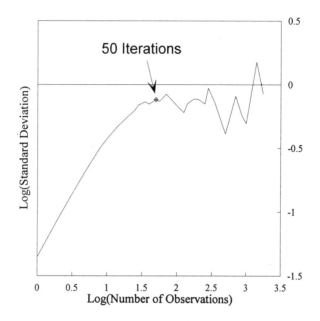

FIGURE 17.4a   Mackey–Glass equation: volatility term structure.

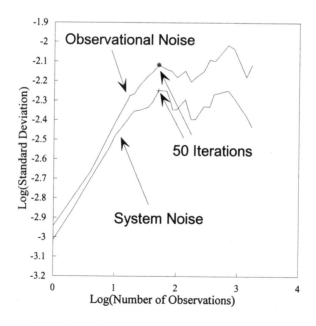

FIGURE 17.4b   Mackey–Glass equation with noise: volatility term structure.

I have done similar analysis for the Lorenz and Rosseler attractors. I encourage readers to try the analysis for themselves, using the final program supplied in Appendix 2 or a program of their own manufacture. The volatility term structure of these chaotic systems bears a striking resemblance to similar plots of the stock and bond markets, supplied in Chapter 2. Currencies do not have this bounded characteristic—a further evidence that currencies are not "chaotic" but are, instead, a fractional noise process. This does not mean that currencies do not have runs; they clearly do, but there is no average length to these runs. For currencies, the joker truly appears at random; for U.S. stocks and bonds, the joker has an average appearance frequency of four years.

SEQUENTIAL STANDARD DEVIATION AND MEAN

In Chapter 14, we examined the sequential standard deviation and mean of the U.S. stock market, and compared it to a time series drawn from the Cauchy distribution. We did so to see the effects of infinite variance and mean on a time series. The sequential standard deviation is the standard deviation of the time series as we add one observation at a time. If the series were from a Gaussian random walk, the more observations we have, the more the sequential standard deviation would tend to the population standard deviation. Likewise, if the mean is stable and finite, the sample mean will eventually converge to the population mean. For the Dow Jones Industrials file, we found scant evidence of convergence after about 100 years of data. This would mean that, in shorter periods, the process is much more similar to an infinite variance than to a finite variance distribution. The sequential mean converged more rapidly, and looked more stable. A fractal distribution would, of course, be well-described by an infinite or unstable variance, and a finite and stable mean. After studying the Dow, we seemed to find the desired characteristics.

It would now be interesting to study the sequential statistics of chaotic systems. Do they also have infinite variance and finite mean? They exhibit fat-tailed distributions when noise is added, but that alone is not enough to account for the market analysis we have already done.

Without noise, it appears that the Mackey–Glass equation is persistent with unstable mean and variance. With noise, both observational and system, the system is closer to market series, *but not identical.* In this study, as in Chapter 15, all series have been normalized to a mean of 0 and a standard deviation of 1. The final value in each series will always have a mean of 0.

Figure 17.5(a) shows the sequential standard deviation of 1,000 iterations of the Mackey–Glass equation without noise. The system is unstable, with

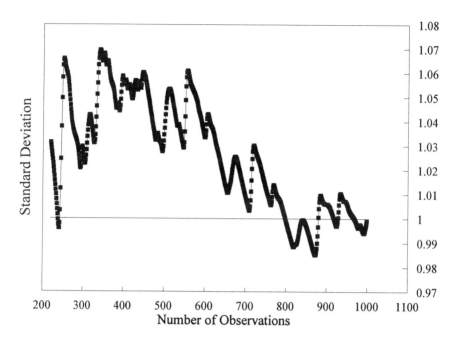

FIGURE 17.5a   Mackey–Glass equation: sequential standard deviation.

discrete jumps in standard deviation followed by steady declines—very similar
to the Cauchy and Dow series studied in Chapter 15. Figures 17.5(b) and
17.5(c) show similar analyses for observational and system noise respectively.
The addition of noise makes the jumps smaller, but they remain, nonetheless,
in both cases. From these graphs, we can conclude that the Mackey–Glass
equation does not have stable variance.

Figure 17.6(a) shows the sequential mean for the observational noise series,
and the no-noise series. The addition of noise has the impact of drawing the
sequential mean closer to 0. Neither series appears nearly as stable as the Dow
and random series seen in Chapter 14, although the observational noise series
is similar, being only 0.02 standard deviation away from the mean. Figure
17.6(b) graphs the sequential mean for the Mackey–Glass equation with system noise. Again, there appears to be a stable population mean, although there
is a systematic deviation. We can tentatively conclude that the Mackey–Glass
equation does not have a stable mean, but observational noise can give the appearance of a somewhat stable mean.

When I performed this analysis for the Lorenz and Rosseler attractors, the
results were comparable. Although empirically derived, chaotic attractors appear to be similar to market time series, in that they have unstable variances.

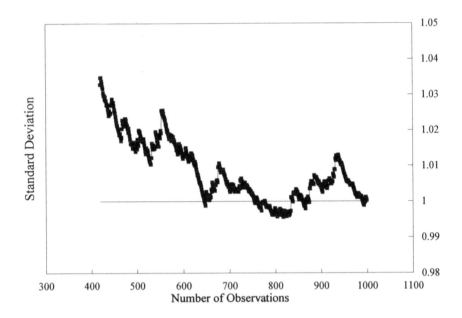

FIGURE 17.5b Mackey–Glass equation with observational noise: sequential standard deviation.

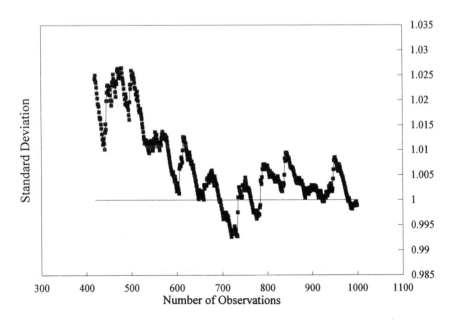

FIGURE 17.5c Mackey–Glass equation with system noise: sequential standard deviation.

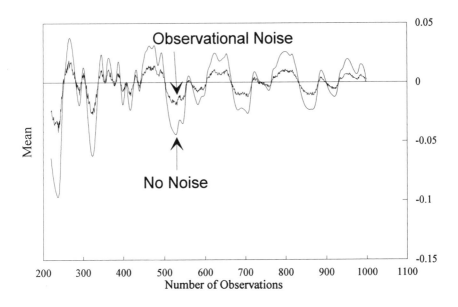

FIGURE 17.6a   Mackey–Glass equation: sequential mean.

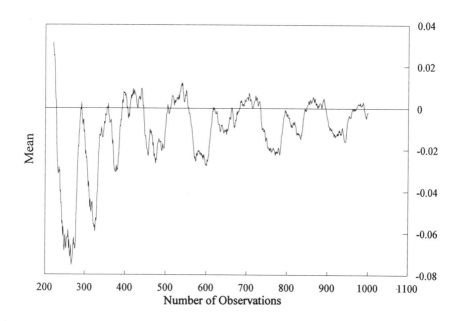

FIGURE 17.6b   Mackey–Glass equation with system noise: sequential mean.

like market time series, chaotic attractors also have unstable means; however, with noise, the systems do resemble market time series. It is possible that long-term market time series are similar to chaotic ones.

MEASURING α

The second characteristic for capital market series is a Hurst exponent of between 0.50 and 1.00. As would be expected, a pure chaotic flow, like the Lorenz attractor or Mackey–Glass equation, would have Hurst exponents close to but less than 1, due to the nonperiodic cycle component. What is the impact of noise on the Hurst exponent of a system?

The Graphical Method

Using the graphical method of Chapter 15, we can estimate α to be approximately 1.57 for the system with observational noise, as shown in Figure 17.7. This gives an approximate value of H = 0.64. Both positive and negative tails are shown.

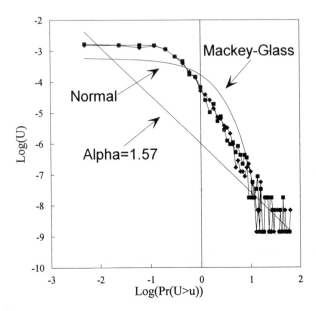

FIGURE 17.7   Mackey–Glass equation with system noise: estimating alpha, graphical method.

R/S Analysis

When we ran the R/S analysis on this system it gave H = 0.72, a substantially higher value than the graphical method. Both values differ significantly from a Gaussian norm *and* they are significantly different from one another. A major discrepancy exists here.

THE LIKELIHOOD OF NOISY CHAOS

The hypothesis of noisy chaos, for our observations, is based on the idea that, because we have so much trouble measuring the system, up to two standard deviations of noise is still not enough to generate Hurst exponents like the ones we saw in Chapter 9. I find that unlikely (although others may not). We have already seen one system with a Hurst exponent that drops rapidly to 0.70—the Weirstrass function, stated in equation (6.2). The Weirstrass function was the superimposition of multiple systems working over multiple frequencies that scale in a self-affine manner. Working within the Fractal Market Hypothesis, it is possible that each investment horizon has its own dynamical system, which is superimposed and added to a longer-term nonlinear dynamical system. Such a system would have dynamics that exist at each investment horizon. Because the frequency distribution at each horizon is similar, we can postulate that the same dynamics are at work, even if the parameters that are important at each horizon vary. This superimposition of many persistent processes at different frequencies is the mirror image of the relaxation processes, which were suggested as the structure of pink noise. It is possible that black noise is also the result of an infinite number of persistent processes at different frequencies, added together in a manner similar to the Weirstrass function. This would be entirely consistent with the Fractal Market Hypothesis.

Finally, we can see why Hurst (and we) have seen so many processes that have Hurst exponents of approximately 0.70. A dynamical system with noise added will drop rapidly to 0.70 in the presence of both observational and system noise. Because some combination of both types of noise is probably in measurements of all real systems, Hurst exponents of approximately 0.70 would be common. Hurst's own data show that to be the case, so we can postulate that noisy chaos is a common phenomenon. Less common would be Hurst exponents less than 0.70. However, at daily frequencies, H values of 0.60 and less are quite common, suggesting the need for an alternative explanation for the "noise."

ORBITAL CYCLES

A final characteristic, which we have already examined, is cycle lengths. In previous chapters, we have examined how the Hurst exponent uncovers periodic and nonperiodic cycles. The time has come to examine this particular characteristic as it relates to dynamical systems.

First, we will examine the well-known Lorenz attractor:

$$\frac{dX}{dt} = -\sigma*X + \sigma*Y$$

$$\frac{dY}{dt} = -X*Z + r*X - Y \tag{17.1}$$

$$\frac{dZ}{dt} = X*Y - b*Z$$

where $\sigma = 10$, $b = 8/3$, and $r = 28$

These parameters are widely used to model the chaotic realm. The cycle of the Lorenz attractor cannot be solved explicitly; however, it has been estimated to be approximately 0.50 second by a method called *Poincaré section.* Although Poincaré section is useful for simulated data, it is less reliable when dealing with experimental data. In this analysis, we used 100 seconds of the X coordinate, sampled every 0.10 second. Figure 17.8(a) shows the log/log plot, and Figure 17.8(b) shows the V-statistic plot. The bend in the log/log plot and the peak in the V statistic are consistent with the orbital cycle of 0.50 to 0.70 second. This estimate is consistent with the estimate from the Poincaré section. However, as we saw in Chapter 6, it is very robust with respect to noise.

In Chapter 6, we saw that varying the cycle length for the Mackey–Glass equation resulted in a break in the graph at approximately that point. Figure 17.9 shows the V-statistic plot for various levels of observational noise. Again, R/S analysis is shown to be very robust with respect to noise.

Once again, it is striking how similar these graphs are to those obtained for the capital markets. In Chapter 6, we stated that changing the sampling interval, and repeating the R/S analysis process, should result in a cycle consistent with the earlier high-frequency analysis. In Figure 17.10(a), we sample the 100-lag Mackey–Glass data used above at every three intervals. The projected

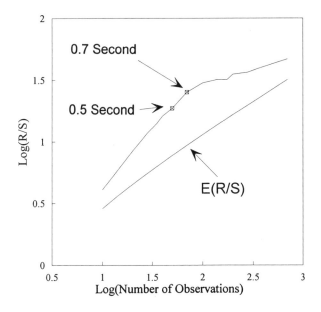

FIGURE 17.8a   Lorenz attractor: R/S analysis.

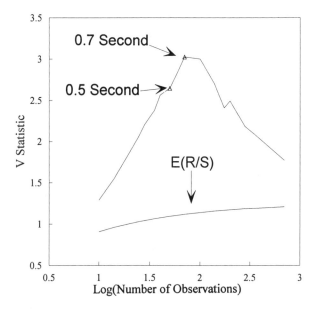

FIGURE 17.8b   Lorenz attractor: V statistic.

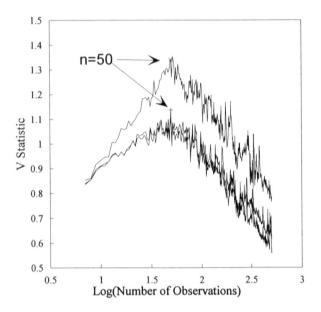

FIGURE 17.9   Mackey–Glass equation with observational noise: V statistic.

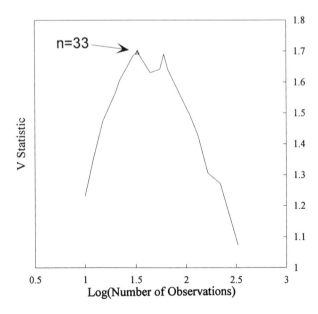

FIGURE 17.10a   Mackey–Glass equation, sampled every three intervals: V statistic.

result should be a cycle of about 33 observations, and the actual result is highly consistent. Figure 17.10(b) repeats the analysis with one standard deviation of noise added. The results are the same.

SELF-SIMILARITY

Noisy chaos has one final characteristic that is consistent with market data: Its frequency distributions are self-similar. After an adjustment for scale, they are much the same shape. Figure 17.11 shows the Mackey–Glass data with no noise, used for Figure 17.1. However, in this case, sampling has been done every three observations, as in the data used for Figure 17.10(a). The shape is still similar to the "log-normal" looking shape that we saw earlier. Figure 17.12 shows the Mackey–Glass equation with observational noise added, used for Figure 17.2. Again, it is sampled at every third observation, and the frequency distribution is virtually identical to the longer time series. We can see that noisy chaos has many of the attributes that we find desirable. In fact, it is likely that fractional noise and noisy chaos are actually the same thing in real

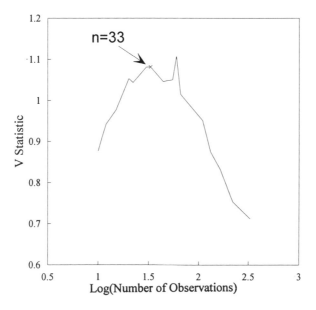

FIGURE 17.10b   Mackey–Glass equation with noise, sampled every three intervals: V statistic.

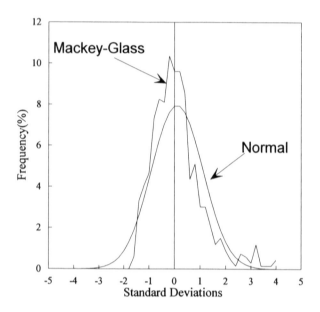

FIGURE 17.11   Mackey–Glass equation, sampled every three intervals: no noise.

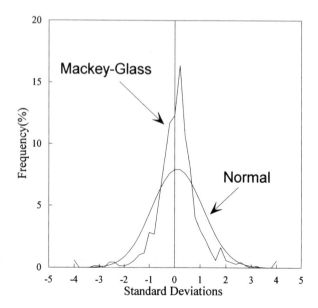

FIGURE 17.12   Mackey–Glass equation, sampled every three intervals: observational noise.

systems. However, the deterministic element is apparent only at very long frequencies. At shorter intervals, the stochastic element dominates. In the next section, I will attempt to reconcile these two seemingly competing concepts, as well as the concept of the ARCH family of distributions, into one collective.

A PROPOSAL: UNITING GARCH, FBM, AND CHAOS

The solution has not been derived mathematically, but we can see what is needed. In the short term, we need persistent Hurst exponents and self-similar frequency distributions. In the long term, we need persistent Hurst exponents, long finite memories, and nonperiodic cycles. It is important to remember that short cycles do not appear stable from the research we have done. Only the long cycle is consistent and stable over all of the time periods studied.

With those results in mind, I would like to propose the following for the stock and bond markets. In the short term, markets are dominated by trading processes, which are fractional noise processes. They are, locally, members of the ARCH family of processes, and they are characterized by conditional variances; that is, each investment horizon is characterized by its own measurable ARCH process with finite, conditional variance. This finite conditional variance can be used to assess risk for that investment horizon only. Globally, the process is a stable Levy (fractal) distribution with infinite variance. As the investment horizon increases, it approaches infinite variance behavior.

In the very long term (periods longer than four years for the U.S. stock and bond markets), the markets are characterized by deterministic nonlinear systems or deterministic chaos. Nonperiodic cycles arise from the interdependence of the various capital markets among themselves, as well as from the economy. Markets that are dominated primarily by traders, with no link to fluctuations in the underlying economy, will not be characterized by deterministic chaos, even in the long term. Instead, they will be dominated by local ARCH effects, and global stable Levy characteristics.

With this approach, we can reconcile the various approaches that have been independently found to produce significant results: ARCH, stable Levy (fractal), and long-term deterministic chaos. The contribution of each process depends on the investment horizon. Short-term trading is dominated by local ARCH and global fractal. Long-term trading is tied to fundamental information and deterministic nonlinearities. Thus, the information set used for modeling and setting strategy is largely dependent on the investment horizon.

18
Understanding Markets

This book has had two purposes. First, I planned it as a guide to applying R/S analysis to capital market, economic, and other time series data. R/S analysis has been in existence for over 40 years. Despite its robustness and general applicability, it has remained largely unknown. It deserves a place in any analyst's toolbox, along with the other tools that have been developed in traditional as well as chaos analysis.

My second purpose centered around outlining a general hypothesis for synthesizing different models into a coherent whole. This hypothesis was to be consistent with the empirical facts, utilizing a minimal amount of underlying assumptions. I called my model the Fractal Market Hypothesis (FMH). I consider this conjecture to be the first cut at unraveling the global structure of markets. The FMH will undoubtedly be modified and refined over time, if it stands up to scrutiny by the investment community. I used a number of different methods for testing the FMH; a prominent tool was R/S analysis, used in combination with other techniques.

A convincing picture began to emerge. Together, R/S analysis and the Fractal Market Hypothesis came under the general heading of Fractal Market Analysis. Fractal Market Analysis used the self-similar probability distributions, called stable Levy distributions, in conjunction with R/S analysis, to study and classify the long-term behavior of markets.

We have learned much, but there is much that remains to be explored. I am convinced that the markets have a fractal structure. As with any other fractal, temporal or spatial, the closer we examine the structure, the more detail we see. As we begin to explain certain mysteries, new unknowns become apparent. We have a classical case of the more we know, the more we know we don't know.

INFORMATION AND INVESTMENT HORIZONS

We discussed the impact of information on investor behavior. In traditional theory, information is treated as a generic item. More or less, it is anything that can affect the perceived value of a security. The investor is also generic. Basically, an investor is anyone who wants to buy, sell, or hold a security because of the available information. The investor is also considered rational—someone who always wants to maximize return and knows how to value current information. The aggregate market is the equivalent of this archetypal rational investor, so the market can value information instantly. This generic approach, where information and investors are general cases, also implies that all types of information impact all investors equally. That is where it fails.

The market is made up of many individuals with many different investment horizons. The behavior of a day trader is quite different from that of a pension fund. In the former case, the investment horizon is measured in minutes; in the latter case, in years.

Information has a different impact on different investment horizons. Day traders' primary activity is trading. Trading is typically concerned with crowd behavior and with reading short-term trends. A day trader will be more concerned with technical information, which is why many technicians say that "the market has its own language." Technicians are also more likely to say that fundamental information means little. Most technicians have short investment horizons, and, within their time frame, fundamental information is of little value. In that regard, they are right. Technical trends are of the most value to short horizons.

Most fundamental analysts and economists who also work in the markets have long investment horizons. They tend to deal more with the economic cycle. Fundamental analysts will tend to think that technical trends are illusions and are not of use to long-term investors. Only by assessing value can true investment returns be made.

In this framework, both technicians and fundamentalists are right for their particular investment horizons, because the impact of information is largely dependent on each individual's investment horizon.

STABILITY

The stability of the market is largely a matter of liquidity. Liquidity is available when the market is composed of many investors with many different investment horizons. In that way, if a piece of information comes through that causes a severe drop in price at the short investment horizon, the longer-term investors will step in to buy, because they do not value the information as highly. However, when the market loses this structure, and all investors have the same investment horizon, then the market becomes unstable, because there is no liquidity. Liquidity is not the same as trading volume. Instead, it is the balancing of supply and demand. The loss of long-term investors causes the entire market to trade based on the same information set, which is primarily technical, or a crowd behavior phenomenon. Typically, the market horizon becomes short-term when the long-term outlook becomes highly uncertain—that is, when an event (often political) occurs that makes the current long-term information set unreliable or perceived to be useless. Long-term investors either stop participating or they become short-term investors and begin trading on technical information as well.

Market stability relies on diversification of the investment horizons of the participants. A stable market is one in which many investors with different investment horizons are trading simultaneously. The market is stable because the different horizons value the information flow differently, and can provide liquidity if there is a crash or stampede at one of the other investment horizons.

RISK

Each investment horizon is like the branching generation of a tree. The diameter of any one branch is a random function with a finite variance. However, each branch, when taken in the context of the total tree, is part of a global structure with unknown variance, because the dimension of each tree is different. It depends on many variables, such as its species and size.

Each investment horizon is also a random function with a finite variance, depending on the previous variance. Because the risk at each investment horizon should be equal, the shape of the frequency distribution of returns is equal, once an adjustment is made for scale. However, the overall, global statistical structure of the market has infinite variance; the long-term variance does not converge to a stable value.

The global statistical structure is fractal because it has a self-similar structure, and its characteristic exponent, α (which is also the fractal dimension) is fractional, ranging from 0 to 2. A random walk, which is characterized by the normal distribution, is self-similar. However, it is not fractal; its fractal dimension is an integer: $\alpha = 2.0$.

The shape of these fractal distributions is high-peaked and fat-tailed, when compared to the normal distribution. The fat tails occur because a large event occurs through an amplification process. This same process causes the infinite variance. The tails never converge to the asymptote of $y = 0.0$, even at infinity. In addition, when the large events occur, they tend to be abrupt and discontinuous. Thus, fractal distributions have yet another fractal characteristic: discontinuity. The tendency toward "catastrophes" has been called, by Mandelbrot (1972), the *Noah effect,* or, more technically, the infinite variance syndrome. In the markets, the fat tails are caused by crashes and stampedes, which tend to be abrupt and discontinuous, as predicted by the model.

LONG MEMORY

In the ideal world of traditional time series analysis, all systems are random walks or can be transformed into them. The "supreme law of Unreason" can then be applied, and the answers can be found. Imposing order on disorder in this manner, natural systems could be reduced to a few solvable equations and one basic frequency distribution—the normal distribution.

Real life is not that simple. The children of the Demiurge are complex and cannot be classified by a few simple characteristics. We found that, in capital markets, most series are characterized by long-memory effects, or biases; today's market activity biases the future for a very long time. This *Joseph effect* can cause serious problems for traditional time series analysis; for instance, the Joseph effect is very difficult, if not impossible, to filter out. AR(1) residuals, the most common method for eliminating serial correlation, cannot remove long-memory effects. The long memory causes the appearance of trends and cycles. These cycles may be spurious, because they are merely a function of the long-memory effect and of the occasional shift in the bias of the market.

Through R/S analysis, this long-memory effect has been shown to exist and to be a black noise process. The color of the noise that causes the Joseph effect is important below, when we discuss volatility.

CYCLES

There has long been a suspicion that the markets have cycles, but no convincing evidence has been found. The techniques used were searching for regular, periodic cycles—the kind of cycles created by the Good. The Demiurge created nonperiodic cycles—cycles that have an average period, but not an exact one. Using R/S analysis, we were able to show that nonperiodic cycles are likely for the markets. These nonperiodic cycles last for years, so it is likely that they are a consequence of long-term economic information. We found that similar nonperiodic cycles exist for nonlinear dynamical systems, or deterministic chaos.

We did not find strong evidence for short-term nonperiodic cycles. Most shorter cycles that are popular with technicians are probably due to the Joseph effect. The cycles have no average length, and the bias that causes them can change at any time—most likely, in an abrupt and discontinuous fashion.

Among the more interesting findings is that currencies do not have a long-term cycle. This implies that they are a fractional noise process in both the short and the long term. Stocks and bonds, on the other hand, are fractional noise in the short term (hence the self-similar frequency distributions) but chaotic in the long term.

VOLATILITY

Volatility was shown to be antipersistent—a frequently reversing, pink noise process. However, it is not mean reverting. Mean reverting implies that volatility has a stable population mean, which it tends toward in the long run. We saw evidence that this was not the case. This evidence fit in with theory, because the derivative of a black noise process is pink noise. Market returns are black noise, so it is not surprising that volatility (which is the second moment of stock prices) is a pink noise.

A pink noise process is characterized by probability functions that have not only infinite variance but infinite mean as well; that is, there is no population mean to revert to. In the context of market returns being a black noise, this makes perfect sense. If market returns have infinite variance, then the mean of the variance of stock prices should be, itself, infinite. It is all part of one large structure, and this structure has profound implications for option traders and others who buy and sell volatility.

TOWARD A MORE COMPLETE MARKET THEORY

Much of the discussion in this book has been an attempt to reconcile the rational approach of traditional quantitative management with the practical experience of actually dealing with markets. For some time, we have not been able to reconcile the two. Practicing money managers who have a quantitative background are forced to graft practical experience onto theory. When practice does not conform to theory, we have merely accepted that, at that point, theory breaks down. Our view has been similar to physicists' acceptance of "singularities," events where theory breaks down. The Big Bang is one such singularity. At the exact moment of the Big Bang, physical laws break down and cannot explain the event. We have been forced to think of market crashes as singularities in capital market theory. They are periods when no extension of the Efficient Market Hypothesis (EMH) can hold.

Chaos theory and fractal statistics offer us a model that can explain such singularities. Even if events such as crashes prove to be unpredictable, they are not unexpected. They do not become "outliers" in the theory. Instead, they are a part of the system. In many ways, they are the price we pay for being capitalists. In my earlier book, I noted that markets need to be far from equilibrium if they are to stay alive. What I was attempting to say is that a capitalist system (either a capital market or a full economy) must dynamically evolve. Random events must occur in order to foster its innovation. If we knew exactly what was to come, we would stop experimenting. We would stop learning. We would stop innovating. Therefore, we must have cycles, and cycles imply that there will always be an up period and a down period.

It has become common for researchers to search for anomalies, or pockets of inefficiency, where profits can be made at little risk. It has been rightly pointed out that a large market will arbitrage away such anomalies once they become general knowledge. The FMH is not like that. It does not find a pocket of inefficiency in which a few can profit. Instead, it says that, because information is processed differently at the various frequencies, there will be trends and cycles at all investment horizons. Some will be stochastic, some will be nonlinear deterministic. In both cases, the exact structure of the trends is time-varied. It is predictable, but it will never be perfectly predictable, and that is what keeps the markets stable. Chaos theory and fractal statistics offer us a new way to understand how markets and economies function. There are no guarantees that they will make it easier for us to make money. We will, however, be better able to develop strategies and assess the risks of playing the game.

Appendix 1

The Chaos Game

This appendix provides a BASIC program that generates the Sierpinski triangle using the chaos game algorithm described in Chapter 1. In my earlier book, I provided a number of BASIC programs, but later received complaints that the programs would not run. The problem is that there are many different forms of BASIC for PCs. This version is called BASICA, and used to be provided by Microsoft with their DOS software. I still use this language for illustrative purposes. If you have access to a different version of BASIC, this program will have to be adapted.

Luckily, it is extremely short. This is all the more remarkable, considering how complex the resulting image is, and shows convincingly how randomness and determinism can coexist. The screen used here is a 640×200 pixel format. The program initially asks for x and y coordinates for starting the program. You can enter virtually any number you like. The algorithm quickly converges to the Sierpinski triangle. Because the program does not plot the first 50 points (they are considered "transients"), the image will be generated anyway. Change the initial coordinates, and you will see that the same image always results, despite the random order in which the points are plotted. In many ways, this program is more impressive on a slower PC, where you can see the image gradually fill in.

The coordinates for the three angles of the triangle in (x, y) notation are (320, 1), (1, 200), and (640, 200). After reading the initial point, the program generates a random number, r, between 0 and 1. We use this random number instead of the dice described in Chapter 1. If r is less than 0.34, it goes halfway from its current position to (320, 1), which is the apex of the triangle. If $0.33 < r < 0.67$, it goes halfway to (1, 200), the left lower angle. If 0.68 < r < 1.00, then it goes halfway to (640, 200), the lower right angle. In each case, it plots the point, generates another random number, and then starts over again. The program is written for 50,000 iterations. The user can use more or less. However, I have found that more than 50,000 fills up the triangle due to lack of resolution, and less than 50,000 leaves a somewhat incomplete image.

```
10 Screen 2   @640×200 pixel screen@
20 Cls: Key off
30 Print "Input x and y co-ordinates:"
40 Print "Input x:": Input x
50 Print "Input y:": Input y
60 cls
70 For i=1 to 50000      @number of plotted points@
80 r=rnd(i)              @generate random number@
90 If r<0.34 then x=x(x+320)/2 else if r<0.67 then
   x=(x+1)/2 else x = (x+640)/2
100 If r<0.34 then y=(y+1)/2 else y=(y+200)/2
110 if i<50 goto 130     @skip plotting first 50 points@
120 pset(x,y)            @plot point@
130 next i
140 end
```

Appendix 2

GAUSS Programs

In *Chaos and Order in the Capital Markets,* I supplied a number of BASIC programs so readers could experiment with calculating correlation dimensions and Lyapunov exponents. I was surprised to discover that some readers assumed that I did most of my research in BASIC, and, for some reason, that lowered my credibility. While I do not think there is anything wrong with using BASIC, I do use other languages for more complicated data manipulation. My current choice is a language called GAUSS, produced by Aptech Systems in Seattle, Washington. GAUSS is a high-dimensional programming language, which I find highly efficient for handling large data files. In *Chaos* . . . , I did not supply a program for calculating the rescaled range, because I did not feel that a BASIC version would be very efficient and I was unsure how widely GAUSS would be used among the intended audience for that book. This book is more technical by design, and it seems appropriate to supply my GAUSS programs here.

The programs are in their most basic format. Users will need to customize them for their own applications. This appendix supplies programs for calculating R/S, E(R/S), the sequential standard deviation and mean, and the term structure of volatility. I typically take the output of these programs and import it into a spreadsheet for graphics and direct manipulation. I prefer spreadsheets for the instantaneous feedback I get from manipulation. Again, how the user decides to manipulate the output is purely a matter of personal preference.

CALCULATING THE RESCALED RANGE

The R/S analysis program can either read from a GAUSS data file or import an ASCII file. It splits the data set into even increments that use both the beginning and end points, as described in Chapter 4. Therefore, you should choose data lengths that have the most divisors. If you input 499 observations, you will get no output. The program in its current form takes a raw data file (say, of prices), and first calculates the log differences. It then does an AR(1) analysis and takes the residual. The AR(1) residual data series is passed on to the R/S analysis section of the program. Thus, the input file should have two more observations than you wish to pass on to the R/S analysis section. If you want analysis on i = 500 observations, you need to input 502 prices.

The program outputs the log(R/S) and the log(i) for the AR(1) residuals, and places them in an ASCII file called *dlyar1.asc*. The ASCII file can be renamed and used as input for whatever package you use for graphics and regression. The V statistic is calculated from this output file. As I said, I prefer to do this in a spreadsheet.

The input file can be either a GAUSS data set or an ASCII file. The GAUSS data set named here is the long daily Dow Jones Industrials series used throughout this book. For shorter files, from other sources, I use an ASCII format. The ASCII input file is called *prices.prn.*

```
@This opening section (which has been REM'd out) reads a
    GAUSS dataset.@
@Open ex=dja1.dat;
p=seekr(ex,1);
sret=readr(ex,27002);
datr=sret[.,1];@

@This section reads an ASCII file as input@
load sret[]=prices.prn;
datx=sret[.,1];
datr=datx;

@calculate number of observations to the lower 100+2@
obv=(int((rows(datr)-1)/100)*100)+2;

@Calculate the log returns@
datn=(ln(datr[2:obv]./datr[1:obv-1]))
obv=obv-1;
```

```
@Take AR(1) residuals@
yi=datn[2:obv]; xi=datn[1:obv-1]; xi2=xi^2;
ybar=meanc(yi); xbar=meanc(xi);
xy=yi.*xi; sxx=obv*sumc(xi2)-(sumc(xi))^2;
sxy=obv*(sumc(xy))-sumc(xi)*sumc(yi);
slope=sxy/sxx; const=ybar-slope*xbar;
datx=datn[2:obv]-(const+slope*datn[1:obv-1]);
clear datn; obv=rows(datx);


@Calculate R/S@
I=9; @Starting value of number of observations for R/S
    calculation@


do while i<obv-1;
i=i+1; n=floor(obv/i); num=(obv/i);
if n<num; goto repeat: endif; @This section checks whether
    we have an even increment of time. If not, we skip to the
    next i.@
x1=reshape(datx',n,i)'; @time series is reformatted
    into n×i matrix, to calculate R/S for periods of
    length i.@
mu=meanc(x1)'; x1=x1-mu;    @sample mean is calculated
    and subtracted@
sig=stdc(x1);                          @sample standard deviations@
sum=cumsumc(x1);                       @cumulative deviations from
                                           mean@
max=maxc(sum); min=minc(sum); @maximum and minimum
                                           deviations from mean@
r=max-min;                             @range calculation@
rs=r./sig;                             @rescaled range@
a=log(meanc(rs)); b=log(i); @log of the average R/S value,
                                           and number of observations,
                                           i@


@Print to File@
printdos "\27[=6h";
c=a ~ b;
output file=dlyar1.asc on;
print c;


repeat: endo;
```

CALCULATING THE E(R/S)

This program calculates the expected value of R/S for Gaussian increments, using the methodology outlined in Chapter 5. In the beginning, there is a starting value for the number of observations, n, and an ending value, e. Like the program for calculating R/S, this program calculates E(R/S) for all the even increments between n and e. In practice, I run R/S on the actual data, and then run this program for the E(R/S), changing e to the total number of observations used for R/S, thus giving equivalent values. This can be modified, and the representative values in Table A2.1, which follows this appendix, were calculated from this program as well.

The output is an ASCII file called ern.asc. It contains two columns, E(R/S) and the number of observations, n. Logs are not taken this time, although the program can easily be modified to do so. In the calculation, we use equation (5.4), as long as n is less than 335. At that point, most PC memories do not hold enough digits for the gamma functions, and the program shifts to equation (5.5), which uses Stirling's approximation.

```
n=9; e=1000; @beginning and ending observation numbers@

do while n<e; n=n+1;
i=floor(e/n); num=(e/n); if i<num; goto repeat; endif;

if n<335;
g=gamma(.5*(n-1))/(gamma(.5*n)*sqrt(pi));
else; g=((.5*n)^(-.5))/sqrt(pi);
endif;

r=0; sum=0;
do while r<n-1;
        r=r+1;
        sum=sum+sqrt((n-r)/r);        @empirical correction@
endo;

ern=g*sum;              @calculation of E(R/S) using empirical
                        correction@
output file=ern.asc on;
p=n~ern; print p;

repeat: endo;
```

CALCULATING SEQUENTIAL STANDARD
DEVIATION AND MEAN

The program that calculates the sequential standard deviation and mean is merely a variation of the one that calculates the rescaled range. The data are continually reformatted into an n × i matrix, but the increment is now a fixed step of length, r. Instead of the rescaled range, only sigma and the mean are calculated. This program uses only the first column; it does not average across all increments of length i. Finally, it does not take AR(1) residuals, which are unnecessary for this kind of analysis. The output is the sequential mean and sigma, as well as the observation number, x.

```
@open ex=dja1.dat; p=seekr(ex,1);sret=readr(ex,27000);
datx = sret[.,1]; obv = rows(datx);@   @GAUSS dataset input
                                       REM'd out@

load sret[] = prices.prn; datx = sret[.,1];
obv = rows[datx];

datr = ln(datx[2:obv]./datx[1:obv-1]); @log returns@
obv = rows(datr);

r = 1; x = 19;  @increments of one observation. start with 20
                observations@
do while x<obv-r;
x = x + r; n = floor(obv/x);
x1 = reshape(datr',n,x)';@reformat data into n by x matrix@
s = x1[.,1]; v = stdc(s); m = meanc(s);  @calculate
sequential sigma and mean@

@print to file@
format 1 8; output file = seqvar.asc on;
print x ~ v ~ m;
endo;
```

CALCULATING THE TERM STRUCTURE OF VOLATILITY

As in the program for sequential mean and standard deviation, the term structure of volatility program uses a major portion of the R/S analysis program, reformatting the data as an n × i matrix, with n the time frame of interest. In this case, we start with daily data, make a 27,002 × 1 vector of prices, and calculate the standard deviation of the changes in the AR(1) residuals. We next go to 2-day data, and create a 13,502 × 2 matrix of prices. Column 1 now contains the price every two days. Then, we calculate the standard deviation of the changes in the AR(1) residuals of column 1. We continue doing that until we run out of data.

In this case, we once again use AR(1) residuals, because we do not want the standard deviation of the longer periods to be biased by inflationary growth. In the shorter intervals, it does not make much difference.

```
@This section reads a GAUSS dataset as input. It has been
    REM'd out@
@open ex=dja1.dat;
p=seekr(ex,1);
sret=readr(ex,27002);
datr=sret[.,1];@

@This section reads an ASCII file as input@
load sret[]=prices.prn;
datx=sret[.,1];
obv=((int(rows(datx)/100))*100)+2; @set observations to
                                    even 100, +2 for AR(1)
                                    calc@

datn=datx[2:obv]./datx[1:obv];   @Calculate log returns@
obv=rows(datn);
```

```
@take AR(1) residuals@
yi=datn[2:obv];
xi=datn[1:obv-1]; xi2=xi^2;
ybar=meanc(yi); xbar=meanc(xi);
xy=yi.*xi;
sxx=obv*sumc(xi2)-(sumc(xi))^2;
sxy=obvI(sumc(xy))-sumc(xi)*sumc(yi);
slope=sxy/sxx; const=ybar-slope*xbar;
datc=datn[2:obv]-(const + slope*datn[1:obv-1]);
obv=rows(datc);

@cumulate AR(1) residuals@
datx=cumsumc(datc[.,1]) + 100;

l=0;x=0;

do while x<=(obv/2);
x=x + 1;
num=obv/x; n=floor(obv/x); if n < num; goto repeat; endif;
    @check if x is evenly divisible@

x1=reshape(datx',n,x); @reshape matrix to desired
                        investment horizon, "x"@
datn=x1[.,1];          @use first column of prices only@
datr=ln(datn[2:n]./datn[1:n-1]); @log return@
s=stdc(datr);          @calculate standard deviation@
@print to file@
format 1,8;
output file std.asc on;
print x ~ s;           @print investment horizon, x, and
                        standard deviation, s@

repeat: endo;
```

Table A2.1 Expected Value of R/S, Gaussian Random Variable: Representative Values

N	E(R/S)	Log(N)	Log(E(R/S))
10	2.8722	1.0000	0.4582
15	3.7518	1.1761	0.5742
20	4.4958	1.3010	0.6528
25	5.1525	1.3979	0.7120
30	5.7469	1.4771	0.7594
35	6.2939	1.5441	0.7989
40	6.8034	1.6021	0.8327
45	7.2822	1.6532	0.8623
50	7.7352	1.6990	0.8885
55	8.1662	1.7404	0.9120
60	8.5781	1.7782	0.9334
65	8.9733	1.8129	0.9530
70	9.3537	1.8451	0.9710
75	9.7207	1.8751	0.9877
80	10.0758	1.9031	1.0033
85	10.4200	1.9294	1.0179
90	10.7542	1.9542	1.0316
95	11.0793	1.9777	1.0445
100	11.3960	2.0000	1.0568
200	16.5798	2.3010	1.2196
300	20.5598	2.4771	1.3130
400	23.8710	2.6021	1.3779
500	26.8327	2.6990	1.4287
600	29.5099	2.7782	1.4700
700	31.9714	2.8451	1.5048
800	34.2624	2.9031	1.5348
900	36.4139	2.9542	1.5613
1,000	38.4488	3.0000	1.5849
1,500	47.3596	3.1761	1.6754
2,000	54.8710	3.3010	1.7393
2,500	61.4882	3.3979	1.7888
3,000	67.4704	3.4771	1.8291
3,500	72.9714	3.5441	1.8632
4,000	78.0916	3.6021	1.8926
4,500	82.9004	3.6532	1.9186
5,000	87.4487	3.6990	1.9418
5,500	91.7747	3.7404	1.9627
6,000	95.9081	3.7782	1.9819
6,500	99.8725	3.8129	1.9994
7,000	103.6872	3.8451	2.0157
7,500	107.3678	3.8751	2.0309
8,000	110.9277	3.9031	2.0450
8,500	114.3779	3.9294	2.0583
9,000	117.7281	3.9542	2.0709
9,500	120.9864	3.9777	2.0827
10,000	124.1600	4.0000	2.0940

Appendix 3

Fractal Distribution Tables

This appendix serves two purposes:

1. It presents tables that some readers will find useful if they delve into stable distributions as alternative proxies for risk, either for portfolio selection or option pricing, as described in Chapter 15.
2. It covers the methodology used to generate the tables. The text of this appendix is addressed specifically to those interested in this level of detail.

In 1968 and 1971, Fama and Roll published cumulative distribution functions for the family of stable distributions. The tables were limited to the symmetric case, where $\beta = 0$. They were the first tables to be generated from algorithms, rather than from interpolation in the manner of Mandelbrot (1963). In this appendix, we will first describe the methodology used by Fama and Roll. We will also briefly discuss other methods developed since 1971. At the end of the appendix, three tables are reproduced from the Fama and Roll paper. It is now possible to generate these tables using some of the powerful software available for personal computers, as well as for workstations. Interested readers can try this as well.

GENERATING THE TABLES

Fama and Roll based their methodology on the work of Bergstrom (1952). In order to implement the Bergstrom expansion, we must begin with the *standardized* variable:

$$u = \frac{x - \delta}{c} \qquad (A3.1)$$

The distribution of u is the stable equivalent of the standard normal distribution, which has a mean of 0 and a standard deviation of 1. The difference is that the stable distribution has mean 0 and $c = 1$. We typically normalize a time series by subtracting the sample mean and dividing by the standard deviation. The standardized form of a stable distribution is essentially the same. δ is the mean of the distribution. However, instead of dividing by the standard deviation, we divide by the scaling parameter, c. Remember from Chapter 14 that the variance of the normal distribution is equal to $2*c^2$. Therefore, a standardized stable distribution, with $\alpha = 2.0$ will not be the same as a standard normal because the scaling factor will be different. The stable distribution is rescaling by half the variance of the normal distribution. We start with the standardized variable because its log characteristic function can be simplified to:

$$\log_e \phi_u(t) = -|t|^\alpha \qquad (A3.2)$$

As we stated in Chapter 14, explicit expressions for stable distributions exist only for the special cases of the normal and Cauchy distributions. However, Bergstrom (1952) developed a series expansion that Fama and Roll used to approximate the densities for many values of alpha. When $\alpha > 1.0$, they could use Bergstrom's results to develop the following convergent series:

$$f_\alpha(u) = \frac{1}{\pi * \alpha} \sum_{k=0}^{\infty} (-1)^k * \frac{\Gamma\left(\frac{2*k + 1}{\alpha}\right)}{(2*k)!} * u^{2*k} \qquad (A3.3)$$

The infinite series is difficult to deal with in reality. Luckily, Bergstrom also supplied a finite series equivalent to equation (A3.3), which could be used when $\alpha > 1$. For $u > 0$, this gives:

$$f_\alpha(u) = -\frac{1}{\pi} * \sum_{k=1}^{n} \frac{(-1)^k}{k!} * \frac{\Gamma(\alpha*k + 1)}{u^{\alpha*k+1}} * \sin\left(\frac{k*\pi*\alpha}{2}\right) + R(u) \qquad (A3.4)$$

R(u), the remainder, is a function of $u^{-\alpha*(n+1)-1}$. That is, for a constant, M:

$$|R(u)| < M * u^{-\alpha*(n+1)-1} \qquad (A3.5)$$

As u gets larger, the remainder R(u) becomes smaller than the previous term in the summation. Equation (A3.4) is asymptotic for large u.

Term-by-term integration of equation (A3.3) gives a convergent series for the cumulative distribution function of the standardized, symmetric stable variable with $\alpha > 1$:

$$F_\alpha(u) = \frac{1}{2} + \frac{1}{\pi*\alpha} * \sum_{k=1}^{\infty} (-1)^k * \frac{\Gamma\left(\frac{2*k-1}{\alpha}\right)}{(2*k-1)!} *u^{2*k-1} \qquad (A3.6)$$

Similarly, integration of equation (A3.4) also yields the following asymptotic series, for large u:

$$F_\alpha = 1 + \frac{1}{\pi} * \sum_{k=1}^{n} (-1)^k * \frac{\Gamma(\alpha*k)}{k!*u^{\alpha*k}} * \sin\left(\frac{k*\pi*\alpha}{2}\right) - \int_u^\infty R(u)du \qquad (A3.7)$$

The integral of the remainder term R(u) will tend to zero in the limit.

In practice, Fama and Roll used equations (A3.6) and (A3.7) when calculating the cumulative distribution functions. The approach was to use equation (A3.6) for small u, and equation (A3.7) for large u. However, in practice, they found that both equations were in agreement to five decimal places, except when α was close to 1. For α close to 1, they used equation (A3.7) when $|u| > -4 + 5*\alpha$, and equation (A3.6) in all other cases.

Finally, Fama and Roll gave the following iterative procedure to determine $u(\alpha,F)$, which I quote in its entirety:

1. Make a first approximation Z to $u(\alpha,F)$ by taking a weighted average of the F fractiles of the Cauchy and Gaussian distributions.
2. If $|Z| > -4 + 5*\alpha$, refine it by using the polynomial inverse of the first four terms of the finite series.
3. Iterate as follows:
   (a) Compute $F - F_\alpha(Z)$.
   (b) Change Z according to:

$$\Delta Z = \frac{F - F_\alpha(Z)}{d}$$

   where d is a weighted average of the Cauchy and Gaussian densities evaluated at the point Z.
   (c) Return to (a) and repeat the process until $F - F_\alpha(Z) < .0001$. The procedure rarely requires more than three iterations.

Table A3.1 Cumulative Distribution Functions for Standardized Symmetric Stable Distributions, F(u)

u	Alpha (α)											
	1.00	1.10	1.20	1.30	1.40	1.50	1.60	1.70	1.80	1.90	1.95	2.00
0.05	0.5159	0.5153	0.5150	0.5147	0.5145	0.5144	0.5143	0.5142	0.5142	0.5141	0.5141	0.5141
0.10	0.5371	0.5306	0.5299	0.5294	0.5290	0.5287	0.5285	0.5284	0.5283	0.5282	0.5282	0.5282
0.15	0.5474	0.5458	0.5447	0.5439	0.5434	0.5430	0.5427	0.5425	0.5424	0.5423	0.5423	0.5422
0.20	0.5628	0.5608	0.5594	0.5584	0.5577	0.5572	0.5568	0.5566	0.5564	0.5563	0.5563	0.5562
0.25	0.5780	0.5756	0.5740	0.5728	0.5719	0.5713	0.5709	0.5706	0.5704	0.5702	0.5702	0.5702
0.30	0.5928	0.5902	0.5883	0.5869	0.5860	0.5853	0.5848	0.5844	0.5842	0.5841	0.5840	0.5840
0.35	0.6072	0.6044	0.6024	0.6009	0.5998	0.5991	0.5985	0.5982	0.5979	0.5978	0.5978	0.5977
0.40	0.6211	0.6183	0.6162	0.6146	0.6135	0.6127	0.6122	0.6118	0.6115	0.6114	0.6114	0.6114
0.45	0.6346	0.6318	0.6297	0.6281	0.6270	0.6262	0.6256	0.6252	0.6250	0.6249	0.6248	0.6248
0.50	0.6476	0.6449	0.6428	0.6413	0.6402	0.6394	0.6389	0.6385	0.6383	0.6382	0.6382	0.6382
0.55	0.6601	0.6576	0.6557	0.6542	0.6532	0.6524	0.6519	0.6516	0.6514	0.6513	0.6513	0.6513
0.60	0.6720	0.6698	0.6681	0.6668	0.6658	0.6651	0.6647	0.6644	0.6643	0.6643	0.6643	0.6643
0.65	0.6835	0.6817	0.6802	0.6790	0.6782	0.6776	0.6772	0.6770	0.6770	0.6770	0.6770	0.6771
0.70	0.6944	0.6930	0.6919	0.6909	0.6902	0.6898	0.6895	0.6894	0.6894	0.6895	0.6896	0.6897
0.75	0.7048	0.7039	0.7031	0.7025	0.7020	0.7017	0.7015	0.7015	0.7016	0.7018	0.7019	0.7021
0.80	0.7148	0.7144	0.7140	0.7136	0.7134	0.7133	0.7133	0.7134	0.7136	0.7139	0.7140	0.7142
0.85	0.7242	0.7244	0.7244	0.7244	0.7244	0.7245	0.7247	0.7250	0.7253	0.7257	0.7259	0.7261
0.90	0.7333	0.7340	0.7345	0.7348	0.7351	0.7355	0.7358	0.7363	0.7367	0.7372	0.7375	0.7377
0.95	0.7418	0.7432	0.7441	0.7449	0.7455	0.7461	0.7467	0.7472	0.7479	0.7485	0.7488	0.7491
1.00	0.7500	0.7519	0.7534	0.7545	0.7555	0.7563	0.7572	0.7579	0.7587	0.7595	0.7599	0.7602
1.10	0.7651	0.7682	0.7707	0.7727	0.7744	0.7759	0.7772	0.7784	0.7795	0.7806	0.7811	0.7817
1.20	0.7789	0.7831	0.7865	0.7894	0.7919	0.7940	0.7959	0.7976	0.7991	0.8006	0.8013	0.8019
1.30	0.7913	0.7965	0.8010	0.8048	0.8080	0.8108	0.8133	0.8155	0.8175	0.8193	0.8202	0.8210
1.40	0.8026	0.8088	0.8142	0.8188	0.8228	0.8263	0.8294	0.8322	0.8346	0.8369	0.8379	0.8389

1.50	0.8128	0.8194	0.8261	0.8316	0.8364	0.8406	0.8443	0.8475	0.8505	0.8531	0.8544	0.8556
1.60	0.8222	0.8300	0.8370	0.8433	0.8487	0.8536	0.8579	0.8617	0.8651	0.8682	0.8697	0.8711
1.70	0.8307	0.8393	0.8470	0.8539	0.8600	0.8655	0.8703	0.8747	0.8786	0.8821	0.8838	0.8853
1.80	0.8386	0.8477	0.8560	0.8635	0.8702	0.8763	0.8817	0.8865	0.8909	0.8949	0.8967	0.8985
1.90	0.8458	0.8554	0.8643	0.8723	0.8795	0.8861	0.8920	0.8973	0.9021	0.9065	0.9085	0.9104
2.00	0.8524	0.8625	0.8719	0.8802	0.8879	0.8950	0.9013	0.9071	0.9123	0.9170	0.9192	0.9214
2.20	0.8642	0.8750	0.8850	0.8941	0.9025	0.9103	0.9174	0.9238	0.9298	0.9352	0.9377	0.9401
2.40	0.8743	0.8856	0.8961	0.9057	0.9146	0.9228	0.9304	0.9374	0.9438	0.9497	0.9525	0.9552
2.60	0.8831	0.8948	0.9055	0.9155	0.9246	0.9331	0.9409	0.9482	0.9550	0.9612	0.9642	0.9670
2.80	0.8908	0.9027	0.9136	0.9236	0.9329	0.9415	0.9495	0.9569	0.9638	0.9702	0.9732	0.9761
3.00	0.8976	0.9096	0.9205	0.9306	0.9399	0.9484	0.9564	0.9638	0.9707	0.9771	0.9801	0.9831
3.20	0.9038	0.9156	0.9265	0.9365	0.9457	0.9542	0.9620	0.9692	0.9760	0.9823	0.9853	0.9882
3.40	0.9089	0.9209	0.9318	0.9417	0.9507	0.9590	0.9666	0.9736	0.9802	0.9862	0.9891	0.9919
3.60	0.9138	0.9257	0.9365	0.9462	0.9550	0.9631	0.9704	0.9771	0.9834	0.9892	0.9919	0.9945
3.80	0.9181	0.9299	0.9406	0.9501	0.9587	0.9665	0.9736	0.9800	0.9859	0.9914	0.9939	0.9964
4.00	0.9220	0.9338	0.9442	0.9536	0.9619	0.9694	0.9762	0.9823	0.9879	0.9930	0.9954	0.9977
4.40	0.9289	0.9403	0.9504	0.9593	0.9672	0.9742	0.9804	0.9859	0.9908	0.9951	0.9972	0.9991
4.80	0.9346	0.9458	0.9555	0.9640	0.9714	0.9778	0.9834	0.9883	0.9927	0.9964	0.9981	0.9997
5.20	0.9395	0.9504	0.9597	0.9678	0.9747	0.9807	0.9858	0.9902	0.9939	0.9972	0.9986	0.9999
5.60	0.9438	0.9543	0.9633	0.9709	0.9774	0.9830	0.9876	0.9916	0.9949	0.9977	0.9989	1.0000
6.00	0.9474	0.9576	0.9663	0.9736	0.9797	0.9848	0.9891	0.9927	0.9956	0.9980	0.9991	1.0000
7.00	0.9548	0.9643	0.9721	0.9786	0.9839	0.9882	0.9918	0.9946	0.9969	0.9986	0.9994	1.0000
8.00	0.9604	0.9692	0.9764	0.9821	0.9868	0.9905	0.9935	0.9958	0.9976	0.9990	0.9995	1.0000
10.00	0.9683	0.9760	0.9820	0.9868	0.9905	0.9934	0.9956	0.9972	0.9985	0.9994	0.9997	1.0000
15.00	0.9788	0.9847	0.9891	0.9923	0.9947	0.9965	0.9977	0.9986	0.9993	0.9997	0.9999	1.0000
20.00	0.9841	0.9888	0.9923	0.9947	0.9965	0.9977	0.9986	0.9992	0.9996	0.9998	0.9999	1.0000

From Fama and Roll (1971). Reproduced with permission of the American Statistical Association.

Table A3.2 Fractiles of Standardized Symmetric Stable Distributions, u

F						Alpha (α)						
	1.00	1.10	1.20	1.30	1.40	1.50	1.60	1.70	1.80	1.90	1.95	2.00
0.5200	0.063	0.065	0.067	0.068	0.069	0.070	0.070	0.070	0.071	0.071	0.071	0.071
0.5400	0.126	0.131	0.134	0.136	0.138	0.139	0.140	0.141	0.141	0.142	0.142	0.142
0.5600	0.191	0.197	0.202	0.205	0.208	0.210	0.211	0.212	0.213	0.213	0.214	0.214
0.5800	0.257	0.265	0.271	0.275	0.279	0.281	0.283	0.284	0.285	0.286	0.286	0.286
0.6000	0.325	0.334	0.341	0.347	0.350	0.353	0.355	0.357	0.357	0.358	0.358	0.358
0.6200	0.396	0.406	0.414	0.420	0.424	0.427	0.429	0.430	0.432	0.432	0.432	0.432
0.6400	0.471	0.481	0.489	0.495	0.499	0.502	0.504	0.506	0.506	0.507	0.507	0.507
0.6600	0.550	0.560	0.567	0.573	0.577	0.580	0.581	0.583	0.583	0.583	0.583	0.583
0.6800	0.635	0.643	0.649	0.654	0.658	0.660	0.661	0.662	0.662	0.662	0.661	0.661
0.7000	0.727	0.732	0.736	0.739	0.742	0.743	0.744	0.744	0.743	0.743	0.742	0.742
0.7200	0.827	0.828	0.829	0.830	0.830	0.830	0.830	0.829	0.828	0.826	0.825	0.824
0.7400	0.939	0.932	0.928	0.926	0.924	0.921	0.919	0.917	0.915	0.912	0.911	0.910
0.7600	1.065	1.048	1.037	1.030	1.024	1.018	1.014	1.010	1.006	1.003	1.001	0.999
0.7800	1.209	1.179	1.158	1.143	1.131	1.122	1.115	1.108	1.102	1.097	1.095	1.092

0.8000	1.376	1.327	1.293	1.268	1.249	1.235	1.223	1.213	1.204	1.197	1.194	1.190
0.8200	1.576	1.505	1.447	1.409	1.380	1.358	1.341	1.326	1.314	1.304	1.299	1.295
0.8400	1.819	1.709	1.628	1.571	1.528	1.496	1.471	1.450	1.433	1.419	1.413	1.407
0.8600	2.125	1.964	1.847	1.762	1.700	1.653	1.616	1.587	1.564	1.544	1.536	1.528
0.8800	2.526	2.290	2.122	1.996	1.905	1.837	1.785	1.744	1.711	1.684	1.672	1.662
0.9000	3.078	2.729	2.480	2.297	2.161	2.061	1.985	1.927	1.880	1.843	1.827	1.813
0.9200	3.695	3.366	2.984	2.708	2.503	2.351	2.237	2.150	2.084	2.030	2.007	1.988
0.9400	5.242	4.379	3.774	3.331	3.002	2.763	2.581	2.444	2.341	2.261	2.228	2.199
0.9500	6.314	5.165	4.370	3.798	3.448	3.053	2.816	2.638	2.505	2.404	2.363	2.327
0.9600	7.916	6.319	5.230	4.453	3.882	3.448	3.127	2.887	2.708	2.576	2.522	2.477
0.9700	10.579	8.189	6.596	5.476	4.659	4.049	3.577	3.234	2.980	2.795	2.722	2.661
0.9750	12.706	9.651	7.645	6.251	5.240	4.485	3.901	3.478	3.160	2.933	2.846	2.772
0.9800	15.895	11.802	9.164	7.359	6.063	5.099	4.357	3.799	3.394	3.104	2.996	2.905
0.9850	21.205	15.300	11.589	9.100	7.341	6.043	5.056	4.283	3.728	3.330	3.191	3.070
0.9900	31.820	22.071	16.160	12.313	9.659	7.737	6.285	5.166	4.291	3.670	3.461	3.290
0.9950	63.657	41.348	28.630	20.775	15.595	11.983	9.332	7.290	5.633	4.375	3.947	3.643
0.9995	636.609	334.595	193.989	120.952	79.556	54.337	37.967	26.666	18.290	11.333	7.790	4.653

From Fama and Roll (1971). Reproduced with permission of the American Statistical Association.

Table A3.3 Fractiles of Standardized Symmetric Stable Distributions, $0.70 < = F < = 0.75$, u(alpha,F)

F	Alpha (α)										
	1.0	1.1	1.2	1.3	1.4	1.5	1.6	1.7	1.8	1.9	2.0
0.7000	0.727	0.732	0.736	0.739	0.742	0.743	0.744	0.744	0.743	0.743	0.742
0.7100	0.776	0.779	0.782	0.784	0.785	0.786	0.786	0.786	0.785	0.784	0.783
0.7200	0.827	0.828	0.829	0.830	0.830	0.830	0.830	0.829	0.828	0.826	0.824
0.7300	0.882	0.879	0.878	0.877	0.876	0.875	0.874	0.872	0.871	0.869	0.867
0.7400	0.939	0.932	0.928	0.926	0.924	0.921	0.919	0.917	0.915	0.912	0.910
0.7500	1.000	0.989	0.982	0.977	0.973	0.969	0.966	0.963	0.960	0.957	0.954

From Fama and Roll (1971). Reproduced with permission of the American Statistical Association.

ALTERNATIVE METHODS

There are other less well-documented methodologies for calculating stable distributions. McCulloch (1985) briefly described these. He referenced an integral representation given by Zolotarev (1966), in addition to the convergent series representation by Bergstrom (1952), used by Fama and Roll.

In addition, DuMouchel had evidently tabulated the distributions in his unpublished doctoral thesis in 1971. I was unable to obtain a copy of those tables, but I did find a description of DuMouchel's methodology in a later paper (1973). DuMouchel took advantage of the fact that the inverse Fourier transform of the characteristic function behaves like a density function. For $0 < x < 10$, he inverted the characteristic function (equation (A3.2)) using the fast Fourier transform (FFT), and numerically calculated the densities. For the tail areas, $x > 10$, he used equation (A3.7) as Fama and Roll do. While easier to calculate, the results should be similar to those of Fama and Roll (1971).

The symbolic languages now available for PCs—for example, Mathcad, Matlab, and Mathematica—should make DuMouchel's method rather straightforward to implement. Other tables are also available. Holt and Crow (1973) tabulated the probability density functions (as opposed to the cumulative distribution functions of Fama and Roll) for various values of α and β. Those interested should consult that work.

DESCRIPTION OF THE TABLES

Table A3.1 is the cumulative distribution function for standardized, symmetric ($\beta = 0$) stable distributions. It covers α ranging from 1.0 to 2.0. The frequency distribution for the standardized values can be found through subtraction, just as for the standard normal cumulative distribution (found in all statistics books). Although $\alpha = 2.0$ is comparable to the normal distribution, these tables will not match because they are standardized to c, not σ, as we stated before.

Table A3.2 converts the results of Table A3.1 into fractiles. To learn what value of F accounts for 99 percent of the observations for $\alpha = 1.0$, go down the F column on the left to 0.99, and across to the value u = 31.82. The Cauchy distribution requires observations 31.82 c values from the mean to cover 99 percent of the probability. By contrast, the normal case reaches the 99 percent level at u = 3.29. Again, this is different from the standard normal case, which is 2.326 standard deviations rather than 3.29 units of c.

Table A3.3 gives further detail of the fractiles for $0.70 \le F \le 0.75$, which is used in Chapter 15 for estimating c, for option valuation.

Bibliography

Akgiray, V., and Lamoureux, C. G. "Estimation of Stable-Law Parameters: A Comparative Study," *Journal of Business and Economic Statistics* 7, 1989.

Alexander, S. "Price Movements in Speculative Markets: Trends or Random Walks, No. 2," in P. Cootner, ed., *The Random Character of Stock Market Prices.* Cambridge, MA: M.I.T. Press, 1964.

Anis, A. A., and Lloyd, E. H. "The Expected Value of the Adjusted Rescaled Hurst Range of Independent Normal Summands," *Biometrika* 63, 1976.

Arnold, B. C. *Pareto Distributions.* Fairland, MD: International Cooperative, 1983.

Bachelier, L. "Theory of Speculation," in P. Cootner, ed., *The Random Character of Stock Market Prices.* Cambridge, MA: M.I.T. Press, 1964. (Originally published in 1900.)

Bai-Lin, H. *Chaos.* Singapore: World Scientific, 1984.

Bak, P., and Chen, K. "Self-Organized Criticality," *Scientific American,* January 1991.

Bak, P., Tang, C., and Wiesenfeld, K. "Self-Organized Criticality," *Physical Review A* 38, 1988.

Barnesly, M. *Fractals Everywhere.* San Diego, CA: Academic Press, 1988.

Beltrami, E. *Mathematics for Dynamic Modeling.* Boston: Academic Press, 1987.

Benhabib, J., and Day, R. H. "Rational Choice and Erratic Behavior," *Review of Economic Studies* 48, 1981.

Bergstrom, H. "On Some Expansions of Stable Distributions," *Arkiv für Matematik* 2, 1952.

Black, F. "Capital Market Equilibrium with Restricted Borrowing," *Journal of Business* 45, 1972.

Black, F., Jensen, M. C., and Scholes, M. "The Capital Asset Pricing Model: Some Empirical Tests," in M. C. Jensen, ed., *Studies in the Theory of Capital Markets.* New York: Praeger, 1972.

Black, F., and Scholes, M. "The Pricing of Options and Corporate Liabilities," *Journal of Political Economy,* May/June 1973.

Bollerslev, T. "Generalized Autoregressive Conditional Heteroskedasticity," *Journal of Econometrics* 31, 1986.

Bollerslev, T., Chou, R., and Kroner, K. "ARCH Modeling in Finance: A Review of the Theory and Empirical Evidence," unpublished manuscript, 1990.

Briggs, J., and Peat, F. D. *Turbulent Mirror.* New York: Harper & Row, 1989.

Brock, W. A. "Applications of Nonlinear Science Statistical Inference Theory to Finance and Economics," Working Paper, March 1988.

Brock, W. A. "Distinguishing Random and Deterministic Systems," *Journal of Economic Theory* 40, 1986.

Brock, W. A., and Dechert, W. D. "Theorems on Distinguishing Deterministic from Random Systems," in Barnett, Berndt, and White, eds., *Dynamic Econometric Modeling.* Cambridge, England: Cambridge University Press, 1988.

Brock, W. A., Dechert, W. D., and Scheinkman, J. A. "A Test for Independence based on Correlation Dimension," unpublished manuscript, 1987.

Broomhead, D. S., Huke, J. P., and Muldoon, M. R. "Linear Filters and Non-linear Systems," *Journal of the Royal Statistical Society* 54, 1992.

Callan, E., and Shapiro, D. "A Theory of Social Imitation," *Physics Today* 27, 1974.

Casdagli, M. "Chaos and Deterministic versus Stochastic Non-linear Modelling," *Journal of the Royal Statistical Society* 54, 1991.

Chen, P. "Empirical and Theoretical Evidence of Economic Chaos," *System Dynamics Review* 4, 1988.

Chen, P. "Instability, Complexity, and Time Scale in Business Cycles," IC^2 Working Paper, 1993a.

Chen, P. "Power Spectra and Correlation Resonances," IC^2 Working Paper, 1993b.

Cheng, B., and Tong, H. "On Consistent Non-parametric Order Determination and Chaos," *Journal of the Royal Statistical Society* 54, 1992.

Cheung, Y.-W. "Long Memory in Foreign Exchange Rates," *Journal of Business and Economic Statistics* 11, 1993.

Cheung, Y.-W., and Lai, K. S. "A Fractional Cointegration Analysis of Purchasing Power Parity," *Journal of Business and Economic Statistics* 11, 1993.

Cootner, P. "Comments on the Variation of Certain Speculative Prices," in P. Cootner, ed., *The Random Character of Stock Market Prices.* Cambridge, MA: M.I.T. Press, 1964.

Cootner, P., ed. *The Random Character of Stock Market Prices.* Cambridge, MA: M.I.T. Press, 1964.

Cox, J. C., and Ross, S. "The Valuation of Options for Alternative Stochastic Processes," *Journal of Financial Economics* 3, 1976.

Cox, J. C., and Rubinstein, M. *Options Markets.* Englewood Cliffs, NJ: Prentice-Hall, 1985.

Davies, R., and Harte, D. "Tests for the Hurst Effect," *Biometrika* 74, 1987.

Day, R. H. "The Emergence of Chaos from Classical Economic Growth," *Quarterly Journal of Economics* 98, 1983.

Day, R. H. "Irregular Growth Cycles," *American Economic Review,* June 1982.

De Gooijer, J. G. "Testing Non-linearities in World Stock Market Prices," *Economics Letters* 31, 1989.

DeLong, J. B., Shleifer, A., Summers, L. H., and Waldmann, R. J. "Positive Investment Strategies and Destabilizing Rational Speculation," *Journal of Finance* 45, 1990.

Devaney, R. L. *An Introduction to Chaotic Dynamical Systems.* Menlo Park, CA: Addison-Wesley, 1989.

DuMouchel, W. H. "Estimating the Stable Index α in Order to Measure Tail Thickness: A Critique," *The Annals of Statistics* 11, 1983.

DuMouchel, W. H. "Stable Distributions in Statistical Inference: 1. Symmetric Stable Distributions Compared to Other Symmetric Long-Tailed Distributions," *Journal of the American Statistical Association* 68, 1973.

DuMouchel, W. H. "Stable Distributions in Statistical Inference: 2. Information from Stably Distributed Samples," *Journal of the American Statistical Association* 70, 1975.

————, *The Economist,* "Back to an Age of Falling Prices," July 13, 1974.

Einstein, A. "Uber die von der molekularkinetischen Theorie der Warme geforderte Bewegung von in ruhenden Flüssigkeiten suspendierten Teilchen," *Annals of Physics* 322, 1908.

Elton, E. J., and Gruber, M. J. *Modern Portfolio Theory and Investment Analysis.* New York: John Wiley & Sons, 1981.

Engle, R. "Autoregressive Conditional Heteroskedasticity with Estimates of the Variance of U.K. Inflation," *Econometrica* 50, 1982.

Engle, R., and Bollerslev, T. "Modelling the Persistence of Conditional Variances," *Econometric Reviews* 5, 1986.

Engle, R., Lilien, D., and Robins, R. "Estimating Time Varying Risk Premia in the Term Structure: the ARCH-M Model," *Econometrica* 55, 1987.

Fama, E. F. "The Behavior of Stock Market Prices," *Journal of Business* 38, 1965a.

Fama, E. F. "Efficient Capital Markets: A Review of Theory and Empirical Work," *Journal of Finance* 25, 1970.

Fama, E. F. "Mandelbrot and the Stable Paretian Hypothesis," in P. Cootner, ed., *The Random Character of Stock Market Prices.* Cambridge, MA: M.I.T. Press, 1964.

Fama, E. F. "Portfolio Analysis in a Stable Paretian Market," *Management Science* 11, 1965b.

Fama, E. F., and French, K. R. "The Cross-Section of Expected Stock Returns," *Journal of Finance* 47, 1992.

Fama, E. F., and Miller, M. H. *The Theory of Finance.* New York: Holt, Rinehart and Winston, 1972.

Fama, E. F., and Roll, R. "Some Properties of Symmetric Stable Distributions," *Journal of the American Statistical Association* 63, 1968.

Fama, E. F., and Roll, R. "Parameter Estimates for Symmetric Stable Distributions," *Journal of the American Statistical Association* 66, 1971.

Fan, L. T., Neogi, D., and Yashima, M. *Elementary Introduction to Spatial and Temporal Fractals.* Berlin: Springer-Verlag, 1991.

Feder, J. *Fractals.* New York: Plenum Press, 1988.

Feigenbaum, M. J. "Universal Behavior in Nonlinear Systems," *Physica* 7D, 1983.

Feller, W. "The Asymptotic Distribution of the Range of Sums of Independent Variables," *Annals of Mathematics and Statistics* 22, 1951.

Flandrin, P. "On the Spectrum of Fractional Brownian Motions," *IEEE Transactions on Information Theory* 35, 1989.

Friedman, B. M., and Laibson, D. I. "Economic Implications of Extraordinary Movements in Stock Prices," *Brookings Papers on Economic Activity* 2, 1989.

Gardner, M. "White and Brown Music, Fractal Curves and 1/f Fluctuations," *Scientific American* 238, 1978.

Glass, L., and Mackey, M. "A Simple Model for Phase Locking of Biological Oscillators," *Journal of Mathematical Biology* 7, 1979.

Glass, L., and Mackey, M. *From Clocks to Chaos*. Princeton, NJ: Princeton University Press, 1988.

Gleick, J. *Chaos: Making a New Science*. New York: Viking Press, 1987.

Grandmont, J. "On Endogenous Competitive Business Cycles," *Econometrica* 53, 1985.

Grandmont, J., and Malgrange, P. "Nonlinear Economic Dynamics: Introduction," *Journal of Economic Theory* 40, 1986.

Granger, C. W. J. *Spectral Analysis of Economic Time Series*. Princeton, NJ: Princeton University Press, 1964.

Granger, C. W. J., and Orr, D. "'Infinite Variance' and Research Strategy in Time Series Analysis," *Journal of the American Statistical Association* 67, 1972.

Grassberger, P., and Procaccia, I. "Characterization of Strange Attractors," *Physical Review Letters* 48, 1983.

Greene, M. T., and Fielitz, B. D. "The Effect of Long Term Dependence on Risk-Return Models of Common Stocks," *Operations Research,* 1979.

Greene, M. T., and Fielitz, B. D. "Long-Term Dependence in Common Stock Returns," *Journal of Financial Economics* 4, 1977.

Grenfell, B. T. "Chance and Chaos in Measles Dynamics," *Journal of the Royal Statistical Society* 54, 1992.

Haken, H. "Cooperative Phenomena in Systems Far from Thermal Equilibrium and in Non Physical Systems," *Reviews of Modern Physics* 47, 1975.

Henon, M. "A Two-dimensional Mapping with a Strange Attractor," *Communications in Mathematical Physics* 50, 1976.

Hicks, J. *Causality in Economics*. New York: Basic Books, 1979.

Hofstadter, D. R. "Mathematical Chaos and Strange Attractors," in *Metamagical Themas*. New York: Bantam Books, 1985.

Holden, A. V., ed. *Chaos*. Princeton, NJ: Princeton University Press, 1986.

Holt, D., and Crow, E. "Tables and Graphs of the Stable Probability Density Functions," *Journal of Research of the National Bureau of Standards* 77B, 1973.

Hopf, E. "A Mathematical Example Displaying Features of Turbulence," *Communications in Pure and Applied Mathematics* 1, 1948.

Hosking, J. R. M. "Fractional Differencing," *Biometrika* 68, 1981.

Hsieh, D. A. "Chaos and Nonlinear Dynamics: Application to Financial Markets," *Journal of Finance* 46, 1991.

Hsieh, D. A. "Testing for Nonlinear Dependence in Daily Foreign Exchange Rates," *Journal of Business* 62, 1989.

Hsu, K., and Hsu, A. "Fractal Geometry of Music," *Proceedings of the National Academy of Sciences* 87, 1990.

Hsu, K., and Hsu, A. "Self-similarity of the '1/f Noise' Called Music," *Proceedings of the National Academy of Sciences* 88, 1991.

Hurst, H. E. "The Long-Term Storage Capacity of Reservoirs," *Transactions of the American Society of Civil Engineers* 116, 1951.

Jacobsen, B. "Long-Term Dependence in Stock Returns," unpublished discussion paper, March 1993.

Jarrow, R., and Rudd, A. "Approximate Option Valuation for Arbitrary Stochastic Processes," *Journal of Financial Economics* 10, 1982.

Jensen, R. V., and Urban, R. "Chaotic Price Behavior in a Non-Linear Cobweb Model," *Economics Letters* 15, 1984.

Kahneman, D. P., and Tversky, A. *Judgment Under Uncertainty: Heuristics and Biases.* Cambridge, England: Cambridge University Press, 1982.

Kelsey, D. "The Economics of Chaos or the Chaos of Economics," *Oxford Economic Papers* 40, 1988.

Kendall, M. G. "The Analysis of Economic Time Series," in P. Cootner, ed., *The Random Character of Stock Market Prices.* Cambridge, MA: M.I.T. Press, 1964.

Kida, S. "Log-Stable Distribution and Intermittency of Turbulence," *Journal of the Physical Society of Japan* 60, 1991.

Kocak, H. *Differential and Difference Equations Through Computer Experiments.* New York: Springer-Verlag, 1986.

Kolmogorov, A. N. "Local Structure of Turbulence in an Incompressible Liquid for Very Large Reynolds Numbers," *Comptes Rendus (Doklady) Academie des Sciences de l'URSS (N.S.)* 30, 1941. Reprinted in S. K. Friedlander and L. Topper, *Turbulence: Classic Papers on Statistical Theory.* New York: Interscience, 1961.

Korsan, R. J. "Fractals and Time Series Analysis," *Mathematica Journal* 3, 1993.

Kuhn, T. S. *The Structure of Scientific Revolutions.* Chicago: University of Chicago Press, 1962.

Lanford, O. "A Computer-Assisted Proof of the Feigenbaum Conjectures," *Bulletin of The American Mathematical Society* 6, 1982.

Lardner, C., Nicolas, D.-S., Lovejoy, S., Schertzer, D., Braun, C., and Lavallee, D. "Universal Multifractal Characterization and Simulation of Speech," *International Journal of Bifurcation and Chaos* 2, 1992.

Larrain, M. "Empirical Tests of Chaotic Behavior in a Nonlinear Interest Rate Model," *Financial Analysts Journal* 47, 1991.

Larrain, M. "Portfolio Stock Adjustment and the Real Exchange Rate: The Dollar-Mark and the Mark-Sterling," *Journal of Policy Modeling,* Winter 1986.

Lavallee, D., Lovejoy, S., Schertzer, D., and Schmitt, F. "On the Determination of Universally Multifractal Parameters in Turbulence," in H. K. Moffat, G. M. Zaslavsky, M. Tabor, and P. Comte, eds., *Topological Aspects of the Dynamics of Fluids and Plasmas,* Klauer Academic.

LeBaron, B. "Some Relations between Volatility and Serial Correlations in Stock Market Returns," Working Paper, February 1990.

Levy, P. *Théorie de l'addition des variables aléatoires.* Paris: Gauthier-Villars, 1937.

Li, T.-Y., and Yorke, J. "Period Three Implies Chaos," *American Mathematics Monthly* 82, 1975.

Li, W. K., and McLeod, A. I. "Fractional Time Series Modelling," *Biometrika* 73, 1986.

Lintner, J. "The Valuation of Risk Assets and the Selection of Risk Investments in Stock Portfolios and Capital Budgets," *Review of Economic Statistics* 47, 1965.

Lo, A. "Long Term Memory in Stock Market Prices," NBER Working Paper 2984. Washington, DC: National Bureau of Economic Research, 1989.

Lo, A., and Mackinlay, A. C. "Stock Market Prices Do Not Follow Random Walks: Evidence from a Simple Specification Test," *Review of Financial Studies* 1, 1988.

Lorenz, E. "Deterministic Nonperiodic Flow," *Journal of Atmospheric Sciences* 20, 1963.

Lorenz, H. "International Trade and the Possible Occurrence of Chaos," *Economics Letters* 23, 1987.

Lorenz, H. *Nonlinear Dynamical Economics and Chaotic Motion.* Berlin: Springer-Verlag, 1989.

Lorie, J. H., and Hamilton, M. T. *The Stock Market: Theories and Evidence.* Homewood, IL: Richard D. Irwin, 1973.

Lotka, A. J. "The Frequency Distribution of Scientific Productivity," *Journal of the Washington Academy of Science* 16, 1926.

Lovejoy, S., and Schertzer, D. "Multifractals in Geophysics," presentation to AGU-CGU-MSA, Spring Meeting, May 1992.

Mackay, L. L. D. *Extraordinary Popular Delusions and the Madness of Crowds.* New York: Farrar, Straus and Giroux, 1932. (Originally published 1841.)

Mackey, M., and Glass, L. "Oscillation and Chaos in Physiological Control Systems," *Science* 197, 1977.

Mandelbrot, B. "Forecasts of Future Prices, Unbiased Markets, and 'Martingale' Models," *Journal of Business* 39, 1966a.

Mandelbrot, B. *The Fractal Geometry of Nature.* New York: W. H. Freeman, 1982.

Mandelbrot, B. "The Pareto–Levy Law and the Distribution of Income," *International Economic Review* 1, 1960.

Mandelbrot, B. "Some Noises with 1/f Spectrum: A Bridge Between Direct Current and White Noise," *IEEE Transactions on Information Theory,* April 1967.

Mandelbrot, B. "The Stable Paretian Income Distribution when the Apparent Exponent is Near Two," *International Economic Review* 4, 1963.

Mandelbrot, B. "Stable Paretian Random Functions and the Multiplicative Variation of Income," *Econometrica* 29, 1961.

Mandelbrot, B. "Statistical Methodology for Non-Periodic Cycles: From the Covariance to R/S Analysis," *Annals of Economic and Social Measurement* 1, 1972.

Mandelbrot, B. "The Variation of Certain Speculative Prices," in P. Cootner, ed., *The Random Character of Stock Prices.* Cambridge, MA: M.I.T. Press, 1964.

Mandelbrot, B. "The Variation of Some Other Speculative Prices," *Journal of Business* 39, 1966b.

Mandelbrot, B. "When Can Price be Arbitraged Efficiently? A Limit to the Validity of the Random Walk and Martingale Models," *Review of Economic Statistics* 53, 1971.

Mandelbrot, B., and van Ness, J. W. "Fractional Brownian Motions, Fractional Noises, and Applications," *SIAM Review* 10, 1968.

Mandelbrot, B., and Wallis, J. "Computer Experiments with Fractional Gaussian Noises. Part 1, Averages and Variances," *Water Resources Research* 5, 1969a.

Mandelbrot, B., and Wallis, J. "Computer Experiments with Fractional Gaussian Noises. Part 2, Rescaled Ranges and Spectra," *Water Resources Research* 5, 1969b.

Mandelbrot, B., and Wallis, J. "Computer Experiments with Fractional Gaussian Noises. Part 3, Mathematical Appendix," *Water Resources Research* 5, 1969c.

Mandelbrot, B., and Wallis, J. "Robustness of the Rescaled Range R/S in the Measurement of Noncyclic Long Run Statistical Dependence," *Water Resources Research* 5, 1969d.

Markowitz, H. M. "Portfolio Selection," *Journal of Finance* 7, 1952.

Markowitz, H. M. *Portfolio Selection: Efficient Diversification of Investments.* New York: John Wiley & Sons, 1959.

May, R. "Simple Mathematical Models with Very Complicated Dynamics," *Nature* 261, 1976.

McCulloch, J. H. "The Value of European Options with Log-Stable Uncertainty," Working Paper, 1985.

McNees, S. K. "Consensus Forecasts: Tyranny of the Majority," *New England Economic Review,* November/December 1987.

McNees, S. K. "How Accurate are Macroeconomic Forecasts?" *New England Economic Review,* July/August 1988.

McNees, S. K. "Which Forecast Should You Use?" *New England Economic Review,* July/August 1985.

McNees, S. K., and Ries, J. "The Track Record of Macroeconomic Forecasts," *New England Economic Review,* November/December 1983.

Melese, F., and Transue, W. "Unscrambling Chaos through Thick and Thin," *Quarterly Journal of Economics,* May 1986.

Moore, A. B. "Some Characteristics of Changes in Common Stock Prices," in P. H. Cootner, ed., *The Random Character of Stock Market Prices.* Cambridge, MA: M.I.T. Press, 1964.

Moore, A. W. *The Infinite.* London: Routledge & Kegan Paul, 1990.

Mossin, J. "Equilibrium in a Capital Asset Market," *Econometrica* 34, 1966.

Murray, J. D. *Mathematical Biology.* Berlin: Springer-Verlag, 1989.

Nychka, D., Ellner, S., Gallant, A. R., and McCaffrey, D. "Finding Chaos in Noisy Systems," *Journal of the Royal Statistical Society* 54, 1992.

Osborne, M. F. M. "Brownian Motion in the Stock Market," in P. Cootner, ed., *The Random Character of Stock Market Prices.* Cambridge, MA: M.I.T. Press, 1964.

Packard, N., Crutchfield, J., Farmer, D., and Shaw, R. "Geometry from a Time Series," *Physical Review Letters* 45, 1980.

Pareto, V. *Cours d'Économie Politique.* Lausanne, Switzerland, 1897.

Peters, E. "Fractal Structure in the Capital Markets," *Financial Analysts Journal,* July/August 1989.

Peters, E. *Chaos and Order in the Capital Markets.* New York: John Wiley & Sons, 1991a.

Peters, E. "A Chaotic Attractor for the S&P 500," *Financial Analysts Journal,* March/April 1991b.

Peters, E. "R/S Analysis using Logarithmic Returns: A Technical Note," *Financial Analysts Journal,* November/December 1992.

Pickover, C. *Computers, Pattern, Chaos and Beauty.* New York: St. Martin's Press, 1990.

Pierce, J. R. *Symbols, Signals and Noise.* New York: Harper & Row, 1961.

Ploeg, F. "Rational Expectations, Risk and Chaos in Financial Markets," *The Economic Journal* 96, July 1985.

Poincaré, H. *Science and Method.* New York: Dover Press, 1952. (Originally published 1908.)

Prigogine, I., and Nicolis, G. *Exploring Complexity.* New York: W. H. Freeman, 1989.

Prigogine, I., and Stengers, I. *Order Out of Chaos.* New York: Bantam Books, 1984.

Radizicki, M. "Institutional Dynamics, Deterministic Chaos, and Self-Organizing Systems," *Journal of Economic Issues* 24, 1990.

Roberts, H. V. "Stock Market 'Patterns' and Financial Analysis: Methodological Suggestions," in P. Cootner, ed., *The Random Character of Stock Market Prices.* Cambridge, MA: M.I.T. Press, 1964. (Originally published in *Journal of Finance,* 1959.)

Roll, R. "Bias in Fitting the Sharpe Model to Time Series Data," *Journal of Financial and Quantitative Analysis* 4, 1969.

Roll, R. "A Critique of the Asset Pricing Theory's Tests; Part I: On Past and Potential Testability of the Theory," *Journal of Financial Economics* 4, 1977.

Roll, R., and Ross, S. A. "An Empirical Investigation of the Arbitrage Pricing Theory," *Journal of Finance* 35, 1980.

Ross, S. A. "The Arbitrage Theory of Capital Asset Pricing," *Journal of Economic Theory* 13, 1976.

Rudd, A., and Clasing, H. K. *Modern Portfolio Theory.* Homewood, IL: Dow Jones-Irwin, 1982.

Ruelle, D. *Chaotic Evolution and Strange Attractors.* Cambridge, England: Cambridge University Press, 1989.

Ruelle, D. "Five Turbulent Problems," *Physica* 7D, 1983.

Samuelson, P. A. "Efficient Portfolio Selection for Pareto–Levy Investments," *Journal of Financial and Quantitative Analysis,* June 1967.

Satchell, S., and Timmermann, A. "Daily Returns in European Stock Markets: Predictability, Non-linearity, and Transaction Costs," Working Paper, July 1992.

Scheinkman, J. A., and LeBaron, B. "Nonlinear Dynamics and Stock Returns," *Journal of Business* 62, 1989.

Schinasi, G. J. "A Nonlinear Dynamic Model of Short Run Fluctuations," *Review of Economic Studies* 48, 1981.

Schmitt, F., Lavallee, D., Schertzer, D., and Lovejoy, S. "Empirical Determination of Universal Multifractal Exponents in Turbulent Velocity Fields," *Physical Review Letters* 68, 1992.

Schmitt, F., Schertzer, D., Lavallee, D., and Lovejoy, S. "A Universal Multifractal Comparison between Atmospheric and Wind Tunnel Turbulence," unpublished manuscript.

Schroeder, M. *Fractals, Chaos, Power Laws.* New York: W. H. Freeman, 1991.

Schwert, G. W. "Stock Market Volatility," *Financial Analysts Journal,* May/June 1990.

Shaklee, G. L. S. *Time in Economics.* Westport, CT: Greenwood Press, 1958.

Shannon, C. E., and Weaver, W. *The Mathematical Theory of Communication.* Urbana: University of Illinois, 1963.

Sharpe, W. F. "Capital Asset Prices: A Theory of Market Equilibrium Under Conditions of Risk," *Journal of Finance* 19, 1964.

Sharpe, W. F. *Portfolio Theory and Capital Markets.* New York: McGraw-Hill, 1970.

Sharpe, W. F. "A Simplified Model of Portfolio Analysis," *Management Science* 9, 1963.

Shaw, R. *The Dripping Faucet as a Model Chaotic System.* Santa Cruz, CA: Aerial Press, 1984.

Shiller, R. J. *Market Volatility.* Cambridge, MA: M.I.T. Press, 1989.

Simkowitz, M. A., and Beedles, W. L. "Asymmetric Stable Distributed Security Returns," *Journal of the American Statistical Association* 75, 1980.

Smith, R. L. "Estimating Dimension in Noisy Chaotic Time Series," *Journal of the Royal Statistical Society* 54, 1992.

Sterge, A. J. "On the Distribution of Financial Futures Price Changes," *Financial Analysts Journal,* May/June 1989.

Stetson, H. T. *Sunspots and Their Effects.* New York: McGraw-Hill, 1937.

Thompson, J. M. T., and Stewart, H. B. *Nonlinear Dynamics and Chaos.* New York: John Wiley & Sons, 1986.

Toffler, A. *The Third Wave.* New York: Bantam Books, 1981.

Tong, H. *Non-Linear Time Series: A Dynamical System Approach.* Oxford, England: Oxford University Press, 1990.

Turner, A. L., and Weigel, E. J. "An Analysis of Stock Market Volatility," *Russell Research Commentaries.* Tacoma, WA: Frank Russell Co., 1990.

Tversky, A. "The Psychology of Risk," in *Quantifying the Market Risk Premium Phenomena for Investment Decision Making.* Charlottesville, VA: Institute of Chartered Financial Analysts, 1990.

Vaga, T. "The Coherent Market Hypothesis," *Financial Analysts Journal,* December/January 1991.

Vandaele, W. *Applied Time Series and Box–Jenkins Models.* New York: Academic Press, 1983.

Vicsek, T. *Fractal Growth Phenomena.* Singapore: World Scientific, 1989.

Wallach, P. "Wavelet Theory," *Scientific American,* January 1991.

Weibel, E. R., and Gomez, D. M. "Architecture of the Human Lung," *Science* 221, 1962.

Weidlich, W. "The Statistical Description of Polarization Phenomena in Society," *British Journal of Mathematical and Statistical Psychology* 24, 1971.

Weiner, N. *Collected Works, Vol. I,* P. Masani, ed. Cambridge, MA: M.I.T. Press, 1976.

West, B. J. *Fractal Physiology and Chaos in Medicine.* Singapore: World Scientific, 1990.

West, B. J. "The Noise in Natural Phenomena," *American Scientist* 78, 1990.

West, B. J., and Goldberger, A. L. "Physiology in Fractal Dimensions," *American Scientist* 75, January/February 1987.

West, B. J., Valmik, B., and Goldberger, A. L. "Beyond the Principle of Similitude: Renormalization in the Bronchial Tree," *Journal of Applied Physiology* 60, 1986.

Wilson, K. G. "Problems in Physics with Many Scales of Length," *Scientific American* 241, August 1979.

Wolf, A., Swift, J. B., Swinney, H. L., and Vastano, J. A. "Determining Lyapunov Exponents from a Time Series," *Physica* 16D, July 1985.

Wolff, R. C. L. "Local Lyapunov Exponents: Looking Closely at Chaos," *Journal of the Royal Statistical Society* 54, 1992.

Working, H. "Note on the Correlation of First Differences of Averages in a Random Chain," in P. Cootner, ed., *The Random Character of Stock Market Prices*. Cambridge, MA: M.I.T. Press, 1964.

Zaslavsky, G. M., Sagdeev, R., Usikov, D., and Chernikov, A. *Weak Chaos and Quasi-Regular Patterns*. Cambridge, England: Cambridge University Press, 1991.

Zhang, Z., Wen, K.-H., and Chen, P. "Complex Spectral Analysis of Economic Dynamics and Correlation Resonances in Market Behavior," IC^2 Working Paper, 1992.

Zipf, G. K. *Human Behavior and the Principle of Least Effort*. Reading, MA: Addison-Wesley, 1949.

Zolotarev, V. M. "On Representation of Stable Laws by Integrals," in *Selected Transactions in Mathematical Statistics and Probability*, Vol. 6. Providence, RI: American Mathematical Society, 1966. (Russian original, 1964.)

Glossary

Alpha The measure of the peakedness of the probability density function. In the normal distribution, alpha equals 2. For fractal or Pareto distributions, alpha is between 1 and 2. The inverse of the Hurst exponent (H).

Antipersistence In rescaled range (R/S) analysis, an antipersistent time series reverses itself more often than a random series would. If the system had been up in the previous period, it is more likely that it will be down in the next period and vice versa. Also called pink noise, or 1/f noise. See *Hurst exponent, Joseph effect, Noah effect, Persistence,* and *Rescaled range (R/S) analysis.*

Attractor In nonlinear dynamic series, a definitor of the equilibrium level of the system. See *Limit cycle, Point attractor,* and *Strange attractor.*

Autoregressive (AR) process A stationary stochastic process where the current value of the time series is related to the past p values, and where p is any integer, is called an AR(p) process. When the current value is related to the previous two values, it is an AR(2) process. An AR(1) process has an infinite memory.

Autoregressive conditional heteroskedasticity (ARCH) process A nonlinear stochastic process, where the variance is time-varying and conditional upon the past variance. ARCH processes have frequency distributions that have high peaks at the mean and fat-tails, much like fractal distributions. The generalized ARCH (GARCH) model is also widely used. See *Fractal distribution.*

Autoregressive fractionally integrated moving average (ARFIMA) process An ARIMA(p,d,q) process where d takes a fractional value. When d is fractional, the ARIMA process becomes fractional brownian motion and can exhibit long-memory effects, in combination with short-memory AR or MA effects. See *Autoregressive (AR) program, Autoregressive integrated moving average (ARIMA) process, Fractional brownian motion, Moving average (MA) process.*

Autoregressive integrated moving average (ARIMA) process A nonstationary stochastic process related to ARMA process. ARIMA(p,d,q) processes become stationary ARMA(p,q) processes after they have been differenced d number of times, with d an integer. An ARIMA(p,1,q) process becomes an ARMA(p,q) process after first differences have been taken. See *Autoregressive fractionally integrated moving average (ARFIMA) process* and *Autoregressive moving average (ARMA) process.*

Autoregressive moving average (ARMA) process A stationary stochastic process that can be a mixed model of AR and MA processes. An ARMA(p,q) process combines an AR(p) process and an MA(q) process.

BDS statistic A statistic based on the correlation integral that examines the probability that a purely random system could have the same scaling properties as the system under study. Named for its originators: Brock, Dechert, and Scheinkman (1987). See *Correlation integral.*

Bifurcation Development, in a nonlinear dynamic system, of twice the possible solutions that the system had before it passed its critical level. A bifurcation cascade is often called the period doubling route to chaos, because the transition from an orderly system to a chaotic system often occurs when the number of possible solutions begins increasing, doubling at each increase.

Bifurcation diagram A graph that shows the critical points where bifurcation occurs and the possible solutions that exist at each point.

Black noise See *Persistence.*

Capital Asset Pricing Model (CAPM) An equilibrium-based asset-pricing model developed independently by Sharpe, Lintner, and Mossin. The simplest version states that assets are priced according to their relationship to the market portfolio of all risky assets, as determined by the securities' beta.

Central Limit Theorem The Law of Large Numbers; states that, as a sample of independent, identically distributed random numbers approaches infinity, its probability density function approaches the normal distribution. See *Normal distribution.*

Chaos A deterministic, nonlinear dynamic system that can produce random-looking results. A chaotic system must have a fractal dimension and must exhibit sensitive dependence on initial conditions. See *Fractal dimension, Lyapunov exponent,* and *Strange attractor.*

Coherent Market Hypothesis (CMH) A theory stating that the probability density function of the market may be determined by a combination of group sentiment and fundamental bias. Depending on combinations of these two factors, the market can be in one of four states: random walk, unstable transition, chaos, or coherence.

Correlation The degree to which factors influence each other.

Correlation dimension An estimate of the fractal dimension that (1) measures the probability that two points chosen at random will be within a certain distance of each other and (2) examines how this probability changes as the distance is increased. White noise will fill its space because its components are uncorrelated, and its correlation dimension is equal to whatever dimension it is placed in. A dependent system will be held together by its correlations and will retain its dimension in whatever embedding dimension it is placed, as long as the embedding dimension is greater than its fractal dimension.

Correlation integral   The probability that two points are within a certain distance from one another; used in the calculation of the correlation dimension.

Critical levels   Values of control parameters where the nature of a nonlinear dynamic system changes. The system can bifurcate or it can make the transition from stable to turbulent behavior. An example is the straw that breaks the camel's back.

Cycle   A full orbital period.

Determinism   A theory that certain results are fully ordained in advance. A deterministic chaos system is one that gives random-looking results, even though the results are generated from a system of equations.

Dynamical noise   When the output of a dynamical system becomes corrupted with noise, and the noisy value is used as input during the next iteration. Also called system noise. See *Observational noise.*

Dynamical system   A system of equations in which the output of one equation is part of the input for another. A simple version of a dynamical system is a sequence of linear simultaneous equations. Nonlinear simultaneous equations are nonlinear dynamical systems.

Econometrics   The quantitative science of predicting the economy.

Efficient frontier   In mean/variance analysis, the curve formed by the set of efficient portfolios—that is, those portfolios or risky assets that have the highest level of expected return for their level of risk.

Efficient Market Hypothesis (EMH)   A theory that states, in its semi-strong form, that because current prices reflect all public information, it is impossible for one market participant to have an advantage over another and reap excess profits.

Entropy   The level of disorder in a system.

Equilibrium   The stable state of a system. See *Attractor.*

Euclidean geometry   Plane or "high school" geometry, based on a few ideal, smooth, symmetric shapes.

Feedback system   An equation in which the output becomes the input in the next iteration, operating much like a public address (PA) system, where the microphone is placed next to the speakers, who generate feedback as the signal is looped through the PA system.

Fractal   An object in which the parts are in some way related to the whole; that is, the individual components are "self-similar." An example is the branching network in a tree. Each branch and each successive smaller branching is different, but all are qualitatively similar to the structure of the whole tree.

Fractal dimension   A number that quantitatively describes how an object fills its space. In Euclidean (plane) geometry, objects are solid and continuous—they have no holes or gaps. As such, they have integer dimensions. Fractals are rough and often discontinuous, like a wiffle ball, and so have fractional, or fractal dimensions.

Fractal distribution   A probability density function that is statistically self-similar. That is, in different increments of time, the statistical characteristics remain the same.

Fractal Market Hypothesis (FMH)   A market hypothesis that states: (1) a market consists of many investors with different investment horizons, and (2) the information set that is important to each investment horizon is different. As long as the market maintains this fractal structure, with no characteristic time scale, the market remains stable. When the market's investment horizon becomes uniform, the market becomes unstable because everyone is trading based on the same information set.

Fractional brownian motion   A biased random walk; comparable to shooting craps with loaded dice. Unlike standard brownian motion, the odds are biased in one direction or the other.

Fractional noise   A noise that is not completely independent of previous values. See *Fractional brownian motion, White noise.*

Fundamental information   Information relating to the economic state of a company or economy. In market analysis, fundamental information is related only to the earnings prospects of a firm.

Gaussian   A system whose probabilities are well described by a normal distribution, or bell-shaped curve.

Generalized ARCH (GARCH) process   See *Autoregressive conditional heteroskedasticity (ARCH) process.*

Hurst exponent (H)   A measure of the bias in fractional brownian motion. $H = 0.50$ for brownian motion; $0.50 < H \leq 1.00$ for persistent or trend-reinforcing series; $0 \leq H < 0.50$ for an antipersistent or mean-reverting system. The inverse of the Hurst exponent is equal to alpha, the characteristic exponent for fractal, or Pareto, distributions.

Implied volatility   When using the Black–Scholes option pricing model, the level of the standard deviation of price changes that equates the current option price to the other independent variables in the formula. Often used as a measure of current levels of market uncertainty.

Intermittency   Alternation of a nonlinear dynamical system between periodic and chaotic behavior. See *Chaos, Dynamical system.*

Joseph effect   The tendency for persistent time series $(0.50 < H \leq 1.00)$ to have trends and cycles. A term coined by Mandelbrot, referring to the biblical narrative of Joseph's interpretation of Pharaoh's dream to mean seven fat years followed by seven lean years.

Leptokurtosis   The condition of a probability density curve that has fatter tails and a higher peak at the mean than at the normal distribution.

Limit cycle   An attractor (for nonlinear dynamical systems) that has periodic cycles or orbits in phase space. An example is an undamped pendulum, which will have a closed-circle orbit equal to the amplitude of the pendulum's swing. See *Attractor, Phase space.*

Lyapunov exponent   A measure of the dynamics of an attractor. Each dimension has a Lyapunov exponent. A positive exponent measures sensitive dependence on initial conditions, or how much a forecast can diverge, based on different estimates of starting conditions. In another view, a Lyapunov exponent is the loss of predictive ability as one looks forward in time. Strange attractors are characterized by at least one positive exponent. A negative exponent measures how points converge toward one another. Point attractors are characterized by all negative variables. See *Attractor, Limit cycle, Point attractor,* and *Strange attractor.*

Markovian dependence   A condition in which observations in a time series are dependent on previous observations in the near term. Markovian dependence dies quickly; long-memory effects such as Hurst dependence decay over very long time periods.

Measurement noise   See *Observational noise.*

Modern Portfolio Theory (MPT)   The blanket name for the quantitative analysis of portfolios of risky assets based on expected return (or mean expected value) and the risk (or standard deviation) of a portfolio of securities. According to MPT, investors would require a portfolio with the highest expected return for a given level of risk.

Moving average (MA) process   A stationary stochastic process in which the observed time series is the result of the moving average of an unobserved random time series. An MA(q) process is a q period moving average.

Noah effect   The tendency of persistent time series ($0.50 < H \le 1.00$) to have abrupt and discontinuous changes. The normal distribution assumes continuous changes in a system. However, a time series that exhibits Hurst statistics may abruptly change levels, skipping values either up or down. Mandelbrot coined the term "Noah effect" to represent a parallel to the biblical story of the Deluge. See *Antipersistence, Hurst exponent, Joseph effect,* and *Persistence.*

Noisy chaos   A chaotic dynamical system with either observational or system noise added. See *Chaos, Dynamical system,* and *Observational noise.*

Normal distribution   The well-known bell-shaped curve. According to the Central Limit Theorem, the probability density function of a large number of independent, identically distributed random numbers will approach the normal distribution. In the fractal family of distributions, the normal distribution exists only when alpha equals 2 or the Hurst exponent equals 0.50. Thus, the normal distribution is a special case which, in time series analysis, is quite rare. See *Alpha, Central Limit Theorem, Fractal distribution.*

Observational noise   An error, caused by imprecision in measurement, between the true value in a system and its observed value. Also called measurement noise. See *Dynamical noise.*

1/f noise   See *Antipersistence.*

Pareto (Pareto–Levy) distributions   See *Fractal distribution.*

Persistence   In rescaled range (R/S) analysis, a tendency of a series to follow trends. If the system has increased in the previous period, the chances are that it will continue to increase in the next period. Persistent time series have a long "memory"; long-term correlation exists between current events and future events. Also called black noise.

See *Antipersistence, Hurst exponent, Joseph effect, Noah effect,* and *Rescaled range (R/S) analysis.*

Phase space   A graph that allows all possible states of a system. In phase space, the value of a variable is plotted against possible values of the other variables at the same time. If a system has three descriptive variables, the phase space is plotted in three dimensions, with each variable taking one dimension.

Pink noise   See *Antipersistence.*

Point attractor   In nonlinear dynamics, an attractor where all orbits in phase space are drawn to one point or value. Essentially, any system that tends to a stable, single-valued equilibrium will have a point attractor. A pendulum damped by friction will always stop. Its phase space will always be drawn to the point where velocity and position are equal to zero. See *Attractor, Phase space.*

Random walk   Brownian motion, where the previous change in the value of a variable is unrelated to future or past changes.

Rescaled range (R/S) analysis   The method developed by H. E. Hurst to determine long-memory effects and fractional brownian motion. A measurement of how the distance covered by a particle increases over longer and longer time scales. For brownian motion, the distance covered increases with the square root of time. A series that increases at a different rate is not random. See *Antipersistence, Fractional brownian motion, Hurst exponent, Joseph effect, Noah effect,* and *Persistence.*

Risk   In Modern Portfolio Theory (MPT), an expression of the standard deviation of security returns.

Scaling   Changes in the characteristics of an object that are related to changes in the size of the measuring device being applied. For a three-dimensional object, an increase in the radius of a covering sphere would affect the volume of an object covered. In a time series, an increase in the increment of time could change the amplitude of the time series.

Self-similar   A descriptive of small parts of an object that are qualitatively the same as, or similar to, the whole object. In certain deterministic fractals, such as the Sierpinski triangle, small pieces look the same as the entire object. In random fractals, small increments of time will be statistically similar to larger increments of time. See *Fractal.*

Single Index Model   An estimation of portfolio risk by measuring the sensitivity of a portfolio of securities to changes in a market index. The measure of sensitivity is called the "beta" of the security or portfolio. Related, but not identical, to the Capital Asset Pricing Model (CAPM).

Stable Paretian, or fractal hypothesis   A theory stating that, in the characteristic function of the fractal family of distributions, the characteristic exponent alpha can range between 1 and 2. See *Alpha, Fractal distribution, Gaussian.*

Strange attractor   An attractor in phase space, where the points never repeat themselves and the orbits never intersect, but both the points and the orbits stay within the same region of phase space. Unlike limit cycles or point attractors, strange attractors are nonperiodic and generally have a fractal dimension. They are a configuration of a nonlinear chaotic system. See *Attractor, Chaos, Limit cycle, Point attractor.*

System noise See *Dynamical noise.*

Technical information Information related to the momentum of a particular variable. In market analysis, technical information is information related only to market dynamics and crowd behavior.

Term structure The value of a variable at different time increments. The term structure of interest rates is the yield-to-maturity for different fixed-income securities at different maturity times. The volatility term structure is the standard deviation of returns of varying time horizons.

V statistic The ratio of $(R/S)_n$ to the square root of a time index, n.

Volatility The standard deviation of security price changes.

White noise The audio equivalent of brownian motion; sounds that are unrelated and sound like a hiss. The video equivalent of white noise is "snow" in television reception. See *Brownian motion.*

Index

DATE DUE

JUL ~~~ ~~~~

DEC 1 3 1995

DEC 1 3 1995

JUN 4